SCORCHED
EARTH

SCORCHED EARTH

The Germans on the Somme
1914–1918

by

**Gerhard Hirschfeld, Gerd Krumeich
and Irina Renz**

Translated by Geoffrey Brooks

Pen & Sword
MILITARY

First published in Great Britain in 2009 by
Pen & Sword Military
an imprint of
Pen & Sword Books Ltd
47 Church Street
Barnsley
South Yorkshire
S70 2AS

ISBN 978 1 84415 973 4

A CIP catalogue record for this book is
available from the British Library

Typeset in Sabon by
Phoenix Typesetting, Auldgirth, Dumfriesshire

Printed and bound in England by
CPI UK

Pen & Sword Books Ltd incorporates the Imprints of Pen & Sword Aviation,
Pen & Sword Maritime, Pen & Sword Military, Wharncliffe Local History,
Pen & Sword Select, Pen & Sword Military Classics and Leo Cooper.

For a complete list of Pen & Sword titles please contact
PEN & SWORD BOOKS LIMITED
47 Church Street, Barnsley, South Yorkshire, S70 2AS, England
E-mail: enquiries@pen-and-sword.co.uk
Website: www.pen-and-sword.co.uk

Contents

Introduction

Total War –
The Writing on the Wall at the Somme

The First World War gave rise to an epoch of worldwide historical change and revolution. What began as a European conflict ended as a global catastrophe: it led to the eclipse of three great empires – the Russian, Austro-Hungarian and Ottoman – and cleared the way for the United States to become a world power. It unleashed the Russian Revolution and made possible a Communist breakthrough worldwide. Neither the rise of Italian Fascism nor German Nazism would have occurred had it not been for the First World War.

All the belligerents called the war 'The Great War' – *La Grande Guèrre, Der Grosse Krieg, Velikaya Voyna*. What made this war 'Great' in the eyes of those who experienced it was the fact that it developed within a very short time into an industrial mass-war in which the casualties ran into the millions and were often enough compounded. Increasingly the soldiers of the Great War became blood offerings to the god Moloch as mechanization churned the battlefields into 'human slaughterhouses' (Wilhelm Lamszus). Shrapnel treated heroes and cowards, the prudent and the reckless alike. It was this indiscriminate mass killing that spawned the indifference to human life which was to have such fearsome consequences for post-war European society. The totalitarian systems of the inter-war period, with their contempt for the individual, their mad schemes for the future reorganization of civilization and technocratic visions linked to a programme of genocide were the direct consequence of this new kind of warfare.

In their headquarters 'far from the guns', generals Falkenhayn, Ludendorff, Foch, Haig and Nivelle cold-bloodedly plotted and carried through their operations in the field

1

involving the acceptable 'sacrifice' of hundreds of thousands of soldiers. Convinced of the superiority of the offensive, and wedded to the new weapons technology, they set aside all ethical considerations in their use of massed armies for attack purposes. The English philosopher and pacifist Bertrand Russell coined it as 'maximum slaughter at minimum expense', summarizing the attitude of the military planners towards the 'losses' in dead and wounded as a mere cost accounting exercise.

In terms of the human casualties the largest and costliest of these Great War operations took place ninety years ago in Picardy, north-eastern France, either side of the Somme river where, from the end of June to the end of November 1916, more than 2.5 million Allied and 1.5 million German troops faced each other. The losses on both sides were correspondingly high: more than 1.1 million men, twice the number at Verdun, were either killed, wounded or taken prisoner. Yet it was not only the enormous loss of life for pitifully small territorial gain (for the Allies) which characterized the first great Battle of the Somme: it was above all the manner in which the British and French armies stormed the initially numerically inferior German forces, before transforming attack and defence in a narrow area into a war of extermination on a previously unimagined scale. These military events on the Somme became the hallmark of industrialized warfare. In the great battle of 1916 alone, the British artillery rained down about 1.5 million shells on a sector of the front twenty kilometres long and two and a half kilometres deep. It was on the Somme that tanks made their debut in 1916, followed, in 1918, on the massive scale by armoured tanks, while both sides tried out new artillery and aerial tactics.

Having regard to the appalling cost of 420,000 British and Empire troops dead or wounded, it is not surprising that for many of these nations the Somme has become synonymous with the suffering of the First World War. For the Germans this stretch of territory became important for a different reason: hundreds of thousands of their soldiers had given their lives on the Somme, and after the retreat of 1917 their fallen had no monument 'in enemy territory' worth mentioning. They had fought an 'heroic resistance', a 'Watch on the Somme' in which the river was considered the German western border: the 'holding out' under protracted enemy bombardment and against a numerically superior opponent became almost immediately a byword for the war experience on the Western Front – the German equivalent of the French maxim at Verdun 'They shall not pass.'

After the war the stoic-heroic Somme soldier, whom the horror and suffering of the battle could never touch, became the graven 'steel-helmet face' of the nationalist soldier of the Weimar Republic. The SS-man continued the tradition in its most radical and inhuman guise after 1933. Nevertheless, as a breeding ground for myth and a place of remembrance for the fallen of the Great War, by the time of the Nazi seizure of power the Somme was increasingly giving ground to Verdun in influence, and after 1945 the trend was irreversible.

The Somme, together with other regions of northern France, had also lain under German domination. Its inhabitants had been rigorously suppressed and their possessions carted off as booty. Finally, during their 1917 withdrawal, the Germans had subjected the whole region to Operation *Alberich*, a retreat involving hitherto unparalleled brutality which left the population in occupation of a wilderness wrought by war. The 'scorched earth policy' first practised on the Somme is an oft forgotten, or easily denied, aspect of a World War which became 'total.' This was probably the reason why for the Germans – contrary to the British – it never developed into a region of national remembrance.

This book is the result of many years' research by the authors into the First World War on the Somme, an aspect of this conflict almost unknown in modern Germany. This volume is neither a belated monument nor an indictment. The authors' main aim has been to assemble a quality selection of primary documents from various points of origin which afford an insight into the military organization of the war and the individual's experience of war routine. Together with official announcements (e.g. Army orders, decrees posted on city walls) are to be found various private testimonies – most originating from the Personal Document Collection at the Bibliothek für Zeitgeschichte (fZ) of the Württemberg Landesbibliothek at Stuttgart. Amongst these are many unknown or previously unpublished letters and diaries as well as numerous photographs.

We wish to thank the administrators of the various literary bequests, the copyright holders and the essayists whose contributions have gone into making the six chapters of the book. We close by introducing the Historial de la Grande Guerre at Péronne, a very successful Great War museum of scientific-academic structure, and the Circuit of Remembrance, a tour of the battlefields and places of remembrance, in order that the reader may know better the war landscape of the Somme and its German past.

Gerhard Hirschfeld, Gerd Krumeich, Irina Renz
April 2006.

Chapter One

The Road to the Somme
German War Policy 1914–1916

By John Horne

In the early hours of 4 August 1918 German forces crossed the border into neutral Belgium. Their objective was the fortified city of Liége blocking the way westwards. The city fell on 7 August but the ring of twelve defensive forts surrounding it offered unexpected resistance. Only after both sides had sustained considerable losses, and the Germans had brought up their siege guns, did the last fort fall on 16 August. The almost one million-strong Army of invasion, consisting of five armies, now moved through Belgium in a great arc to reach northern France. The aim of the operation was to encircle Paris and drive the French Army towards the two German armies waiting at the frontier of German Alsace-Lorraine, where the French would be 'wiped out.' After this had been accomplished, the Germans would then move off to the east and attack the French ally, Russia.

The Move that Failed

The German plan almost succeeded. The French commander-in-chief pursued the goal of invading Lorraine blindly. Although he knew that the German right flank could cross the Ardennes in southern Belgium quickly, he ignored information accumulating from his military intelligence that the main weight of the German push would fall much further north, on the Meuse and central Belgian plain. Not until the weak French left flank, supported only by a small British expeditionary corps (BEF), began to pull back in the face of a superior force of three German armies did Joffre recognize the danger. With great presence of mind he used the French railway system to transfer the major part of his troops from north to south and so oppose the German move on Paris.

Here, on the Marne at the beginning of September 1914, the weaknesses of the Great War Plan, based on a modified version of the Schlieffen Plan, became apparent. In the years immediately before the war the German attack plan had been changed to reduce the number of army corps on the right flank. These had been transferred out to reinforce the borders of the then German provinces of Alsace and Lorraine, and to the east of the Reich to counter a possible invasion by Russia, whose forces had been given improved mobility by means of an improved railway system. This transfer weakened the German flank and forced the overstretched right wing to turn short of Paris instead of encircling it from the west as planned. This exposed the German armies to an attack on the flank by French forces coming up from the capital. Even after the adjustment there remained a dangerous gap between the German 1. and 2. Armies, and the BEF moved into it. Joffre ordered a common thrust against the exhausted Germans, who had come 500 kilometres in three weeks of heavy fighting. The German advance thus stalled.

Generaloberst Helmuth von Moltke had always stood in the shadow of his famous uncle who, as victor in the Franco-Prussian War of 1870, had been co-architect of German unity with Bismarck. Theoretically Moltke, who had set up his HQ at Charleville-Mézières in the French Ardennes, had overall command, but he was greatly isolated by poor telephone and radio communications, and particularly by his disinclination to use stand-by aircraft to maintain contact with his commanders in the field. In despair he gave the Chief of Signals, Oberstleutnant Richard Hentsch, the task of linking up with the commanders of the weary and thus endangered flank and so coordinate their further activities. Knowing the likely consequences of a rout, on 9 September Hentsch ordered the commanders of 1. and 2. Armies to break off the attack and pull back. This order was confirmed by Moltke next day. The entire Army now embarked upon the ordered retreat, pursued by British and French forces, along an axis to the north centred on the Département of Aisne. What the French were later to call the 'Miracle of the Marne' had destroyed the German war plan. Moltke suffered a nervous breakdown and was replaced by the Prussian Minister of War, Erich von Falkenhayn.

The war along the River Aisne now showed its true face. The fighting to that point had been the bloodiest in history by far, with casualties higher than the two sides would suffer again until the Somme. The reason was that industrialized killing by machine guns, new kinds of shell with longer flights and high-explosive artillery shells had changed the battlefield into a bloodbath. Unprotected infantry were especially exposed in frontal attacks. Although the German General Staff and the military planners of all major powers knew of these improvements pre-war, they neglected to update the operational tactics in the field, relying instead on attack and the training of conscripts by career officers in the hope of avoiding high casualties and keeping the war fluid. When the Germans reached firm ground above the Aisne they began to dig a trench system which was practically invulnerable when defended by artillery and machine guns. Over the next two months the two sides attempted to surprise their opponents on the flanks. For this purpose they had to attack the trenches where, as a rule, the Germans held the best positions. In this way the retreating 2. Army occupied the heights between Albert and Péronne in the north-east of the Somme Département in Picardy, and dug into the dry chalky ground against the advancing French. After a final attempt by the Germans to 'outflank' the Allies in Flanders and so resume the attack on Paris, the front came to a halt in November 1914. The trenches became a static system stretching from the English Channel to the Swiss frontier. Military technology had created for the defenders a decisive advantage.

The failed campaign in the west converted the German presence in Belgium, Luxemburg and north-east France into that of an occupying power. This also occurred in the east, where in 1915 the Germans won substantial territory in the Baltic and

Polish regions of Russia. Germany mastery over parts of Europe further inspired the war-aim fantasies of numerous military men, politicians and businessmen. The brutality shown by German troops to the civilian population on their arrival placed a heavy burden on this mastery in Belgium and France.

War Atrocities and Occupation

Immediately after hostilities began, during the attack on Liége, German forces became convinced that Belgian civilians were offering more or less open resistance. This did not appear to consist of isolated incidents by individuals, but rather an organized civilian resistance instigated by the Government and local authorities including the mayors and clergy. German intelligence troops who had infiltrated the border region of French Lorraine before the general invasion shared this belief. After the main military thrust, the assumption that considerable resistance was coming from partisans (known as *franctireurs*) led at once to mass hysteria. The belief was unfounded but gripped the entire invasion Army and was current in Germany itself. In indignation Reich Chancellor Bethmann-Hollweg and the Kaiser reproached the French and Belgian Governments. The *franctireur*-myth was based on experiences in 1870 when German-Prussian troops had encountered this kind of resistance in France. The German officer corps disapproved deeply of any civilian involvement in military hostilites. On account of the perceived threat, the commands ordered counter-measures which resulted in excessive brutality being shown. Numerous towns and villages were destroyed, civilians were hanged collectively, or used as human shields in the fighting or deported to Germany. About 6,500 Belgian and French civilians died as a direct result of the German invasion. The Berlin Government rejected categorically the Allied accusation that German troops had acted in contravention of the 1907 Hague Convention and committed atrocities, and laid the blame squarely on Belgian and French civilians. The inhabitants of the regions involved, of whom more than 1.5 million had fled meanwhile, were shocked when the German invasion turned into an occupation in the autumn of 1914.

The distrust and fear of the civilian population towards the Germans led to the introduction, by the latter, of an occupation administration based on martial law. The disproportionately harsh punishment of actual and alleged offences, and the taking hostage of local dignitaries to guarantee the safety of German troops had been the initial reaction of Moltke the Elder to the resistance of French civilians in 1870, and it now became current occupation routine. The practice was also introduced, for punishment and as a preventive measure, of deporting citizens of the occupied countries to Germany for internment in Army barracks emptied by the mobilization. There is no exact number count of these political internees but there were certainly tens of thousands of Belgian and French deportees, amongst them women, children and the elderly. The practice was maintained throughout the war.

By 1915 the area of Europe occupied by Germany and its allies had grown significantly and at the beginning of 1918, after the collapse of the Russian Empire and its secession from the Entente, was practically comparable to the conquests of Nazi Germany a quarter of a century later. Germany's mastery in Europe was distinguished by a variety of administration types: for example, most of Belgium and Poland was ruled by a Governor-General accountable directly to the Kaiser, while the Army administered the north-eastern territories along the Baltic coast like a giant colonial domain. In areas directly behind the German lines, however, the so-called *Etappengebiet* or military area, the safety and supply of troops was of major importance and resulted in an especially repressive regime for the inhabitants.

This was the case in ten French départments with a total population of two million partially or wholly occupied by the Germans, and also in that part of Belgium which lay directly behind the Flanders front.

While the Governments-General of Belgium and Poland pursued political and cultural programmes which were intended to convert these territories in the long run into component parts of a new German Order, the treatment of occupied France was at first dictated by strict military necessity. Brussels became a pleasure centre for German troops on leave, a 'Little Paris', as a substitute for that 'City of Lights' still beyond the German reach. In contrast, Lille, the largest town in occupied France, was not much more than a gigantic military workshop and transit camp. From October 1914 it was ruled with an iron hand by a military Governor (Generalmajor Karl von Graevenitz) and the commandant of fortified Lille (General Wilhelm von Heinrich). After the Prefect of Départment Nord had been condemned and expelled from Lille, the military commander allowed the mayors to remain in office only as spokesmen for the civilian population. The consultants for the population in these predominantly Catholic areas were therefore primarily local priests and regional bishops. Freedom of movement was curtailed completely. The communes were required to provide financial concessions in the form of new taxes immediately. Men of military age, between seventeen and fifty, were enlisted for compulsory work service. Naturally the military authorities billeted German officers and certain men in private houses, while businesses and firms were subjected to strict controls and obliged to keep German troops constantly supplied. The military presence was overwhelming as a result of the German troop build-up on the Western Front. Oppressive upon the local inhabitants was the requirement to greet German officers, the replacement of French street signs with German ones and the introduction of 'German local time' an hour ahead of the French. Even the most minor details of daily life were strictly regulated: those who resisted were threatened with draconian penalties.

Total War in the West

The enforced standstill on the Western Front had a dynamic effect on the German occupation, for the inability to win 'total victory' made more urgent an increasingly 'total' war policy. The imposition of a naval blockade of Germany by Great Britain which cut off imports of food, raw materials and supplies important for the war effort was answered by the German Government's refusal to admit responsibility for supplying food to the peoples of occupied France and Belgium. The justification was the Allies' refusal to allow food to be imported to these regions. The argument was good to some extent although the affected regions had rich farming lands whose produce was being sequestered for the needs of the German armies. The result was a negotiated compromise involving an enormous international effort whereby food and clothing were brought into the occupied areas and distributed by volunteer help organizations. The action was headed by the American businessman and later US President Herbert Hoover, and supported with great reluctance by the Allied Governments.

The Allied fear that the Germans would be placed in a position where they could use local resources for their war effort was well justified. The initially widespread plundering of food, cereals and household objects had changed by 1915 into a systematic exploitation of the industrial resources of the occupied territories with substantial effects on the living standards of the people. From the outset machines and eventually even entire factories were dismantled and taken to Germany. In France and Belgium the occupied territories embraced some of the most highly developed industrial zones of Europe, now put to use serving the interests of the German war economy. Between the autumn of 1914 and the spring of 1915 an acute shortage of ammunition existed amongst all belligerents, and the amounts of ammunition fired in the initial battles could not be made good by industry – even with the massive support of the armies. Hoping to wrest the advantage from the enemy in order to revive the offensive by the use of industry and technology, it was no coincidence that the German Army used chlorine gas for the first time in April 1915 at Ypres, to which the Allies replied in kind in the autumn. It was also no coincidence that in 1915 the British developed a prototype of the 'Little Lillie' tank used operationally for the first time in 1916 on the Somme. The British naval blockade enabled the Allies to fall back on the wealth and production capacity of the United States and on raw materials from all parts of the world while preventing Germany from doing the same. This also applied to agricultural products required to feed industrial workers and German soldiers, and it was not surprising that Germany should attempt to compensate for the Allies' access to international industry by attempting to force through a military-based economy which met resistance in Germany itself. This was especially obvious amongst the local civilian labour force. Initially the German military made it obligatory for age-eligible males to work locally, on the basis that men of equivalent age in most enemy countries were conscripted for military service. From 1916 however, forced labour from France and Belgium was at work digging trenches and constructing semi-industrialized zones with streets, railways, camps and storage depots everywhere to the rear of the front line where previously there had been nothing. When the shortage of labour became acute, more than 50,000 Belgians were deported for work to munitions factories in Germany. The Germans considered that they were 'in good company', for the Allies employed workers from China and the colonies. The French, for example, introduced more than a quarter of a million civilian workers from Africa and South-East Asia for employment behind the front, in agriculture and also in armaments production. The inhabitants of the occupied territories were practically prisoners, however, and had no choice, which as a rule was not the case with workers from the colonies.

The 1907 Hague Convention respecting land warfare prohibited an occupying power from forcing the population under its control to work directly for its war effort and against its own nation. The German military made the infringement worse when, in April 1916, it led off old men, women and girls at Lille, some at gunpoint, to work on the land. The measure was originally intended to reduce the high unemployment in the town, but the action roused strong feelings because the menfolk considered it their duty to protect the women, and they feared the worst.

The French Government appealed to world opinion, as the Belgium Government in exile had already done with regard to the deportation of Belgian workers to Germany. In view of this further damage to its public image the German Government was obliged to abandon both measures, although labour from eastern Europe continued to be sent to work in Germany. Within Belgium and the occupied territories of Northern France forced labour remained the rule, and behind the front local men were accommodated increasingly under harsh conditions in the camps.

In November 1914 the last German attempt to keep the war mobile failed at Ypres. Within the OHL (*Oberste Heeresleitung* = Supreme Army Command) and the Kaiser's political entourage a crisis developed, as two opposing strategies crystallized. Paul von Hindenburg and his Chief of Staff and close colleague Erich Ludendorff, who together had beaten off the Russian invasion in August 1914 and now commanded German forces in the east, favoured a defensive tactic of holding the trenches along the Western Front while the Russian Army in Poland was eliminated by newly formed units. This reversal of the Schlieffen Plan would make victory possible in the West. Erich von Falkenhayn, Chief of the General Staff (as successor to Moltke) on the other hand was of the opinion that a total victory was not possible. Instead he proposed concluding a separate peace with Russia (with relatively favourable conditions for the Czar) and to concentrate on separating the British (whom he considered to be Germany's real arch-enemy) from the French.

Falkenhayn's reasoning and proposals were categorically rejected by Reich Chancellor Bethmann Hollweg, who was still opposed to a diplomatic solution at this point, and also by Hindenburg and Ludendorff, in whose eyes it bordered on high treason. Whilst their plans to rid themselves of Falkenhayn failed at the intervention of the Kaiser, who distrusted Ludendorff's ambitions, the crisis showed distinctly that peace negotiations by the political and military elites would be seen as a gesture of defeat and that therefore there could only be a military solution. Falkenhayn was left with no option but to reinforce the Western Front against the unceasing French attacks and the numerical superiority of Allied forces. He ordered the laying of parallel lines of trenches and the defence of the conquered terrain without regard to casualties. The German defensive lines would be strengthened by enlarged accommodation and concrete bunkers similar to those on high ground at Thiepval in the Somme region.

In 1915 however the front remained quiet except for sporadic outbreaks of fighting and numbers of landmines exploding.

With the support of the BEF the French began launching major offensives on both sides of the extended main sector of the Somme front, in the north in May and September in the entire Artois coal basin region and in February in the hills of Champagne. These battles were very costly in lives for both sides, mainly because of Falkenhayn's insistence that every metre of territory lost had to be won back. Joffre considered the offensives to be military defeats for his inability to penetrate the German front. The result undoubtedly convinced Falkenhayn that a breakthrough in the west was increasingly improbable for either side and the victor would be he who exhausted the enemy's forces by a 'war of attrition' and deprived his enemy of the will to go on.

Falkenhayn's basic assumption that the war could openly be won in the west was apparently refuted by further events in 1915. The increasingly obvious inferiority of Austro-Hungarian troops pitted against the Russian Army which, at the beginning of 1915 had overrun large areas of Polish Galicia, the north-eastern territory of the dual monarchy, forced Germany to come to the aid of her ally. In a common counter-offensive during the late spring and summer led by the newly-formed 11.Army under August von Mackensen, the Russian armies were thrown back 200 to 400 kilometres to a line which they then held until 1917. Ironically this was Falkenhayn's greatest victory. The subjugation of Serbia, the successful defence of Austria against an invasion by Italy, which meanwhile had entered the war on the side of the Entente, and the Allied landings at Gallipoli (repulsed by a Turkish Army under German command) turned 1915 into a year of German victories in eastern and southern Europe. On the other hand the situation in the west remained unchanged. The Russians began to recover from their setback and showed no inclination to sue for peace. From December the Chief of the German General Staff therefore concentrated his attentions once more on bringing the war with France to a successful conclusion.

Convinced that Russia had been seriously weakened by its early offensives, Falkenhayn wanted to force the French to sign a separate peace. He believed that in that way he could isolate Great Britain and undermine her ability to continue the war in Europe alone, for Falkenhayn was of the opinion that Britain was Germany's main enemy. It was his intention to let the French pursue an objective from which they could not withdraw without at least suffering a psychological defeat after having been subjected to long barrages of artillery fire causing them great losses of unique advantage to Germany.

The town of Verdun lying in a river basin, enclosed by heights along the Meuse to the north and east, was the selected objective. A rapid, successful conquest of these heights would provide German artillery with a favourable location from where to pour down fire on the French infantry congregated in the city. Despite the initial massive bombardment, the ten German infantry divisions failed to take the heights along the Meuse. Therefore, from mid-March 1916 Falkenhayn justified the Battle of Verdun as an attrition strategy, in the sense of a demographic gamble whose objective it was 'to bleed France to death.' But Falkenhayn had underestimated the resistance of the French public and Paris Government, which saw this struggle from the beginning as a monumental war of national defence. He also failed to divide the Alliance.

When the major Anglo-French offensive on the Somme began on 1 July 1916, it ended the German offensive on the Meuse. The Somme was the proof that the French Army had in no way 'bled to death' at Verdun. The Somme offensive also demonstrated that the British were capable of transporting a mass army to the Western Front and maintaining the industrial effort in Britain. Meanwhile the logic of the total war had escalated. Gigantic quantities of ammunition had been expended at Verdun and for the first time the large-scale and lasting use of new weapons and equipment such as the flame-thrower or the German 'coal-scuttle' helmet was seen. Falkenhayn now pressed for unrestricted U-boat warfare in the battle for desperately needed food supplies and war materials, but he failed to persuade the Kaiser.

OHL began to consider a drastic reorganization of weapons production by a military control of the German labour market. At the same time the conflict was exposing major weaknesses in Government policy making. The smouldering political crisis was resolved at the end of August 1916 when Ludendorff and Hindenburg finally forced the Kaiser to sack Falkenhayn. After the generals themselves had taken over OHL, the military became the real power in the State and thus cleared the way for increasingly radical war measures both internally and externally. These included extensive control over, and exploitation of, the populations in the occupied territories of Belgium and Northern France.

Georg David Bantlin (1879–1961) (Fn 1)
Sanitätskompanie 3, Inf. Div. 26, XIII Armee-Korps

In Civilian Life a Sanatorium Physician from Wyck/Föhr[1]

DIARY

14 October 1914 (Roncq)

A day on the march. Lille is in German hands: the division is advancing northwards between Lille and Roubaix (Cysoing, Ascq, Mons-en-Baroel, Marcq-en-Baroel to Roncq). Unfortunately I do not have enough maps, as not sufficient were delivered. The mild wind has brought rain which patters down incessantly on our fairly laconic column. It is a strange area which we are passing through. Here we cannot understand why they talk of the people pulling back in France. Our entire march route looks like an elongated village or town, or more accurately a mixture of both, for the housing district of small town or village character alternates with magnificent villas in fine parkland. Here and there one sees large factories, but they lie still. The inhabitants come out, curious and somewhat anxious, the female section, despite everything, rather flirtatious on the street. Happily everything is intact, just a few barricades at the entrance to places remind us that we are at war. When one looks at how the region is laid out it is noticeable that the villages all have just the one street and no great depth either side. This is why they all seem to hang together to a certain extent. Directly behind the street very rich agricultural land begins, consisting of meadows or the towering poplars characteristic of the region, and meadowy woodland.

As QM, I rode ahead in order to obtain quarters in Roncq, a town of 7,000 inhabitants. This is not so easy when one thinks that in such a place we have to accommodate two large Staffs, one infantry regiment, two artillery-munitions columns, one artillery detachment and two field medical companies, therefore 4–5,000 men and 6–800 horses. But one has experience of this and we even managed to get all the men under cover in quarters bedded on straw, twelve to a living room, saloon or kitchen and each officer has his own bed. The horses are the most difficult and finally we stabled them in a factory. On 15 October we took advantage of the Brigade Staff leaving and billeted ourselves in sixes in the mansion of a rich manufacturer Desumerot (weaver). As almost the entire population has remained at home, fortunately, so here with the gentleman of the house, and life is just like being on manoeuvres. We eat in a magnificent dining room with a view out over grandiose parkland. To reach the diner one passes through huge wing doors and descends a couple of marble steps. Glorious wines and carefully prepared dinners eaten with marvellous cutlery taste rather different to field-kitchen soup on a tin plate with tin spoon.

Our attire makes us strangers in the cared-for surroundings. Our hobnail boots tread on fine Persian carpets, our weather-beaten uniforms appear in marked contrast to the silk-decorated armchairs, Flanders leather wallpapering and old candelabras, the richly-guilded hearths, around whose mantles are arrayed delightful bronzes and old porcelain. Each officer has his own elegant room with glorious bed and washbasin. In this luxury we shall probably pass a few days, for the division (26.) has the task of defending the Lys sector ahead, while to our left XIX Korps etc. is turning across to link up with the army which besieged Antwerp. It is hoped to drive the British into the marshes with their armoured cars. As to what else is going on in the world we have no clue. We have had no post or newspapers since 3 October. The railway track, mostly provisional, was used at first only for troops and equipment, not post. So one just has to be patient.

At midday I made a forbidden and therefore all the more interesting drive with Oberstabsarzt Buhl in the horse and cart to Lille fifteen kms away. The fortified city had held out three days against our artillery fire. It has been in German hands for two days. The British, of whom there were more in Lille than

French, have fled or been captured. A bombarded city has a grotesque, sad and often rather comical look about it. Besides the well-preserved Exchange (except for its windows, of which the entire city has suffered) and the main gendarmerie house, in the streets leading to the main railway station there are only rows of four-storey walls, gigantic in their height, which incline this way and that so that you tiptoe past lest the vibration brings down the entire structure on your head.

The contents of the various floors are heaped in confusion on the ground floor. This is all that remains of what were once houses, large cafés, etc. Luckily all the important buildings have survived, the Museum of Fine Arts, the St Maurice church. The Prefecture looks odd. A shell exploded on the great front step sending a thousand splinters everywhere but only minor damage was caused. The explosive effect of our shells must be immense. One sees many ruined houses which must have been collapsed inwards with the blast. Streams of people are moving through the boulevards again: many worried faces – no wonder, when one sees and hears the destruction, many missing lie buried in the cellars – but then again women cooking, closed shops alongside re-opened cafés and elegant businesses which look really miserable and strange in the dull light of a few candles at dusk (the gas supply has not yet been resumed). Like passing through a mediaeval city by night, our small horse returned us and our lanterned cart to our quarters.

Ludwig Berg, Catholic Theologian

The Author was a Catholic Priest attached to the Kaiser's Great HQ.

DIARY[2]

14 October 1914 Bapaume
On this farm there is nothing more to eat or drink. Sick officers from the military hospital are billeted here. They need rest.

Arrival with Major of the French from Berlin and young lieutenant from Magdeburg. To the military hospital in the school. Here about 0730. Heard soldiers' confessions and visited officers.

Many seriously wounded, one with both legs amputated: many amputees laid out in the hall, in the blood, on sacks of straw on the ground . . . all want to return to Germany.

Bapaume, c.60, sick with typhus!

0730. Ate with the wounded from their soup cauldron . . . a Protestant wanted to tell me something at all costs to relieve his conscience despite my objection that I am a Catholic priest.

After that to M. Le Doyen (Dechant): the Stabsarzt told me that he would not be very pleasant this evening because somebody had stolen wine from his cellar. Anger against Germans and their barbarism, and thus conduct of the war and actions everywhere. He always very good. Walked with me to a house in a wood to where a priest had come after being driven out of the village. Initially lady of house not very forthcoming, afterwards extremely good. Made hot beef-soup and fried eggs. Red wine on the table. Tea to finish off. Gave me large room with good bed. The priest, like Dechant, was very critical of Germans. They could not distinguish between religion and nation, between the needs of the wounded and what inhabitants are guilty of in war. Always: war against Catholic clergy in Belgium, just as here.

Finally alone with expelled priest at supper, because he will not let himself be convinced. The sister who accompanied me to the bedroom, and had had a lot of conversation with the lady of the house, told me in the bedroom: 'I do not agree with what the priest told me.' Good convent soul, who said directly: This Government (i.e. French) was very bad, continual repression of clergy, Government relationship in Germany she liked. But the idea of Protestantism remains the enemy, irreconcilable for now. The whole afternoon the thunder of the guns quite near, about eight to nine kms away. Frequent rapid fire. In the morning I held mass in the chapel of the orphanage to the thunder of the guns.

Large motor was loaded with wounded and left. On the way: French trenches behind hedges, on the highway gun emplacement firing through hedges, possibly without being observed.

In the locality itself soldiers, baggage, a large military hospital with about six doctors: one a Berlin professor! On the streets many French guns, French uniform greatcoats, in the hospital courtyard empty cartridge pouches and backpacks of wounded soldiers. On the lorry previously, barrels of fuel, German wounded.

In the last room (of the military hospital) were nine with head wounds: 'There, ours, shot through head, unconscious. No point taking them.' Nearly all Protestants. One dying, he was in the chapel, three very serious. On the motor groans and cries of wounded. Noted personal details and then left.

I to fuel pump at Bapaums and off to the front.

The evening before from 8 to 1 ready to march, instruments and pharmaceutical packed. Fearsome barrage by our artillery, attack beaten off again. Our infantry much too light on the ground, one every ten steps, distance between the lines maximum 500 to 600 metres sometimes from fifteen to two hundred, enemy opposite in trenches, attack spotted once with (periscope?) and beaten off. In yesterday's attack more dead and wounded, a soldier told me he had been shot through his steel helmet and cartridge pouch.

French few infantry, but aircraft and artillery! Slaughter animals, cook, camp life. Presents go down well. Distributed fairly. Amongst these gifts women's stockings, which are very long. Real tobacco. (. . .) The French have very good provisions, in their backpacks jam, clothing, meat! Our soldiers are allowed to empty packs and take everything. 'The bullets cast for you turn you into dust.' Terrible battle near Arras. Bodies of French dead piled two and three high as shield.

Gustav Sack (1885–5 Dec 1916)
Unteroffizier Dec 1914, later Leutnant: Bavarian
Inf.Regt.I (Bav.Inf.Regt.24 from June 1916), Bav.Inf.Div.I

In Civilian Life a Writer

Correspondence with his wife Paula Sack, Hamburg[3]
(The author addressed his wife as 'Karl')

20 October 1914 (Vernandovillers)
So, my dear Karl, the first letter from the trenches. On Friday morning after eight days the crazy travelling came to an end. I

was still cooking the bird, which at this time showed a strong need for bouillon cube (soup), then we marched two hours to village quarters, from there on the Saturday to another, and on Sunday afternoon we were assigned by regiment and went at once into the trenches.

It is not really a trench. It is in a thick mixed wood with much undergrowth on whose edge every three to five metres each man has his hollow or protective hole with a gun rest against the enemy infantry line only 200–300 metres distant and side protection against the enemy artillery barrage expected hourly. For the most part dug-in, on the ground, straw and an old sack into which one crawls and a heap of clods for a pillow. Quite habitable but devilish cold. Menu is: 0700 a mug of tea or coffee, difficult to tell the difference, 1200 another one and towards 2300 the lid of a field cauldron filled with strong soup, additionally pumpernickel bread in the breadbag. I have got smokes. I have seen no enemy. Shells and shrapnel, theirs and ours, passes continuously overhead, the former quite close, usually explodes in the village. Rifle fire now and again – that is all. The only thing I need is handkerchiefs. For almost eight days I have been blowing my nose into the same red handkerchief which, with the passage of time, – I have a cold – has a really strange smell. Therefore as presents: handkerchiefs and soap! Duty is light – one hour sentry by day and at night two hours plus one hour listening duty. Yesterday morning I was seized by an incredible fit of melancholy, additionally totally apathetic, a pipeful of tobacco brought me back to my senses. It getting damp, darker, starting to rain, piddling a bit. In ten days there will be a storm – so they say! And the siege of Paris will last over the winter. I love and kiss you. Your Karl. Shrapnel just fell 'extremely' near. Karl, thumbs up! My beard is long and is getting fiery red. Greet my parents!

26 October 1914 (Péronne)

Are you still alive? You are still alive! Everybody gets letters and dozens of parcels, only I, who deserve them most of all, get nothing! Days still quiet and behind the front – that means a couple of kilometres – as army reserve. We are about half an hour from Péronne in quarters and make our daily stroll in this boring nest which has nothing but cognac, always cognac and coffee, and meat, of which I ate another pound again today, and I, whom field fare repels. I had a beef-steak done for me here in the café,[4] a whole pound for me! Outside, music in the square, the whole nest, which by the way hosts a house of pleasure,[5] everything eaten up, totally field-grey: my knowledge of French is better, incidentally, than I thought. As for the war – it is quite, quite different, and more crazy than you can imagine.

Kiss Karl.

31 October 1914 (Hardecourt)

So (sketch) my dearest Karl, I have been laid low with diarrhoea in the reserve trench, with the support platoon, another three days. They have excavated almost a small town in the ground here, the vertical snakelines (i.e. in the sketch) are the communications trenches, the others protective trenches, to the right the scrape-hole in which your husband, half sheltered against rain and metal splinters, passes the night. One sees nothing even though the wicked foe is only 3–400 metres ahead, but one hears all the more: before and behind us the artillery roars, the shells explode – one gets used to it. Additionally the aircraft come humming and the larks take not the least notice. When is mail arriving? It is truly time, my love. It is 1300, I have not eaten yet, and must eat something.

Kiss Karl.

2 November 1914 (Hardecourt)

(. . .) My darling, I have quite forgotten what I wanted to write in reply to your last (fourth) letter. You can see that I 'like you' from the fact that nearly every day I write you between one and three letters – I hope that at least half arrive! But Karl, my good friend, you must not be a sourpuss – first because you really have no (better) reason and then – the shells whistle, hum, sing, hiss constantly above me and explode each time with the same infernal noise and always very close. And I am freezing! Tonight from 1900 to 0700 outside on sentry – good moon, cotton wool clouds, good sunrise, partridges nearby, everywhere very picturesque, but cold, cold and hungry!

See if you have enough money, dearest Karl – a tin of sardines, a sausage, chocolate etc. – and a drop of alcohol!! Specially since my parents do not write me any more – no letter, no parcel, no chocolate, no sausage! And the stamp only costs ten pfennigs. The sun has come out and we can dry things a bit in our dug-outs. Karl, the filth sticks to us. Have a look round to find me a place like this in Hamburg! F. has got us on a lead. Another day in the trench, tomorrow evening for four days to the rear. Always here and there.

Dearest, will you send me something nice? Knit me a pair of thick woollen gloves? Yes? I am lying here in my scrape-hole, leaning halfway out, have put my pack down on the trench floor and use it to write on, and one after another they step over pack and letter on their way to the latrine, which is near but fortunately with a favourable wind! You should also send me some opium against the diarrhoea. Not morphine, naturally, my child.

There are certainly better, more solid husbands than I, you can therefore try it again. I would not like to imagine it, not at all. But I must not fall, we have to earn money first, swap, to get to Copenhagen etc. But you can't imagine how modest I live now – a bed – I had no bed for three weeks – a cup, a chair, washed clean, a mirror, a cup of tea from our suddenly mis-shapen teapot – all unimaginably beautiful things. I should like to receive a light wound, and then you can look after me. In that case I would like to be transferred to a military hospital in the Rhineland, not Munich, I would be sick if I were brought to Munich. Karl, in perhaps six months and then – no more sour-puss, for you are and remain my Karl.

Kiss Karl.

5 November 1914 (Hardecourt)
My Darling

Today the seventh day in the trench: we look like pigs: a layer of filth about a centimetre thick – not exaggerating – sticks to greatcoat, uniform jacket and trousers, and the article about Nietzsche[6] is, if intended, infamously bad. Better the one about Löns,[7] pity about him, one of the few nice scribblers because he is honest and harmless, yesterday rain, outside in front of the trench on 'listening sentry.' If the disgusting newspapers say we are gaining ground slowly, that means we have dug fifty to sixty metres closer to the enemy in two nights!

Yes, the cigarettes were good, my love. And how delightful were the sausage and anchovy butter!! I received your fat letter in the Gabelsbergerstrasse as I wrote to you in the last letter, in case you didn't receive it. No more peppermints, my angel, now we are not sweating. Yes, my mother sent me a bobble-hat and cigars, the ear-warmers are very welcome. Karl, slowly, now and then I am getting some fun out of the thing – so far no bullet fired, only artillery and artillery. In the stupid, cloying, wet trenches often enough exquisite, amusing scenes. For the time being am not writing to my parents. They want me to come home 'so that we can think about a safe career for you.' Thank you, always the same. The day after tomorrow there will be finally and definitively a four-day rest. Washing!! A couple of acceptable comrades: a Dr Davidson, Assistant in Byzantine Studies at Munich, the archetype academic snob, and an artistic director from Posen who is dead certain to be the first for bombardment with the 'Refraktair.'[8] Also the Hauptmann, Professor at University of Strasbourg and Turnschaftler: there-fore association brother, will probably, has even thought about how he can get me a quick promotion.

Tell me how many letters approximately you have received from me. Must be twenty to twenty-five. The Bavarians are unbelievable, indescribably stupid, enormously stupid – sacra-ment! sacrament! is all they know. Please also send me some 'Japanese Closet Paper.' I have almost used up my three packs since I suffer from diarrhoea every third day.

Is the bird still alive? Do you know what the best thing is? When I travel from Munich to Hamburg in the food waggon, telegram ahead. And then we knock some back! Karl, do you love me? Now the sun has come out a bit. I have a terrible fear that one night my hole in the ground will collapse on top of me – ghastly feeling!

Kiss Karl.

17 November 1914 (Hardecourt)
Dearest Karl

It is a disgrace, everything is being whisked away. At the

moment all we have to eat is mustard, anchovy butter, milk, chocolate and two sausage sandwiches – nothing else! I am starving! I cannot stomach the field diet – at night a bowl of horrible soup – I have diarrhoea and live on bread and a little water. There is nothing else for it but to keep it coming. A parcel daily! Bacon, sausage, mustard, anchovy butter, milk, sardines, chocolate, cigarettes and caraway – must. Debts are immaterial, during the war I have not written a word and 'write something great about one's war experiences' is of no use. Understood? The 'Paralyse'[9] for example is something great! Many thanks for the large handkerchief, which I will use as such. Today finally relieved for a few days. It was appalling: rain, frost, filth and again inexpressible filth. Warmest, and tomorrow letter!

Gustav.

31 December 1914 Afternoon, (in the Hardecourt Trench)
(. . .) This is, by God!, the most awful New Year's Eve which I have ever let slip by me: I always used to be flaked out at New Year, but not like today . . . ! First, quite superficially: our meal consisted of bread, plentifully available, but wet through and soggy, spread with salt, and cold coffee from last night plus your figs for breakfast. Tonight at midnight I will drink your health from the small flask of punch – the other one is empty. More, after it froze last night it pissed down again, disgustingly thin, and grey and incessant – enough to make you weep. And everywhere the trench walls – strengthened with such effort – fall in – swamp, filth, a pigsty. If it keeps raining it will come through our roof eventually, and then we can bathe in mud like the pigs. Do you know, incidentally, that these holes are so low, cross-legged on the ground one can just sit upright in them. Did I also tell you that there have been rows of dead French soldiers in front of our positions for the last fourteen days? Recent conscripts, quite young, fresh boys, fourteen days in the filth and rain, nobody buries them, these black rotting lumps. Last night a patrol brought us sardines and tins of jam which are in all the French breadbags. One feels half guilty at opening them, half disgusted, but at least they covered the boys over. But – *dulce et decorum est, pro patria mori*. Ghastly, totally ghastly. If only one could drink oneself senseless! And then, why have I

not received a letter from you on the last day of this strange year? (. . .)

1 February 1915, Vanguard near Ferme Hem (Hem Monacu)
Dearest Karl

Out once more on the Somme – it is really wonderful, except one thing: there must be an end to it. Yesterday it snowed, and with my tribe of nomads armed with wire-cutters we roamed through the village in search of barbed wire to cut free from hedge and bush. After that the poor doctor and I went back to the pretty young girl from the day before yesterday – in this village there are only females, about twenty of them – bringing for the hungry serving wench – for she is a delightful serving girl – pumpernickel bread and coffee. It is a good thing we are leaving this ferme tonight! Not that I could develop a taste for this slim creature – she is sixteen to seventeen years old, very slim with wonderful eyes and a devastating coquettishness – but it is unsettling! Imagine it: she is the first female whom we womanless gypsies have met in over three months, and she comes in a delightful package. If one had this girl, one would keep looking her over – brown, grey, green, just like you! and kiss the thin, meagre shoulders. But we just threw snowballs at each other - are you jealous, Karl? I will write a short novel[10] about this small girl from the marshes – she fits so wonderfully into this beautiful, that is, eerie, swamp landscape.

25 June 1915 (Hardecourt)
Dearest Karl

You may congratulate me! I wrote to you this morning that I was sitting outside my dug-out under a cape in the rain writing my letter – at midday a shell fell on the very spot, devastated the front wall and there, where my verandah – that is what I called it – used to be, is a ravaged hole, my strips of cape fluttering in the treetops. I was inside the dug-out on my field bed at the time having some really unchaste thoughts when the beastly thing hit and hurled me against the wall. What a mess it made of my little booth! Most of all I am sorry that the glass in the frame of the photograph in which you look so sparkling is broken. Therefore I congratulate you from my heart, my Karl, especially because a quarter of an hour before I was sitting on the very spot shaving: I would have been torn into a thousand pieces. Why am I so cruel as to tell you that in a letter?

Karl, I really believe it smells like peace. Man, dear God! What I would not give to be walking with you in October in a sunlit wood (. . .)

30–31 August 1915 (Hardecourt)
(. . .) The British are a gang of criminal swine, every day a wounded man (with the diabolical hollow-casing bullets: aluminium nose and jacket, lead centre. Because of the empty space between the nose and the centre, when it hits the thin jacket breaks down and the lead nucleus splays causing bestial injuries) and now – we are back in Hardecourt, my angel – they have shoved us into the village: these are villages which the French want spared, so few of them are left standing they are rarer than salami. So one is constantly on the move, with one leg in the cellar so to speak. (. . .) Otherwise, it is autumn, is it not? Karl, if we – the Germans I mean – want peace, we could have it at once if we accept what is said in Grey's[11] open letter to the Reich Chancellor – see especially the concluding point! – but the bigwigs are simply big-heads and megalomanic and have not earned enough yet, and until they do the patient, sheep-headed man in field-grey remains in field-grey and a hero. Karl, there is nothing more disgusting than these times! Karl, so what – the Inselverlag is publishing Hindenburg? What do we have to hope for? Goodnight my love,

Karl.

Paul Kessler (1883–1978) Field-Post Secretary, Garde-Inf.Div.2

In Civilian Life, Post-Office Manager at Lahn: BfZ N98.1

Letter to his wife Elise Kessler at Lahn.

26 November 1914 (Lille)
I have been back with my Bavarian friends for the last two days. I get on very well with them. I am the only Reichspost official to

be accepted into their closer circle: of the others, none of the Prussians has yet got to see the quarters of a Bavarian colleague. I am supposed to be going to 2.Army, to which I have been transferred, but have preferred to report sick here on account of my leg: perhaps I can remain. I am still walking with a stick. *Un officier blessé* I hear them say occasionally with gentle regret. In my quarters I have had dizzy spells again. I am living in the house of a doctor who is in the field and whose wife is away. There is only an aged housekeeper and she has been in this house thirty-two years. She told me tearfully that she herself has two sons serving and has heard nothing from them for six months because no correspondence can get through of course. At the moment I am sitting in the doctor's study as I write to my Datz. In here I also do my French studies from the Backpack Dictionary[12] which a colleague lent me. Here are some extracts from the text:

'Arranging Quarters: "Are you the owner of this house? I wish to billet myself here, my valet and I. Show me at once to my room. What, this dirty hole, I shall search out another for myself. Open all doors immediately. (Sketch of a pistol). Ah, yes, I shall have this one. First of all dry my things: I shall now sleep for two hours. Avoid making any noise during this period. Afterwards knock on my door and I shall have something to eat. I am holding you responsible for everything. If you start anything I shall have you shot."'

The book is published by Oberleutnant Weltzien, War Academy, Berlin! Cheers, thank God not to be on the other side. I have never used this tone and can only add that that has served me well so far. People have more trust in you and are much more forthcoming. One can be friendly yet remain on one's guard (. . .).

Wilhelm Münz (1895 – 2 July 1916)
Gefreiter, later Unteroffizier, Rsve-Inf-Regt 119/Rsve-
Div.26.

In Civilian Life Candidate for Rectorship at Schornbach (BfZ
N.Knoch: Pressel)

Letters to Pastor Pressel of Schornbach

Highly esteemed Pastor!

If the seriousness of the situation were not obvious to me
by the roar of exploding shells and infantry bullets constantly whistling past I might think myself on a geological trip
to the caverns of some limestone mountain. I have already spent
the first four days cowering two metres below ground testing the
flexibility of my joints. We are therefore more mole than human,
for only at night may we leave our underground habitation and
stretch our legs to our heart's content. That is also when we
receive our mail.

It is very moving how people in all parts of the homeland send
us things. Please accept my warmest thanks for your parcel with
its welcome contents, also for the leaflet of 22 November which
I received at Jules before leaving!

Finally I have achieved my dearest wish, to be in the forwardmost front line! We are about seven kilometres from Albert to
the right of the great army road in a small valley basin between
Ovillers and La Boisselle, opposite the French trenches which are
on a low elevation about 700 metres away. Unfortunately until
further notice our activities are defensive: our infantry does not
fire. This means that the Frenchmen blithely show their
delightful faces in broad daylight while for us to do the same
invites a small sending of copper. Our main task is to calmly
repel the frequent night attacks of our opponents.

As we learned from Air-Signals the night before last, on the
next favourable night the enemy will attempt to break out.
When one is on lonely sentry duty by night and sees in the
distance the muzzle flashes of the enemy artillery, and almost at
once hears a dull thump close by, Psalm 91 is the only comfort.
Only by firm trust in God's help can one remain quietly at one's

post and hold one's nerve. And despite our sad sighs with regard
to the coming Christmas period, we seek comfort in our Fate
and do not present ourselves to the enemy in his land as soft
German men and boys. We shall celebrate Christmas patiently
far from home, where it will look nothing like it is here! Ovillers
is, for example, a place the size of Schornbach which has been
razed to the ground. We must defeat the enemy! Meanwhile I
wish all your intimate family circle a happy Christmas and send
to you, and your esteemed lady Pastor and dear children my
warmest thanks.

10 February 1915 (Ovillers)

Your military package was ten weeks in transit, but arrived
safely! It was quite reasonable that the post would not send
through all the large packets at once, and in any case over
Christmas the enemy artillery ruined our appetites. With more
satisfied faces than at Christmas, my ten 'sleeping comrades'
tucked into the cakes and pastries. I shared it out amongst them,
for in view of the current cereals regulations I would have been
unworthy to be called German if I had eaten all the Christmas
confectionery myself. Instead of one, eleven German warriors
were thinking of you on a 'tea visit' with thanks in their hearts.
Please accept also my warmest thanks for the nice lines.

As I learned from my parents, it seems that my brother
published true life accounts from the infantry returning from the
trenches in the Argonnes Forest. Until then I had compelled him
to keep silent about it. It is in fact true: we look terrible, and the
health of many has held out far longer than they expected. For
two reasons I thought it best to remain silent: for one thing,
these experiences are best recounted later with some humour,
and for the other to avoid causing unnecessary distress to the
people at home.

For the French opposite us things are apparently different.
A section of the French trench had collapsed after a day of
torrential rainfall at a point at least 1,000 metres from us. Any
Frenchman who wanted to pass through this point had to leave
the trench and run for his life, since we would take this opportunity to display our prowess with the rifle. One of our sentries
said that he fired at a Frenchman who jumped back into the

trench, making a great splash on all sides. When one thinks that a trench is between two and three metres deep, and this one was at least a kilometre away, one can imagine how much water it held. Whatever the case, the sentry had eagle-eyes. It is nothing like so bad with us, and if anybody complains we say, 'Do you know how high the plume of water over there rose when that Frenchman jumped in?'

One does not fear the wet, soft earth. I often have a private chuckle when I remember my first day in the trenches. I moved here and there very cautiously, avoiding every puddle and carefully removing immediately every tiny piece of mud from my uniform. Yet now when I see myself covered from head to toe with earth and filth I am content and happy, for it is better 'camouflage' than our field-grey. The main thing is that after ten days in the trench we do at least have the opportunity to wash thoroughly. This 'bath' always comes as a visible relief! From the civilian point of view we need to wash ten times a day, for we are currently miners: at the word of command excavating bombproof shelters.

Such a shelter is built in the following way. First of all come fairly stout planks for the shoring-up, above them are arranged tree trunks for the roof, then three to four metres of natural earth and finally an earth/straw mixture. The shelters are a maximum of one metre wide to reduce the danger from direct hits. This is necessary as apparently the enemy artillery will attempt to achieve what the French artillery failed to do on 17 December. Thus the French opposite are preparing another attack. They have brought up their *Turkos* (colonial troops from North Africa) who are supposed to overwhelm us in the night attack. (In the mist yesterday we captured a French patrol which made this statement.) In the present cold spell these colonial troops may not have the desired inclination to go all out for us, but should they come, with God's help, we shall warm them up a bit!

Perhaps you will be interested to know more about La Boiselle, which is 200 metres to our left, and often features as a 'hot spot' in the French daily reports. La Boiselle lies on a low ridge well forward towards the French trenches. When they held it, it was of strategic interest for the French because they could bring to bear on us 119ers persistent fire to the flank. Since we captured it we are now spared this evil, while our artillery can fire down pretty accurately on the Bapaume-Albert military road, which we now have under observation from the elevation.

When I arrived, the French still had half of La Boisselle, but they were pushed back to the south-west exit by a night attack of the 120ers. Despite tremendous opposition from artillery, our people captured it. Our artillery now concentrated heavily on this edge of the village forcing the French to pull out temporarily. No sooner had our boys moved in than the enemy artillery forced them out again, and the fighting raged back and forth in the so-called 'shell yard' of La Boisselle. (In one assault, amongst others Pioneer-Lt. Constantin Eberhard von Schorndorf, a former classmate of mine, fell on 27 December.)

Soon afterwards the French were once more in possession. About two and a half weeks ago 3.Battalion/119 made a night attack at about 2300. It was stealthy and succeeded. Eighty French were captured and about the same number killed. Bavarian fortifications engineers now undermined the place while the infantry held the trench until 0700 next morning. Then we evacuated it for the French to reoccupy, not without losses. We let them settle in nicely until 1300, and on the dot there was the huge explosion we expected and the 'shell yard' blew up. That put an end to the toing and froing. Apparently the town cemetery is going to be next.

Whenever we were in occupation of the town, the French fell back on the cemetery. Our artillery would then force them out. I found out today that it is deserted, although both parties continue to shell it. While the opposing sides at La B. used to be only thirty to fifty metres apart and maintained constant attacks, the French have now been driven back to their own line. The 120ers had at first the task, as we did, of merely holding the trench at all costs. This was more difficult for them because they were attacked more frequently. Our best wire entanglements are the dead Frenchmen lying about 100 metres from our trench since 17 December. Even the British apparently prefer not to attack over the corpses of their dead allies, therefore the 'Turkos' will have to. Well, we are ready for them. The best thing is that the General Staff can nearly always give us warning of an enemy attack beforehand. It is a mystery to me how they always know.

Accordingly, it seems the French will launch a frontal attack on 15 February. That day the church bells will ring throughout all France and a general fast will be observed to make their victory more certain. Well, we hope they come! Our enemies cannot do better than attack. Enemy losses under normal circumstances are a maximum of 1:5. On 17 December it worked out at about 1:30. When one thinks that we have been working since 28 September on defensive measures, one can imagine what is going to be required to take a trench. Probably only artillery firing endless direct hits could eventually so reduce our numbers as to force us to evacuate. But that is scarcely conceivable, for we are fighting for Justice and Freedom and a Higher Power guides the enemy shells, guides them to a safe place where they do us no harm. The French artillery for example fires daily at least 100 shells into a small valley between Ovillers and Pozières. Probably they think some of our artillery is there. However, it has only a dummy battery and we take great delight in seeing the enemy's shells and shrapnel hitting that valley every day.

We hope therefore on 15th, with God's help, to send the enemy packing with a bloody nose and bring our dearest in the homeland one step closer to an honourable peace! Again, with heartiest thanks, may you and your lady wife and dear children accept the greetings from enemy territory of your grateful

W Münz.

29 April 1915 (Bapaume)

(. . .) I will honour the memory of my dear father by always trying to be like him. Above all he is a shining example to me by his loyal performance of duty!

On the night of 7/8 May we will probably transfer to another trench, probably at Beaumont, two regiments' breadth to the right of Ovillers. There we will function as 2.Army Reserve, previously we were corps reserve. Therefore we shall eventually have the chance in Flanders to pay the British a visit. We take pleasure in relieving our comrades out there. We have had a long time here to settle our nerves and compose ourselves inwardly. Amongst other things we have recently formed a choir so that, on the evening before we leave, we can perform melodies from the homeland in front of the Commanding-General's and our regimental commander's quarters. For next Sunday we have arranged a welfare church concert for the families of the fallen of Res.Regt 119: organ, songs and violins! We also had a well-stocked library here. So now something can be expected of us. And you may be sure that each of us will do his duty! With God we shall go forth again! (. . .)

Letter to Eleven-Year-old Trudel Pressel at Schornbach

12 September 1915 Trenches (Beaumont)
Dear Trudel!

I was enormously pleased that you should think of me in the trenches on your birthday. I wish you everything good retrospectively for your birthday. May you be healthy with your dear parents and brothers and sisters! When a big bucket of black coffee was placed on the table, we opened the biscuits from your parcel. Thank you ever so much, and especially for your lovely letter!

I would like to make you a present of it, but right now I do not even have a tiny photo of the trench to send you. Nor can I fulfil your wish, of which your dear Papa told me, to get you some Belgian stamps, therefore you will have to make do with my description of our trench in place of a birthday present.

First of all of course you wanted to know how far our trench is from the French trenches or rather, as they are now, the British trenches. Just imagine us taking a walk along the high street in Schornbach to the oil mill. The street would be our trench, and the 'old stream' running parallel would be the British one. My position would be where the road forks towards Mannshaupten, therefore I am on the right edge of the street and the British on the 'oil mill stream' over there below the bridge. See how near they are! It would be very easy for them to come over during the night, but between the two lines of trenches the British and Germans have huge wire obstructions (two sketches follow). They are simple wire and iron frames strung with barbed wire. You have to imagine these filling all the space between the trenches except for fifteen to twenty metres in the centre. Now you can see why simply coming across to us is not so easy, for with every step the wire twangs, and the sentries who hear it shoot at once, while flares are fired which light the terrain bright as day. In Stuttgart that happens now and again when they fire rockets. Our flares are quite similar. You will have seen pictures of what a trench looks like. (Soon I will send you a few of ours.)

You should not imagine that we are always in the trench at ground level. No, those not on sentry duty, i.e. not watching the British trench, stay in the underground room protected against shells and bullets. Steep steps lead down from the trench into the dug-outs. Just like the steps in your home from the glass doors down to the cellar, only our steps are steeper and so low that one has to go bent double. My dug-out is about as big as your verandah and five metres down. In the centre, like in a small garden outhouse, is a table with wooden trestles. We have fixed pictures on the panelled walls. Down there we sit and read and write by the light of a candle hung above the table by a wire. It is a shame that you cannot pay us a flying visit to see inside for yourself. How about if I called across to the British: 'Stop your shooting for a while, Trudel from Schornbach wants to look round our trench today!' But you know, if I did shout that across, they would send lots and lots of shells over during your visit, and so it is probably best if I stay here until we have taught the British better manners. Once we make them into better people, the bells of peace will peal out and then, dear Trudel, perhaps I will return to Schornbach if God protects me against the enemy's bullets. With the wish that that day will soon come and we meet again, I send you my warmest greetings.

Your Wilhelm.

30 September 1915 Trenches (Beaumont)
Dear Pastor!

For the September issue of the community letter and the two latest editions of *Durch Kampf zum Sieg* my warmest thanks!

Events here at the moment find us naturally on the back foot at the hot spot of the new Anglo-French offensive. We were ready to receive an attack, for three days we (i.e. our whole Division) was under bombardment by British heavy and light artillery. Apparently it was only to deceive us locally, for two days later the whole Western Front came to life, not just here. Noteworthy that we were told of the new offensive the previous evening: 'An enemy patrol captured near Arras stated that tonight the British and French will attack the front at five places!' We already knew that the evening before! At 0400 it started about eight kilometres to our right near Roclincourt. We had been at maximum alert since three, our artillery and mortars too.

At the shout of 'Hurrah!' from one of the sentries ahead of the trench we would have stood and hurled our hand grenades: at the firing of a red flare our shells and landmines would have torn great gaps in the lines of the advancing British! It is always a wonderful feeling when we sit together in a refuge awaiting an enemy attack! But as the new offensive has already shown, our enemies have finally recognized that it is almost impossible to take a German trench without artillery preparation beforehand. Therefore as per our new Order of the Day: seventy hours' constant artillery bombardment before! That is something awful! If two of our divisions evacuated their trenches and pulled back to a line two kilometres rearwards, it would be completely understandable. In such a case the enemy would not have taken 'trenches' but only 'a cemetery of comrades dead and buried alive.' The artillery is decisive. The attacker's artillery has a superiority in guns. Yet the great autumn offensive of our Western opponent has already collapsed, although we must remain on alert for further attempts. To God alone the glory!

27 December 1915 (Beaumont/Somme)
Dear Pastor!

Many thanks for your Christmas greeting which I enjoyed! Now Christmas 1915 is over. Here it was all quiet. The mood in our dug-out, with the Christmas tree at the centre all lit up, was solemn and for me again a really unforgettable experience (. . .)

Already I have known much pain and disappointment during this war! When, together with my brother Hans, I volunteered in August 1914, my sense of duty and feelings for the Fatherland were accompanied by the wish to have the war change my character inwardly. I imagined it so well: with a loud Hurrah! attacking alongside one's comrades in a rain of fire – coming through safely with God's help – an experience in life like that one would never forget! Instead I have been thirteen months in the trenches, and more or less always in the same place. I have experienced much, and it has probably made a great impression on me, but through the frequent repetition I feel rather 'blunted' within myself (. . .)

Anyway, the evening after next we are off for ten days to Mir . . . (Miraumont). We hope it will be ten days' rest. The endless wading through the mud, and shovelling the mud, can be a bit tiring. Additionally my platoon has continual British shelling to put up with. Only single rounds, but the shooting gets you worst when you are digging.

We provided the motive for it ourselves. On 19th our Pios (Pioniers) had to blow up one of our long mine galleries as the British were again mining through to our trench. Blowing up the twenty-one metre deep gallery, which reached right up to the British trenches, had a colossal effect! It created a new valley! One should be sorry for the people who were in the stretch. One can imagine nothing worse than such an explosion: the ground suddenly folds beneath one – one has time to reflect – and then everything goes up in bits and pieces and comes down in bits and pieces to be covered over with earth immediately. Lucky the men who die at once! That would not happen in a mobile war. How happy we would be to take our place in a German offensive and risk our lives in an attack. Perhaps we shall have the chance soon! And then we may hope that with an energetically executed penetration of the Anglo-French front we bring the hotly desired peace a step closer. The important thing is that we can shout:

'The land is free and the morning breaks
Even if we had to win it by dying!' (. . .)

Walther Vogt (1888–1941) Feldunterarzt, Inf.Div.35.

In Civilian Life a Doctor at Marburg/Lahn

Letter to His Parents at Marburg/Lahn

27 October 1915 (Serancourt)

We moved into Serancourt yesterday, a charming little Somme town. Our quarters are the best we have ever had or seen anywhere. In the large archaic private house of the director of a large sugar factory (also mairie) (Fn 14) is our officers' mess and in his bureau the local *kommandantur*. Our Rittmeister rules here like a small king over a Reich numbering 1,000–1,500 inhabitants.

There is fabulous order and discipline in all institutions. Absolutely everything is under carefully organized military control. Supplies of wheat, oats, hay, straw, coal, wood, fruit, vegetables, factories, machines, mills, the entire Somme-Canal with its installations, everything is under military administration.

The supplies having been registered, each inhabitant received his winter apportionment for the prescribed period and the huge harvested excess was then impounded. This is now administered not only by the local *kommandant* but a large Economic Committee formed of corps officers working together with AOK. Any kind of requisitioning is absolutely forbidden. Poultry, cattle, horses, the numerous magnificent large white oxen, all in the hands of the inhabitants, are registered precisely, all products such as eggs, milk, vegetables, fruit are bought from the inhabitants by the Committee except for that allowed for regular domestic consumption.

Bread cereals for the civilian population are delivered by a Spanish-Dutch company to specified mills and this is for the exclusive use of the inhabitants, not even we officers can buy white bread from the baker. It is a very complicated and often fastidious organization down to the smallest detail. Of astonishing thoroughness and purpose. For us wild warriors from the east, at first surprising and often amusing, and even more often uncomfortable, but very important as a food source for homeland and Army.

Only in an extremely strict and economically-administered occupied territory is it possible to work out such high farming benefits without harming the population. The entire farming economy, including cultivation, seeding and threshing the harvest, is done by soldiers or inhabitants under military supervision. Oxen and horses belong to the inhabitants, but work for everybody. The corps bridge-trains now serve as a wholesale goods business, the two lieutenants have their own business centres.

I am the doctor for the locality engaged at the moment in setting up a surgery. I share lodgings with a Lt Claussen, a nice well-educated magistrate from Hamburg, whom I have known well for some time. We live in the lovely villa of a person of independent means, we each have a bedroom with an incomparable, enormous French bed and share a living room, which serves as a dining room, very tastefully furnished with heavy oak furniture, marble fireplace with small iron grate, colourful old-French plates adorning the walls, electric light, in short all very comfortable. A good piano in the lounge. I think we would like to hold out here until the war's end, we have seen enough of the war itself. Please send me music sheets, Brahm's Requiem, Rhapsodies, ballads, piano pieces (. . .)

Notes:
1   Bibliothek für Zeitgeschichte, Württemberg (BfZ) No 6.1.
2   Ludwig Berg: *Pro Fide et Patria* (War Diaries 1914–1918) publ. Frank Frank Betke and Almust Kreile, Cologne 1998.
3   Gustav Sack: *Prosa, Briefe, Verse*, Munich 1962.
4   Cafe Moellon.
5   Freuderhaus.
6   Friedrich Nietzsche.
7   Hermann Löns.
8   Drama by Sack.
9   Prose by Sack.
10 This eventually received the title 'Eva'.
11 Edward Grey, British Foreign Minister.
12 Tornister Wörterbuch: German-French backpack dictionary with imitated pronunciation, new version by Viktor E Weltzien, Oberlt, 26 Inf.Regt., attached to War Academy, Berlin Schöneberg: several reprints by Mentor Verlag.

Chapter Two

The German Occupation
of Northern France

This volume covers not only the fighting on the Somme from 1914 to 1918, but also the German relationship with the population in the occupied territory. Whilst adhering to the usual understanding of the terms 'front' and '*Etappe*' (the military region behind the front) there are some difficulties in differentiating between the two. According to the terminology of the time, the 'front' or 'area of operations' was distinguished from *Etappe* in that the latter embraced the whole territory between the fighting front and the German border. The establishment of a rather civilian-type *Generalgouvernement* as installed in occupied Belgium was not planned for northern France, not least because the 'Germanization' ideology was less appropriate there than in the Flemish part of Belgium. Occupied northern France therefore remained a war zone although the borderlines between 'front' and *Etappe* could change daily.

The operational area was the region immediately along the north-south line of the front, while the *Etappe* stretched to the Belgian border. The towns and villages in this region were classified as *Etappenhauptorte* and *Etappenorte*. The region was run by a so-called *Etappeninspektion* or inspectorate which controlled the *Kommandantur* of each sub-region. The administrative chief for *Gouvernement Lille* was the *Etappenkommandant* of Lille, from 18 October 1914, Generalmajor Karl von Graevenitz. The *Kommandantur* supervised the city administration and was responsible for coordinating the difficult relationship with the civilian population in the entire *Etappe*.

The relationship between an occupying power and the population was regulated fundamentally by the Hague Convention of 1907. This laid down that the occupying army had to allow the reinstatement of public order and public life under local civil law, provided there was no major obstruction to doing so. Self-evidently, plundering by soldiers was forbidden. The army of occupation could require services and supplies from the population for its upkeep, but these always had to be paid for. The civil rights of the occupied people and their honour – a rather vague though frequently used expression – were not to be violated and private property was to be respected. Nevertheless the occupying Power could seize all funds and private property of an enemy *State* insofar as this State could use it to finance or prosecute the war. The occupying Power was in no way the owner, but only the tenant, of public buildings and State lands and properties thereon.

The main problem, a defect of logic in the Hague Convention, was its failure to appreciate that an occupied territory is controlled and administered by the occupying Power as a sovereign Power while the population remains legally bound to the original Power. In effect this meant that in northern France, for example, the German military could not force the population to engage in 'hostile actions' against the French, therefore their own forces, and the allies of France. But what were 'hostile actions'? On the whole, as the war became 'total', activities relevant to the war spread into nearly all areas of life and industry. The concept of what was important for the war effort was therefore as comprehensive as discretionary, and developed constantly into areas of dispute between the occupying authority and the representatives of the French State. The mayors as elected representatives of the populace and conversation partners of the occupying authority stood increasingly in the crossfire of criticism of the two sides.

Civilians in Northern France – Two Diaries

Professor Annette Becker, Historian,
University of Paris X-Nanterre

The following diary entries[1] compiled by two inhabitants of occupied northern France illustrate clearly the problems and difficulties which the occupation caused 'locally' and the reactions in the *Etappen* areas to the fighting on the Somme often 'so close you could hear it.' Diarist David Hirsch, an elderly Jewish businessman from Roubaix, and Maria Degrutère, a Catholic schoolmistress from Lille, are very representative of those sections of the population forced to remain in the zone of German occupation, sections constituted exclusively by men too old for mobilization, women and children. The diary entries are composed of experiences of daily life at war and under occupation: of fear and expectation of hostility, and not least the rumours and propaganda circulated by both sides.

The inhabitants of areas under military occupation were in a unique situation. They felt that they were at the front, but cut off from the French nation at war. Their experiences under German occupation were extraordinary because to some extent they were living two wars at the same time: the war known to most French civilians on the German side of the battle line, and another war within a war zone surrounded by death and destruction, marked by psychic burdens and material shortages. Additionally the French living in the *Etappe* were the target of a very heavy propaganda offensive, where civilians formed the captive readership of newsprint published by the occupying authority, and only rarely had access to French newspapers. Information was therefore mixed with rumour and wishful thinking.

The main goal of Allied propaganda was to portray the Germans in occupied territories as those 'Huns' who had left a bloody trail through Belgium and northern France in 1914, emphasis being placed on the 'wilful destruction' of the Library at Liége and Rheims Cathedral. The Germans for their part went to great lengths to prove in proclamations and publicity of all kinds that they had always acted within the Hague Convention and done nothing other than suppress illegal revolutionaries acting contrary to the rule of war, the so-called *franctireurs*, or armed citizenry. Moreover – and this was especially important for the region of the Somme fighting – they pointed to their efforts to protect French cultural treasures against British and French shelling.

Mentioned and agonized over again and again in the diaries is the matter of the deportations – described by the Germans as 'displacements' and 'transplants', euphemisms to minimize the nature of the activity – of men, women and children from Lille at Easter 1916. This was a traumatic event accompanied by much protest and well documented at the time. Decades later it had not been erased from the memory and led to strong polemic against the 'Huns.' In the occupied territories, the events at Lille were mixed in people's memories with the brutal deportations of Belgian workers by the German occupiers in the autumn of 1916, which led to an outcry even from the public in neutral States. The documents, some published during the war, respecting the events of Easter 1916 show that in this action the occupiers had made a major advance towards total war.

The Germans viewed the deportations as a necessity of war which were accordingly allowed under international law: the 'displaced civilians' were only moved out of Lille and its environs to improve the grave food situation in the villages caused by the British naval blockade, and so avoid the unrest that was to be expected as a consequence. The French were convinced that their own war aim was exclusively to protect home territory and beat off an attack considered grossly unjust. Whether soldier or civilian in a war forced on France, the people wanted to prove themselves worthy. The slogan valid from August 1914 to November 1918 remained: 'We suffer, but we suffer for France.'

Maria Degrutère, Lille Schoolmistress
DIARY

11 October 1914, Sunday
I attended mass at six and returned, all quiet. I attended mass again at seven. At the gospel there was panic when announced that the Germans were coming. A mass evacuation following. At about 9.15 the firing began and lasted until midday. I spent the morning in the cellar, the afternoon was almost quiet, one could hear the guns in the outlying districts. At eight in the evening I went up to the flat to rest, at nine-thirty the firing started again, louder. Raced down to the cellar, the children fast asleep in their cots. Sat up all night. About six the firing stopped for a few hours. It was a terrible night.

12 October 1914
Infantry fighting in the environs, near the East Cemetery and the fortified ring. At six (evening) ran out for milk and bread. Firing began again at eight with greater intensity, lasted until two on Tuesday morning. Spent day and night in the cellar, did not even leave for the bathroom or meals.

13 October 1914
Lille surrendered Monday night at five-thirty. The Germans marched in to music through the burning houses. About 4,000 shells had been fired into the city. Surrounding Lille were 40,000 Germans and 120 guns, against 2,000 French with three or four guns. The most important quarter of the city was in flames, about 1,200 houses affected. Damage estimated at two billion francs. Occasional artillery fire. Spent part of the day in the cellar, part on the ground floor, and the night half in the cellar and half in bed. Many German regiments were moving up and down in the Madeleine district returning from the parade in Lille. Four hundred French and Algerians captured in Lille were marched through city.

14 October 1914
Life almost normal, night in bed, noise of guns in environs.

Houses blown up with dynamite to prevent the fire spreading because the Germans have shut off the water.

15 October 1914
Grandparents left, repaired broken windows. Had a look at the ruins of Lille. At night numerous convoys came through.

16 October 1914
The Germans are in la Madeleine. Clocks put to German time. No vehicles allowed on the streets after eight in the morning.

19 October 1914
Through the night and in the morning German cavalry and infantry marched past, music and singing. They took over the whole street including the pavements. Went to Marcq to give classes. I was all by myself, alone amongst them. A really peculiar feeling. A British aircraft flew past overhead. After dinner we saw an aerial fight between two aircraft. There is no more butter or lard, and no meat. The butchers are selling cuts of goose.

20 October 1914
La Madeleine occupied. Soldiers and horses billeted with townspeople. There is no electricity. Weapons handed in at the City Hall by the inhabitants of Madeleine were taken away, the Germans loaded them on a four-wheeled cart. By night there was excitement in the Rue du Chaufour, in Fives, in the Rue du Jardin de l'Arc. They even went so far as to break the Persian blinds to get into the houses.

21 October 1914
Sightseeing the ruins of Lille. Sound of artillery very close all day. Fight between one British and four German aircraft. Much machine-gun fire. Three Germans rang doorbell and asked for accommodation.

28 October 1914
Arrival more troops: 3,500 men are coming to La Madeleine. Empty houses are being broken up by troops. Soldiers buy wine

and biscuits with local currency. A German strutted in Jeanne's laundry room.

31 October 1914
Noise of artillery nearer. A new poster announced that we are under German administration, describes various ordinances. One hundred and thirty British prisoners and many German wounded came through. Cars and motorcycles requisitioned. Kaiser Wilhelm stayed in Lille and was driven through La Madeleine.

29 November 1914
The family was together with the Germans. They ate all day but were very nice. Always the same artillery fire, fearful. The Germans left the house at seven in the evening. Those with M. Vermaere gave Suzan chocolate. Fire broke out in the Faidherbe secondary school.

24 December 1914
A really sad Christmas dinner. Instead of mussels we had a piece of fatty horse flesh but were happy enough to have something. The Germans celebrated Christmas in every way possible. A Christmas tree in every place they are billeted, in the churches celebrate mass, have banquets, etc.

17–18 January 1915
Nothing new, complete quiet everywhere. On 8 January the Germans shot M.Damons of St André for lending soldiers civilian clothing. He protested his innocence. The war for one's daily bread goes on.

3 September 1915
The Germans have ordered a census of Lille and La Madeleine. One has to write on a strip of paper stuck to the floor the name and age of all family members. It is very annoying because Jeanne now has to go home to sleep. The Germans have just requisitioned copper and wine from Mme.F. They took almost 4,000 bottles leaving only 250 and did not provide a requisition docket.

8 September 1915
The Germans have forbidden the sale of potatoes. There is none to be found anywhere, and therefore unrest in the market. Fortunately every fourteen days we receive rice, beans, maize, lard and every week beef or salted bacon from the American Committee. Were it not for that we would starve to death because the bread ration is inadequate and butter, like meat, cannot be bought.

4 November 1915
Because the Germans like the piano, and I want to avoid having them in my living room, I have taken the piano out and put it in the tiny study. They seem happy with that (. . .)

8 November 1915
In Lille the Germans shot a sixteen-year-old, Léon Trulin, who lived in the Rue Jeanne Mailotte in La Madeleine. He was a member of a spy ring. Other young people, including Gonti's son, were sentenced to forced labour. It appears they took photographs of the trenches. M. Brackers d'Hugo has also been sentenced for concealing weapons. Between 7 and 12 November we heard a dreadful cannonade. Rifle fire very near, which kept us awake all night. It happens from time to time, then there are quiet moments again.

March 1916
Life is getting slowly more intolerable. There is no more butter, eggs or milk, no meat and not even potatoes. We have bread but very poor quality. The shops are empty. Horseflesh costs ten francs a kilo and old cheese eight francs. No more vegetables, no shoes, no cloth (. . .). Our staple is rice and it is very difficult to feed the children. After the Germans requisitioned all the cows, sheep, pigs and poultry, now they want the rabbits. There is no fuel, a candle costs from fifty centimes to one franc.

2 March 1916
All dog-owners have to register their animals and pay a tax of forty marks. Our town looks like a ruin after they took away the lamps. The inhabitants are forbidden to have a light indoors,

luckily we have thick curtains to prevent a light showing outside. This is all very sad.

14 March 1916

Food is more scarce and dearer (. . .) The Germans have closed all shops and impose a fine of 200 or 300 marks on anyone who sells more than the maximum set by the *kommandant*. Higher prices yet are feasible. As the Belgian frontier is sealed down tight one finds nothing more in the stores which remain open. There is only dry bread, rice and a little horseflesh. That is especially bad for the children and invalids, and of these at the moment we have plenty.

19 March 1916

The Germans are imposing a dog tax of ten, twenty or thirty marks. A certain number of unpatriotic people are paying up, but many kill even the valuable dogs. The mayor of Lille put down his three dogs worth 4,000 francs. They are also killing police dogs and St Bernards, these are really major sacrifices.

20 March 1916

The Café Hèquette has been evacuated by its owners to become a German clothing store for their troops in transit (. . .) The Germans have started impounding chicory. They came down our street and looked over the houses with an outhouse, they want the boarding. They requisitioned the Brabant and Brunswick parks for their poultry. They searched all cellars and, in the house opposite, found twelve bottles which an invalid had been hiding.

22 March 1916

For some weeks now we have heard hardly any shelling.

30 March 1916

First distribution of fresh meat by the American Committee. The prices are still very high but we are glad of it nevertheless. There is 200 grams per person but that will not go round, unfortunately not even for us. Luckily Martha is a cashier at one of the three butchers and with help of a cart we also got meat, which pleased us very much. Salted and pickled herrings were also distributed, one per person. There is a huge number of people to be attended to, and one can queue all day.

April 1916
We had to queue the whole day for the little that is on sale and being distributed by the Committee. Everybody needs bread, milk (. . .) They are even confiscating the grass in the luxury gardens on the squares, from hedgerows etc.

10 April 1916
(. . .) Went to Roubaix. Saw 1,800 French civilians arrested on the street and brought at bayonet point to the railway station. Family members followed the group crying. Very sad to see. A number of men were also captured.

18 April 1916
Men and women are being taken away from Lille because they cannot be trusted to go independently. Bishop Charost and M. Delesalle (Mayor of Lille) have written letters of protest to the *Gouverneur*. Food cannot be bought. Sugar and horsemeat is no longer available.

23 April 1916 Easter
What a sad Easter. Food ever scarcer, for dinner rice and bread as we cannot find anything else. The weather does not help, incessant rain and the cellars beginning to flood. At night the Germans woke up everybody in the district to collect the census slips. Not satisfied with that, meanwhile they sent whole families, who wanted nothing else than to be at home, to other occupied regions. They did that at Roubaix, Tourcoing, Lille. It began at Fives. Everybody had to be ready. They were given ninety minutes to pack thirty-five kilos including kitchenware. To prevent any uproar machine guns were placed in the streets, before the departure they were fired into the church and school. Everywhere great excitement and panic. In every respect life is getting ever less pleasurable. The deportations from Lille lasted a week, every day German soldiers (twenty per house) arrived at three in the morning in one or other district with bayonets fixed,

forced everybody to get up and took away the men and especially women and girls aged twenty to thirty-five, and nobody knows to where. The scenes are indescribable, hours of anxiety and panic for the mothers whose children have been wrenched away from them. Several people fainted and collapsed, others were sent mad, some attempted to argue in perplexity with the officers. Several of our friends went through this horror. It makes us sick to think of such a thing happening in our district La Madeleine. It is a sight to tear at your heart-strings. We are being led like criminals to the scaffold. On Easter Sunday we could not attend mass because the church was occupied by troops.

1 May 1916
The Germans have put the clock forward one hour. Terrible confusion because nobody has experience of this. Everybody must be indoors by seven, the patrols start five minutes earlier. Everybody has to rush to get indoors.

3 May 1916
Proclamation orders that the hangars (American aid depots) must declare their entire inventories to the Germans. New panic because many people believe the Germans intend to confiscate gold, silver and valuable documents of interest.

16 May 1916
Another proclamation ordering a second requisitioning of wine.

18 May 1916
A poster ordered all poultry-owners to declare their flock. It does not look like they will be confiscated, but the Germans want the eggs, and if they do not get enough we will have to buy-in eggs to make up the shortfall.

29 May 1916
The Germans ransacked our house for metal objects, and especially copper. They impounded the kitchenwares, the copper corners of the porch frame, ceiling lamps, coppered umbrella stand, furniture, scales, pots, weights, etc.

5 June 1916

Poultry-owners are duty-bound to supply the Germans with one egg per three hens daily. If that is not done the hens have to be surrendered or eggs bought-in to make up the deficiency, which is nearly impossible.

20 June 1916

The Germans are demanding a new war levy of 47 million francs for Lille, Tourcoing and district, of which 23 million must come from Lille, 1.6 million francs from the Madeleine quarter, etc. The Mayor of Lille wrote a wonderful letter to the German military *Gouverneur* protesting against this new injustice. As it happens we have no more money, but the Germans are forcing us to pay under threat of the heaviest reprisals against the entire population. So we sent two million of the six million demanded for 1 July.

27 June 1916

Shoes are only to be had for mad prices. They are on offer at fifty-eight francs the pair, therefore the Americans are sending us 30,000 pairs for women and children for a population of 660,000. These cost eleven to twenty-five francs a pair, four to eleven francs for children's shoes, but there are not enough to go round. It is a shame. Soon we will all be walking barefoot.

29 June 1916

A new poster is advertising for farm workers. Accommodation and sufficient food will be provided. The people of Lille are very wary for fear that it forebodes more forced evacuations, and many of those affected are very unhappy. We hear the guns now night and day, frighteningly loud.

1 July 1916

For some days a series of aircraft have been flying over. The Germans fire at them with large-calibre guns and a lot of these shells fall in the city and explode, causing very many incidents. Two shells hit St Sauveur's Church during evening prayers, killing a small girl. In the ensuing panic many children were trampled underfoot, forty-two injured. A lady was killed in her room in the Rue des Augustin and several houses were demolished. (. . .) Things are really very bad in our city. Today we are still alive, but one never knows what will happen from one half-hour to the next. That is worse than the occupation.

Another proclamation about the rabbit population: the penalty for killing a rabbit is 1,000 marks and three months jail. Meat is scarce and costs thirty marks a kilo. (. . .) No more food is coming from Holland, and therefore we have become vegetarians, but the price is insanely expensive. (. . .) The Germans have ordered the confiscation of all fruit in private possession (. . .)

21 July 1916
Aircraft fly over every day and are fired at. Very often the shells do not explode in the air, but cause casualties and material damage on the ground (. . .)

23 July 1916
Mme.Ruear has been given fifteen days in the citadel for receiving letters from her husband. The diet in her cell is 250 grams bread daily, water and a little rice. Poison gas came down in the St André district, therefore posters have appeared regarding precautions to be taken. Amongst other things one should hold a wet handkerchief to the face (one would think we are at the front). The Germans put their gas masks on (. . .)

14 August 1916
A poster has appeared regarding the appropriation of copper, bronze and brass from private households. Fresh outrage because these materials are of direct use to attack our armies. Therefore the towns of Roubaix, Tourcoing and Lille are proposing not to prepare lists. The deacon of the St Christophe diocese at Tourcoing has been sentenced to ten years'military imprisonment for recommending to clergy not to prepare lists. The Prefect and Mayor of Lille protested, always a new upset. Gradually we are being stripped of everything we own. There is no advantage living in an occupied country if one is to live like a pauper. Every day a new punishment, and we are deprived of all our freedoms and all necessities. Children cannot fly a kite

any more because it is seen as a signal. Somebody lit a match at night and was fined twelve and a half marks by a passing patrol because at night it is forbidden to carry any means to make a light (. . .).

16 August 1916
Anybody who has a bank box can only use it with permission of the Germans and accompanied by a German.

28–29 September 1916
A new poster has announced that a voluntary evacuation into unoccupied France may be allowed but only women who will be supported in France, children separated from their parents, and the sick, particularly TB sufferers, qualify. There are no details about travel costs and the means, but because life here is really oppressive many people have put down their names, at least 900 in the Madeleine district, 600 at Marcq etc.

2 October 1916
A poster has ordered the Mayor to remove from unoccupied houses all clothing and shoes of absentees. This is because there are none on sale and the sendings (of the American Committee) are insufficient. The *Kommandantur* has required the Madeleine district to supply 150 workers. As the community cannot do so, it has to pay a fine of 1,000 marks daily. When the fine was not paid on time the first day, hostages were taken. As an additional punishment the community has had its vegetable distribution stopped and the Germans are taking all mechanical farming equipment until the required workers are produced.

3 October 1916
Great confusion in the district over a new poster in which all female workers aged from eighteen to forty-five are ordered to be listed, together with men up to age fifty-two. Everybody is uneasy because it is assumed that work service plans are being made. Another poster has ordered all those who have not yet done so to make a list of linen, jute, rubber, copper, tin, zinc, oil, etc., cars, bicycles and motorcycles. In a word, everything

imaginable, and with a fine of 50,000 marks or ten years in prison for non-compliance. In this way the country will soon be sucked dry.

5 October 1916
A new poster orders the population to clean their frontages, and those of absent neighbours before 0800 each morning, this makes a total of five posters in three days. From about seven until ten in the evening twenty shells fell on Lille. We heard the report as they were fired and the whistle of the shells as if they were coming straight for us. It was peculiar, and one dares not sleep. When the shelling stopped we went to bed, but fully dressed in case it became necessary to flee (. . .).

16–17 October 1916
In Roubaix and Tourcoing all young men aged from seventeen to twenty-five have been held, in Lille a number of men, with orders to bring a blanket, clogs, clothing and food for two days. It is a truly sad sight to see the mothers and wives in tears accompanying their children or husbands, while others sing the *Marseillaise*.

27 October 1916
A house search at our place. Two Germans turned the house upside down, cellar, outhouse, all the furniture was examined, everything broken apart. They took a small copper jug away from the outhouse and a small disconnected gas meter. Mme.Cordonnier had to pay a fine of fifty marks for hiding copper objects. They rummaged in the coal bunker and latrine trench, really degrading.

1 November 1916
A number of industrial workers from Lille, Roubaix and Tourcoing have been taken to Germany as hostages because of the German-French hostilities. These people were informed at midday mass and led off at 1700. Some of the women are at least fifty-five (. . .). They are now checking identity cards at all Lille city gates.

27 November 1916
Visit by two military police about estimating the value of the copperware found in the outhouse. Mama has to go to the *Kommandantur* tomorrow at 1430 to pay a fine of five marks, we got off lightly, several of our neighbours had harsher punishment (. . .). Life is a pain whichever way you look at it. We cannot remember what meat tastes like, we live on vegetables, rice and American bacon. Fortunately every fourteen days we receive a kilo of potatoes per person for thirty pfennigs.

6 December 1916
Twenty per cent of the people who signed up in November can return to unoccupied France. Children under four go free, from four to ten, half fare. The journey costs sixty-nine francs in 2nd Class and forty-six francs in 3rd Class to Schaffhausen. Thirty kilos luggage is allowed per person (. . .). Everything has to be given to the Germans who seal it and return it at the border. One is not allowed to take money. It is even said that travellers were not allowed to carry hand luggage or food, we gave postcards with photographs of the family to friends to pass on but the Germans would not allow this. It made us very sad (. . .)

25 December 1916
A miserable Christmas.

David Hirsch, Businessman of Roubaix
DIARY

7 January 1916
Three days ago eggs were on sale in Lille. There is no more toilet paper, we use the official posters instead.

9 January 1916
General von Castelnau, returned from the Orient, forecasts victory with mathematical precision. No more gunfire.

11 January 1916
At 0330 on Tuesday there was the single dreadful noise of a hit,

an ammunition depot between Porte de Douai and the rear part of St Sauveur railway station blew up. The Germans say it was an accident, the people of Lille say it was hit by three British shells. The whole district behind the station looks terrible. There is talk of 400 to 500 dead, more than half of all windows in Lille have been shattered, even some in Roubaix (. . .). Enormous blocks of stone collapsed on the Place de la Republique.

12 January 1916
The German official communiqué speaks of a casemate which exploded south of Lille. Seventy civilians died and forty were injured in the explosion. The German communiqué states that the people of Lille blame the British for causing the explosion with their shelling. In Lille the *Kommandantur* has issued a poster offering 1,000 marks reward for the capture of those responsible for the disaster.

13 January 1916
As always, nobody reproaches the British, in contrast to what the Germans would like, and who perhaps blew up the magazine themselves.

9 February 1916
It is rather comical to be forced today to watch a great nation like Germany dismantling all the piping in Desbonnet's little factory.

10 February 1916
One hears the guns infrequently. A proclamation posted at Wattrelos states that no person may approach or cross the frontier on pain of death. This morning a young married woman (twenty-two years of age, two children) was shot while returning from Belgium. It is said that soldiers let her through without firing and then the officer ordered them to kill her.

24 February 1916
In the Woëvre near Verdun in the East, the Germans attacked along a ten-kilometre length of front. At some places they advanced three kilometres. They took 3,000 prisoners. At 2300 we heard lively firing, as when they shoot at aircraft.

25 February 1916
The push towards Verdun has continued, they have taken some villages near Verdun. The British have shelled the St André district with a few rounds. Some Germans and several French were killed and not a few wounded.

27 February 1916
The Germans had ordered the Mayor to ring the church bells to celebrate the capture of the protected fort at Verdun. We heard this evening that we had retaken it. Perhaps for this reason the bells remained silent. We heard artillery from 2300 until 1500 this afternoon.

28 February 1916
The German offensive before Verdun seems to have been stopped. They are now saying that our attacks on the fort, which they took the day before yesterday, were unsuccessful (. . .).

7 March 1916
Despite great intensity the German attack on Verdun has been held up for the second time. Food is scarcer everywhere, there is no meat, potatoes, butter or eggs.

10 March 1916
The Germans lied in maintaining that they had captured Fort Vaux. They did not have it at all, and today they say that the French have recaptured it. The French communiqués state that the Germans never had it. Can it be that they need a fictitious victory to influence public opinion to invest in their War Loan, launched on 4 March? Otherwise all quiet. We are not hearing the guns at the moment.

18 March 1916
Both the Germans and ourselves are claiming to have captured the 'Dead Man' to the west of Verdun. There are two spot heights, 295 metres and 265 metres on this mountain. We took the higher one. For some days the Germans have made no kind of progress in the area around Verdun. More than 600 ID cards were taken from the men who demonstrated at the food shops.

So the Germans know who demonstrated and can react harshly.

19 March 1916
Posters announcing ten years in prison for looting food shops. Any gathering in front of the shops is forbidden.

29 March 1916
Mortality is higher than usual. In normal times, two graves at readiness are enough in Roubaix, and now we have six. Not a potato can be found, not even at 125 francs for 100 kilos. The Germans have advanced a little at Malancourt near Verdun taking 500 prisoners.

4 April 1916
On the subject of German mentality: the NCO with the job of inviting the French to the *Kommandantur* is a great person. He spent about twenty years in the La Vilette district of Paris and speaks the Parisian dialect. He tells those who arrive: 'You are probably all wetting yourselves for fear of being shipped off to Germany, aren't you? But what use could they make of a bunch of scared rabbits like you people!'

The military court at Namur has sentenced about a dozen people to terms between one month's jail and eight years' penal servitude for failing to report the presence of a French Army captain.

6 April 1916
Yesterday evening 200 to 300 people, young men and women, were taken forcibly for tree felling in the district around Valenciennes, undoubtedly for making trenches. A poster at the town hall announces that there is an office of information for families concerned as to the fate of loved ones. In the Reichstag the Chancellor declared that the Germans will keep Poland and organize Belgium in such a way that their populations will no longer have anything to fear from this neighbour.

7 April 1916
At 2300 last evening, in a house-to-house search, 900 men were brought out and taken early this morning to the station for tree

felling or potato planting or – for deportation to Germany? Many young persons were arrested in the street, all the wood is being taken away from Leroy's and they told him that 'even small amounts are being used for trenches.'

8 April 1916
It is said that young people of about eighteen are being recruited for work in Germany. Yesterday the Germans went to houses in the Rue d'Epeule which they had listed, and took away the young people. At midday and during the evening until eleven we heard loud artillery fire.

9 April 1916
Beginning of Easter week. The Germans are continuing to deport people. A number of them have been brought to a concentration camp near Sedan, the others are working as tree-fellers in the woods. One female accompanies every thirty men as cook.

10 April 1916
Two thousand French civilians were taken off at midday.

11 April 1916
This morning we had to look on while 700 men and women were brought out. They say they are being sent to Saxony. We have heard the artillery. They keep saying that in about ten days all the men will be shipped out of Roubaix. The German administration has ordered the Roubaix city administration to draw up a list of all its employees.

12 April 1916
During the night there was a little gunnery. In Roubaix there is a sort of departure neurosis, all men believe they are going to be rounded up even though nobody has said anything. Therefore they spent three parts of the day packing in case they have to go.

20 April 1916
There was great excitement last evening in Roubaix. Posters were put up announcing that the Germans would transfer a

proportion of the inhabitants to unoccupied France because of difficulties feeding them here, these difficulties having been caused by the British. Each person may take 30 kilos and should begin to make preparations for departure. French troops have made progress in the area of Caillette Wood near Douaumont. The British have captured about 800 metres of trench near Ypres.

21 April 1916

They have begun taking away about 1,200 to 1,500 inhabitants, mainly unemployed and about three per cent women as camp cooks.

22 April 1916

The removal of men and women continues. During the night a whole district was cordoned off and towards 0300 they made house-to-house calls informing those who were to report three hours later at Motte in the Rue d'Alger, from where lorries would take them to Sedan, so it was said.

23 April 1916 Easter

In the Caillette Wood near Verdun we have advanced a little, also in the south at Douaumont and Haudremont. In Roubaix the tension has not died down because men and women are still being taken. It is the same in Lille, contrary to all the laws of war and human rights, especially with regard to the women.

24 April 1916 Easter

At 0630 the Germans gathered at the Hindenburg barracks (i.e. the Motte factory) all the young aged between sixteen and seventeen, on the pretext of exchanging their ID cards: a large number of them were detained and their parents informed that they should prepare their packs.

25 April 1916

This morning our district looks very strange. The Germans are said to be coming to take people away. Since 0500 the district is very tense. Old Léonie asked Caroline in tears to give souvenirs of herself to her employer's children should they be taken (. . .)

The many trams heading for the Motte factory are full of people singing the *Marseillaise* and *Le Petit Départ*, principally the men have packed. One hundred and forty people from (the Roubaix district) Tugotins went off singing the *Marseillaise* bravely, they have been practising and sang as a choir in a deeply moving way (. . .)

26 April 1916
They are continuing to take people away. Relations between Germany and the USA are very tense because of the way the Germans are running the U-boat war and torpedoing ships without warning. They say a poster is coming which will cause us much grief.

27 April 1916
The Germans have been to Alfred's district. He was locked up in the Hindenburg Barracks (Motte factory) but later released because he proved he had employment. It is said that the deportations are at an end and the security troops are withdrawing from Roubaix tomorrow. Great consternation in Lille about the deportations and stupid rumours are circulating, the worst being the rumour that women are being called to the *Kommandantur* to have their breasts removed.

14 May 1916
After everything I have read and heard I ask myself if France is ready for the big offensive. It seems that we have not amassed enough ammunition. Arras has been totally evacuated since January. Seventy per cent of its houses have been destroyed by the constant artillery bombardment.

29 May 1916
In Germany there is a grave shortage of food, amongst other things it is reported that a German soldier in charge of food supplies stole some to send to his parents. Yesterday assault troops asked women coming from the French supply depots to sell them all they had (. . .).

31 May 1916
Joffre (C-in-C French Army) is said to have predicted that the war could end at any moment and that in any case by September the occupation here in the north will be over.

15 June 1916
The Spanish-American Committee has sent from America a really enormous amount of women's and children's clothing, shoes, shirts, material, curtains, etc., etc., about fifteen lorry-loads. Amongst others somebody sewed into the collar of a man's shirt: 'In the esteem of a Canadian lady for her forebears, 1,000 woollen shirts.'

27 June 1916
New proclamations remind us of the old prescriptive measures which have been too widely ignored: forbidden to carry packets over five kilos. The Commanding-General has replied to the Mayor of Lille saying he does not accept the Mayor's interpretation of the Hague Convention and orders him to pay the War Levy. If this is not done, the inhabitants will suffer more so than if it is paid.

28 June 1916
We understand that a Great Offensive has begun at Roye towards Nesle. We have heard a lot of artillery fire.

Note:
1   Extracts from: Annette Becker (publ): Journaux de combattants et de civils de la France du Nord dans la Grande Guerre, Villeneuve d'Ascq (Nord) 1998.

Chapter Three

The Battle of the Somme 1916

Gerhard Hirschfeld

In October 1914 (the 'Race to the Sea'), after brief but fierce fighting against the French Army, the Germans established themselves along the Somme. With the beginning of trench warfare from about mid-November 1914, a seventy-kilometre long front line came into existence, increasingly strongly fortified, which stretched on the north-south axis through the villages of Gommecourt, Beaumont-Hamel, Thiepval, Fricourt, Maricourt, Curlu (following a bend there in the Somme) to Dompierre, Fay, Chaulnes and Maucourt. For twenty-one months, 2. Army under General Fritz von Below expanded its infantry and communications trenches north and south of the river, 'wired up' woodlands and barricaded villages abandoned by their populations. In some places they created bunker-like refuges and soldiers' accommodation (such as the 'Swabian Fort' at Thiepval) or dug underground galleries – often up to twelve metres deep.

Artillery fire was exchanged regularly, mines were used (Fricourt, Fay) and attacks made against enemy trenches, but the only major battle between Germans and French, in June 1915 at Serre in the north of the Somme region, made no significant change to the front. At the end of January 1916, 11.Bavarian Inf.Div. captured the small village of Frise at the entrance to the Somme bend. When the Allied offensive began in July 1916, the Germans had north of the Somme, under the command of General Hermann von Stein, commanding-general XVII Army Corps, five full strength divisions plus two-thirds of 10.Bavarian Inf.Div. South of the river under General von Pannewitz, commanding general XVII Army Corps, were four divisions, a Garde-Corps with subordinated Landwehr division and behind these. to the east, three reserve divisions and one-third 10. Bavarian Inf.Div.[1] The total strength of the German force (including the technical units) on the Somme was initially 300,000 men. Opposing them in trenches on the eve of the offensive were 500,000 British and 200,000 French troops. Many participants and also entire units of these armies were colonial or from the British dominions of Australia, New Zealand, Canada and South Africa.[2]

Prelude

The decision of the Entente to attempt the breakthrough in 1916 and put an end to trench warfare, and the war of attrition, was taken in December 1915 in a conference at Chantilly north of Paris. The Germans were to be attacked simultaneously in all theatres in order to give them no opportunity to transfer their reserves from one front to the other. The exact location and time of the General Offensive in the west was not agreed at Chantilly, and not until 14 February 1916 did the respective commanders-in-chief, Joffre and Haig, agree on eastern Picardy. Especially from the French point of view, the Somme region was chosen for its topography and the nature of the landscape. The hilly terrain and chalky ground promised a firmer subsoil than the heavy mires of Flanders – and the fact that there, at the seam between the Allied armies as it were, a close military cooperation between them would be possible from early on. Joffre and Haig agreed initially that the French would lead the main assault with the British playing only a supporting role. The strength of the French Army operating south of the Somme river was set at forty divisions with 1,700 heavy guns.

The German attack on Verdun on 21 February 1916 with bitter fighting and very heavy casualties north of the city and west of the Meuse put a stop to the Allied plan. The number of operational French divisions on the Somme was cut at once to twenty-two and for the attack itself the C-in-C French 6th Army, General Marie Émile Fayolle, was left with only twelve whole divisions for the fifteen kilometres of front under his control. The main weight of the military operations scheduled to begin around 1 July now lay with the BEF. Haig attempted in vain to postpone the start of the offensive to mid-August so as to bring up reinforcements and additional artillery, but Joffre insisted on Haig keeping the agreed date because of the dangerous situation in which the French Army found itself at Verdun. On 23 June, German forces 78,000-strong made their (final) major assault north-east of the city of Verdun.

The German military leaders had been expecting for some time a large Allied *Entlastungsangriff* ('relieving attack' to use the term coined by the Chief of the General Staff, Falkenhayn) in the Somme region. That the attack was actually 'desired', as Falkenhayn wrote in his memoirs, 'is to be doubted having regard to the situation at Verdun and on the Russian front.'[3] Whereas the German armies in 1916 at Verdun and Galicia (the Brussilow Offensive) had no lack of heavy guns and ammunition, and bomber and reconnaissance aircraft were used regularly in combat, 'they were wished for on the Somme with a thousand curses', the Great War chronicler Stegmann[3] wrote bitterly in 1921. General von Below, facing the Allied offensive, had asked in vain for 2. Army to be strengthened, and made repeated requests 'for reserves, artillery and aircraft.'[4] Falkenhayn awarded absolute priority to the attack on Verdun, however, and more importantly underestimated the British resolve to make the great gamble in northern France in the summer of 1916.

The Battle

The British and French opened the Battle of the Somme on 24 June with a preparatory barrage. The opening phase began with British light field howitzers bombarding the German wire defences and surface trenches. Two days later an incesssant, massive barrage by the entire artillery began along the central front line north and south of the road from Albert to Bapaume. For over a week 1,537 guns fired more than 1.5 million shells at the German trenches. At some sectors (Fricourt) the British used small quantities of poison gas and phosphorous as an accelerant,[5] but the effect of the bombardment as a whole fell short of the expectations of the British and French Chiefs of Staff, and the fears of the Germans. The British in particular were short of heavy artillery – their 467 guns were distributed rather sparsely along the twenty kilometres of attack front. Heavy rain and poor visibility had an additional negative effect on gunnery accuracy and prevented complete destruction of the German infantry and communications trenches and above all the very solid, partially concrete-built or reinforced bunker dug-outs.

The poor 'softening up' effort by the artillery and unfavourable weather were not the only factors to bring the success of the Allied offensive on the Somme into question, for the operational and tactical ideas of the two British generals commanding the operation were incompatible. While Haig, C-in-C of the BEF, had planned a rapid push 'to the third line' of enemy trenches, and so roll up the system, allowing a general breakout northwards, General Henry Rawlinson, C-in-C 4th Army, which carried the main weight of the attack, had initially only very limited goals. Rawlinson, advocate of a tactic known as 'bite and hold', aimed to make the infantry advance dependent on the penetrative success of the artillery: he was thinking of concentrated attacks by ground troops with the artillery following later if necessary.[6] The result was a fatal compromise because Haig lacked authority over Rawlinson, Allenby (3rd Army) and Gough (Reserve Army) subordinated to him on the Somme.

Convinced that the enemy positions and machine-gun posts had been adequately softened up by the week-long bombardment, on the morning of 1 July British and French infantry units stormed the German trenches. 1 July 1916, officially the first day of the 1916 Battle of the Somme, became the bloodiest day in British military history. The BEF lost 57,470 men, of whom 19,240 were killed, the remainder wounded, prisoner or missing.[7] The losses were particularly high on the left flank where VIII Corps, in its attack on Serre and Beaumont-Hamel, ran into the forward German line. 36th Ulster Division, later famed for its bravery, took the heavily fortified 'Swabian Fort' at Thiepval but was forced to withdraw after losing contact with neighbouring divisions.

The attack on the right flank, where units of the 4th Army achieved all targets set for the day (Mametz, Montauban) was more successful. The older generation of British military historians blamed Haig for the catastrophe, principally for his untimely operational concept and his 'Mass and Morale' fixation (John M. Bourne). The British media retain this negative impression of Haig. In November 1998 the *Daily Express* branded him 'the man who led millions to their deaths.' Other historians prefer to find an explanation for the disaster of the first day in the huge numbers of often raw soldiers (Kitchener's Army) being thrown into the fray direct from training. The popular BBC production of 1999 'The Great War' considered that a contributory factor had been the manner in which the infantry divisions crossed No Man's Land, marching upright and in closed ranks into the German machine-gun fire.

The Australian military historians Robin Prior and Trevor Wilson pointed out in a recent book involving very detailed research into the Battle of the Somme that probably only twelve (but possibly another five) of the eighty British battalions which 'went over the top' left their trenchs to converge on the enemy positions in a straight line and at a common tempo.[8] The other battalions came up to the German front under cover of darkness, or the men had more or less spontaneously re-formed in No Man's Land into small fighting groups practising various tactics of attack. Even that had served the British infantry poorly, however. Whenever German machine gunners had been able to fire directly into the attacking infantry the latter had been exposed to a lethal hail of bullets, and mortars, no matter how they advanced. The decisive error of the British and therefore the cause of the enormous losses on the Somme on 1 July was accordingly an inadequate preparatory artillery bombardment for the ground troops to follow, and the inaccurate and ineffective fire directed towards the German machine gun and gun emplacements, which were able to put up a barrier of preventive fire of unexpected scale when the time came.

That such an attack could be prepared and carried through successfully was proven on 1 July by the French south of the Somme. Supported by the 688 guns of their heavy artillery and attacking only along a sector fifteen kilometres in length,

Fayolle's 6th Army reached all its objectives (north of the Somme as far as Hardecourt and south to Fay). 1.Colonial Corps reached the main German defensive line and won ground temporarily. Over the next few days French troops consolidated their territorial gains and in some places even managed to push the front line five kilometres eastwards towards Péronne. Even the French were far from achieving the desired breakthrough on the Somme, however. On 12 July, General Fayolle, C-in-C 6th Army, noted in his diary: 'This battle never had a goal. We cannot speak of a breakthrough. And if there is no breakthrough, what was the point of the battle?'[9]

Despite the disproportionately high losses and the comparatively minor gains in territory neither the French nor British High Commands considered calling off the offensive even though the two Chiefs of Staff, Joffre and Haig, were increasingly at odds regarding the future direction and objectives of the ongoing operation. Soon there could be no talk of coordinated proceedings: from now on British and French conducted their respective attacks without agreeing the operational and tactical details with each other beforehand. Instead of large-scale offensives and encirclements of the enemy, the French and British forces became increasingly committed to minor battles with high losses to win every elevation, every scrap of woodland and every village. After the introductory attacks of both armies on a broad front, this now converted into the second phase of the battle. It lasted from mid-July to mid-September 1916.

Later, military historians would describe the bloody fighting conducted by enormous masses of men and materials as 'wastage battles' (*batailles d'usure*).[10] An example of this was the capture of Pozières and the ruins of a mill near the village by I.Anzac Corps between 23 July and 5 August. The 'victory' on the communications highway between Albert and Bapaume was bought for the price of a third (about 23,000 men) of the three Australian divisions in this sector. The advantage to the Allies was an important exit trench in the central battle area. The costly Anzac raid on Pozières – together with the disaster at Gallipoli – later became the foundations of the road to Australian independence from Great Britain.

The German defenders on the Somme were clearly inferior to

the Allies in numbers and weaponry. By the end of August, the British had sixty-two, and the French forty-four divisions, a total of 106 infantry divisions against fifty-seven and a half German, and the head count in the latter was not only considerably less, but some German divisions in the field were counted several times over.[11] The more than 1,500 guns of the Allied armies at the beginning of the battle were opposed by 598 light and 246 heavy artillery pieces. Still greater was the Allied superiority in aircraft at reconnaissance units (aircraft and balloons), and also in fighters and bombers. Reich archive historians calculated this initial disparity at 3:1 in favour of the British and French side.[12]

The German High Command reacted to the Allied offensive with a comprehensive rearrangement of their units on the Somme (19 July). From now on von Below commanded exclusively the new 1. Army operating north of the river, General Max von Gallwitz led 2. Army on the southern sector of the front with overall control of both armies. This was only a provisional measure, for on 28 July the Somme armies (together with 6.Army stationed between Lille and Arras and led by Generaloberst Freiherr von Falkenhausen) were placed under Army Group *Kronprinz Rupprecht von Bayern*. This was a desperately urgent solution to relieve the 'worn out divisions' by fresh units on a broader ground base. None of these 'new' infantry divisions – according to the declared targets – was henceforth to spend more than fourteen days' fighting, while artillery units, of which as a rule lesser demands were made, would be exchanged after every four weeks.

The wide-reaching shuffling and re-groupings of the German armies in the west shortly before the dismissal of Falkenhayn and the setting up of 3.OHL under Hindenburg and Ludendorff (29 July) reflect the great extent of uncertainty in the German military High Command, and also the gradual realization of the true enormity of the battlefield in the Somme region.

On 15 September, tanks made their debut in warfare for the first time. The thirty-six (of forty-nine deployed) British Type Mark I tanks which attacked German positions north-east of Pozières were not very successful, but did cause considerable consternation amongst German infantry, which had nothing similar. In the offensive mid-month, and in a major attack on

25 September, units of the French 6th Army were again involved, and British and French forces penetrated the front at Thiepval, Martinpuich, Combles, Rancourt, Cléry-sur-Somme, Barleux and Chilly in the south to push the German front a few kilometres further eastwards, but the hoped-for major breach of the front eluded them.

The removal from the line of exhausted units, eventually practised on the grand scale, constant replenishment of the initially far too small supply of ammunition and the building up of previously weak air reconnaissance and bomber groups enabled the Germans to compensate gradually for their former inferiority. The formation of fighter-aircraft units (*Jagdstaffeln*) expressly for the purpose made it possible by mid-September to put an end to the air superiority of the Allies at the Somme. The twelve warplanes, single-seater fighters of Hauptmann Oswald Boelcke's Jasta 2, won almost legendary fame. Boelcke alone shot down forty enemy aircraft, twenty of them over the Somme. He was decorated with the *Pour le Mérite* and died a hero's death at the end of October 1916 near Bapaume.

The third and last phase of the Battle of the Somme began at the end of September 1916, breaking down into countless minor battles. Many of the local attacks by the Allies failed (especially the British attack on the Warlencourt height, and the French in the St Pierre-Vaast Wood), or had only limited success. From mid-October the autumn weather brought a change for the worse as persistent rain transformed the battlefield into 'a landscape of primaeval mud' (Ernst Jünger), a giant sewer in which men, horses and vehicles stuck fast and could hardly move forward. 'Everywhere deep shell craters, most filled to the brim with water. At their rims one edges through the mud. The trunks of trees, fallen and ragged with shrapnel, over which one has to climb. A ghastly assortment of about six corpses, cut to pieces, covered in blood and mud, one with half its head missing: a little further on a blown-off leg, a couple of bodies so forced together that below the layer of mud the individual corpses cannot be distinguished,' wrote regimental physician Hugo Natt in November 1916.[13]

In mid-November 1916, after a temporary improvement in the weather, the last major attack by the British 5th Army (until

1 November the Reserve Army) under General Gough along the Ancre river was considered a disappointment, despite the capture by 51st Scottish Highland Division of Beaumont-Hamel which had been so hard-fought previously on 1 July. The French, who in September had reached Bouchavesnes north of Péronne with heavy losses – their farthest penetration eastwards of the German line, were little able to consolidate their territorial gains in this locality, and made no breakthrough.

The towns of Bapaume and Péronne, the hard-fought objectives of the French and British attacks, remained securely in German hands. The Battle of the Somme 'slowly burned out', as a popular German military chronicler described it.[14] Neither side achieved any noteworthy success: new military technology was tried out by both sides, new operational strategies and tactics were developed or rejected. Both sides claimed to emerge from the battle the victor – the price which they paid to do so was fearsome.

The Balance Sheet

The 1916 Battle of the Somme was far and away the bloodiest battle of the Great War. Between 24 June (commencement of the artillery bombardment) and 25 November (provisional end to the fighting), the British lost a total of 419,654 men dead, wounded, prisoner or missing, the French 204,353 and the Germans about 465,000.[15] Thus the Allies' losses were substantially higher than those of the German defenders. The British losses exceeded the worst estimates of their military leaders. The Somme destroyed, in the long term, the fighting ability of twenty-five British divisions;[16] put another way, every second British soldier who fought on the Somme was either so seriously wounded as to be unfit for future military service or failed to return at all.

For the Germans, the Battle of the Somme represented an enormous 'bloodletting' from which the Western Army, already weakened in the offensive before Verdun, would not recover. The Reich archive military historians summarized the Somme losses later: 'The existing old nucleus of German infantry trained in peacetime bled to death on this battlefield.'[17] To replace these experienced soldiers, amongst whom were numerous senior NCOs, there now arrived fresh and often inadequately trained recruits, whose chances of survival were accordingly that much slimmer. Responsibility for the extremely high losses lay not least with the German High Command, which at the beginning of the Battle of the Somme had insisted that the forward trenches be held at all costs. The German front line, as a rule heavily manned, could only be vacated voluntarily with the express authority of High Command.[18] This restricted to a major extent, if it did not actually render impossible, the mobility of the German infantry in the front line.

In view of the immense losses caused by the long artillery bombardment and the increasing refusal of many German soldiers to fight only 'in line', a new tactical concept, the so-called 'Stormtroop tactic' was introduced on the Somme. Developed by Ludendorff before he entered 3.OHL, and officially accepted by 2. Army at the end of August, the tactic involved small operational units set up ad hoc at regimental level and commanded by officers with good front experience. By this means did the German infantry on the Somme, despite the oppressive Allied superiority in artillery, increase its fighting prowess if only temporarily. The experience of service in small elite groups led by a proven front-line warrior created a new kind of soldier, converted by Ernst Jünger into an enduring monument in his memoir *In Stahlgewittern* based on his own experience of the Somme. Jünger sketched a mythically exaggerated, stoic warrior and 'true hero' of the Great War no longer susceptible to the horror and suffering of the battle. This anti-bourgeois, ultra-militaristic type of soldier was found in the 1920s literature and the ideology of the military nationalism of the Weimar Republic before 'Steel-helmet Face' (Gerd Krumeich) came to embrace the experience of 'total battle.' By extension the SS-man was its most radical and inhuman expression.

In a certain way the myth of the heroic 'Somme Warrior' of post-war Germany corresponds to the 'heroic image of the warrior' current even today in British military history writing, more precisely the British infantryman whose skill, courage and readiness to sacrifice himself were qualities evident on the Somme.[19] Yet the 'first day' of the battle, 1 July 1916, showed that those soldierly virtues could not determine the outcome of an attack. The Great War was an industrialized civil war whose material battles in Flanders, at Verdun or on the Somme were fashioned and decided principally by mass-produced large-calibre guns and the new possibilities of technology such as warplanes. This fact was first recognized by those who fought there. At the beginning of October 1916, Vizefeldwebel Hugo Frick, attached to a reserve division on the Somme, wrote to his mother in Germany: 'It is no longer a war, but mutual destruction by the power of technology. What hope has the soft human body against that?'[20]

Otto Maute (1896–1963), Driver, Machine-Gun Company, Inf.Regt 180/Reserve-Div.26.

In Civilian Life a Factory Worker.

Letters to His Family at Tailfingen/Balingen

23 June 1916 (Warlencourt)

Am writing to you again after having my baptism of fire so to speak. With three drivers we had to take two four-horse waggons at ten in the evening after 1. and 2. platoons riflemen arrived in trenches. From Warlencourt, as the village is called, we rode via Le Sers, Courcelette to the positions and stopped at the running trench of the third line to unload guns and ammunition. About then the British fired some rocket flares, after which the artillery of both sides opened up. For the first time I heard the whistle of the shells which hit nearby. We came under fire because we were in the vicinity of the German artillery position. Naturally it was impossible to quieten the horses. As soon as we had finished unloading the waggons I headed back. We got to Warlencourt at about 0330.

I will tell you some things about the railway journey. I have written to you every time we were at a new position.(. . .) In Bapaume we de-trained, you can find the town on the map. From Bapaume it was a one-hour drive here. Once we settled in, everyone started to write. On Tuesday we were inspected at Miraumont by the divisional commander Generalleutnant

Freiherr von Soden. On Wednesday we were inspected by the regimental commander. His name is Oberstleutnant Fischer. Yesterday we did not have much to do except look after our horses. Then at ten in the evening we went to the front. Today I prefer not to go out because the British are shelling like mad. Otherwise it is not so bad here, better than Müsingen. The food is adequate, in the field one gets a loaf of bread every second day. Write soon telling me what it is like at home. How is the farm, have you begun with the hay yet? Behind the front we are reaping everything. Arras is not far from here. Now you know where I am. Write soon and send something for my thirst.

25 June 1916 (Warlencourt)

Today is my first Sunday in enemy territory. One notices nothing strange about it. Just as we arrived they said the British are going to open an offensive and this seems to be starting. Since yesterday morning their guns are firing like I never heard before, it is a proper bombardment. Yesterday evening we had to go with three four-horse waggons to the trenches but got only as far as Pozières, where we were ordered to turn back because the approach road was under heavy fire. When we got back we could not unharness the teams, we had to stay at alarm-readiness. All the others had already harnessed up. We could not sleep for all the cannon fire going on. This morning we learned that the village of Miraumont is being evacuated. This is only half an hour between us and the front. Naturally we have packed everything so that if anything happens all we have to do is harness up and attach the team. This artillery barrage is hitting all the trenches. Naturally our guns reply, last evening one ammunition column after another went to the front positions. It is not impossible that the British will penetrate our front line and we will have to move out. Things with us are so different from yourselves at home, where everybody can take a Sunday stroll as if there were no war. Here nobody can leave the farm. Our Regt.180 is with Reserve-Regt.119, which has many Tailfinger people such as Scharr, Rieper, Eppler von Truchtelfingen (. . .) There are almost no civilians left in our village, on the farm where we are is only one woman whose husband is a soldier, and her fourteen-year-old son. (. . .)

2 July 1916 Warlencourt

Yesterday was hot. The artillery fire which started on Saturday last week and especially at night was incessant. It stopped suddenly at midday yesterday. Then came the long-expected British attack. They attacked the front line of our division directly and broke through at Regt. 99. They got to our artillery positions. Then 10.Bavarian Inf.Div. was thrown in. In the counter-attack our people ejected the British from our trenches and then took the first British trench. While this was going on it remained quite quiet except that the ammunition columns drove like the furies. Then the wounded came in, the lightly wounded walked, the serious cases were on waggons or in ambulances. At midday we harnessed up our horses, then I had to go to Bapaume for ammunition. I drove like the wind. The British fired over us into Bapaume. They left the Bapaume-Albert road untouched, but we were showered by flying fragments the size of your fist, and it made us think because they landed only two to three metres away. What would it be like to receive a direct hit from a ship's thirty-cm gun? The ammunition then had to be taken to the trenches, I did not have to go because I had fetched it.

According to the wounded, our regiment had heavy losses in the attack, but Regt.99 came off worse, they say fifty per cent. During the night the shelling resumed. We kept the horses harnessed up all night and had a good night's sleep alongside them. This morning all the windows of the house facing the lower stall were shattered by splinters, there were a lot in the farmyard. Later when it quietened down we unharnessed and cleaned the horses, but harnessed them up again at midday, as they are now.

During the week, four of the villages ahead of us were evacuated. They were firing into them with phosphorous shells. The night before last Miraumont was burning brightly throughout the night when I had patrol. At home you simply have no idea of what war is like. This evening we have packed everything in case we have to leave as eight days ago. British prisoners brought in today are the first I have seen. Today an aircraft crashed in our neighbourhood. When you write to me you must not put the village name or I will be in hot water. I really should not have written this. I am not, as I wrote you last time, near Arras, but Albert. That is about ten kilometres from here. The local village commandant is also named Maute. He is a junior lieutenant and the son of a factory owner from Spaichingen. Father, if you know him, please let me know. Despite everything all is well with me, we have food so that I have never eaten so much meat, if this were Germany I would not want to go home(. . .).

6 July 1916 Warlencourt

I also have to tell you not to put *Northern France* or *Warlencourt* on the envelope for it is forbidden to write where one is. You also have to advise the Post Office that it has to be left off. The service office told me that the village name is unnecessary and forbidden. I will receive everything, just write road and street number. Yesterday I ate in the forwardmost trenches. We took provisions to Courcelette, and then we had to take them to the running trench, two hours away. You have no idea what that means, the trench was so full of water it reached my trouser pockets. I had to drag my boots through it, it is a pure quagmire. A farm had been completely levelled by the shelling, the trench was obliterated. We received artillery fire along this 500-metre-long stretch. The air pressure of the shells as they exploded tossed us each time on our backs to the floor. One after another we jumped below and were sweating so much that it trickled down our legs. Suddenly a shell whistled over and we thought we had breathed our last, luckily it was a dud. It bored into the ground about five to six steps away. After that we went into a dug-out to rest. Afterwards we made our way through the trench. Where the trench had collapsed under the shelling we had to run because the British had the gaps under MG fire. Finally we reached the kitchen dug-out where we handed over the things. We stayed there thirty minutes and looked at the British trenches. Then we went back, and since the artillery was silent we left the trench, where you could easily drown, when we were half an hour from the front and we crossed open country. There I saw another corpse. We got back dog-tired at six. I had to change completely, my boots were full of mud. We had to wash trousers, socks, everything. You can see that it is often difficult but we also have nice days like today. Last eveing everybody on provisions transport duty had a piece of Swiss cheese and meat for supper. Although it is very dangerous, it is not so bad in the field. I am therefore still happy and remain healthy(. . .). I do not need money, I have more than I ever had in civilian life.

1 August 1916 (Grévillers)
Written on first anniversary of my mobilization (. . .) Every second day everybody has to ride to the trenches. Each time we use two four-horse and one or two two-horse waggons. Then we have to make from here via Irles and Miraumont to Grandcourt where there is a field-railway station, and we have to go to that station to load up: hand grenades, wood for dug-outs and barbed wire. Then we go to the trenches and make the trip two or three times. The road there is naturally not even, just rough track made by lots of traffic and full of shell holes, and because we go by night we have to keep a sharp lookout. When we get to the destination we unload as quickly as possible because this location and the road beyond it are heavily bombarded. When I was there the last time at Grandcourt, two waggons ahead of me a shell hit an ammunition waggon which burnt out with the horses and drivers. Few splinters reached us. In that we had more luck than we can understand. We never get back until six in the morning, always covered in dust. It is damn hot. Yesterday and today aircraft bombed Grévillers, today four men were killed and thirty wounded by bombs. One of our drivers was wounded so that now we have lost three, two being struck by horses and this one. Otherwise I am still enjoying it. Tomorrow we go to the provisions yard, and at midday we will go with the horses to pasture and stay there.

7 August 1916 (Favreuil)
Scarcely had I written to you on the 3rd and handed it in, than a bomber squadron flew over our village Grévillers and dropped one after another ten bombs, killing five and wounding fifteen, also eight horses lay wounded in the street. Next day at the same time they came again and dropped bombs. This time one of our drivers was wounded in the hands and feet by splinters. The same day (4th) at 0730 eight shells came over one after the other and all hit in and around the church. The church clock stopped

at the precise moment, and half the tower collapsed. Now there was a withdrawal. You cannot imagine it. The whole village was stuffed with the military. Ambulances were driving around as if demented. First we got the horses out of course. Quite a lot had been killed or injured, also from blocks of stones or beams. We received the order to harness up. We left at 0100 after everything was packed and loaded on the waggons. We went now to some villages further back and passed through Biefvillers, Favreuil to Beugnâtre. There we stayed on 5th and 6th. Then we came forward a little to Favreuil where we are now, but we are in barns. Naturally we have a longer journey to the front because it is much further, well beyond Bapaume. But it is good we left Grévillers because meanwhile the British shelled it to a ruin. Today we had the funeral of two fallen comrades from our company. We brought them from the front, and today they were buried in the local cemetery. Both were killed by a shell. Otherwise I have no news.(. . .)

10 August 1916 (Favreuil)
(. . .) I have to tell you that I was nearly killed last night. As every evening we left here (Favreuil) with two four-horse waggons to collect materials from Grandcourt station for the trenches and had arrived, and were about 400 metres out of St Pierre-Divion where we had to go. We had loaded iron and steel, naturally it weighed a lot, suddenly shrapnel hit amongst us. At once all four horses went down, my lead-rider and I were hurled into the horses, I got tangled up and the shrapnel balls kept coming while I was trying to get clear. Then we two drivers and the guard who was with us slipped under the waggon, and then three or more pieces of shrapnel fell amongst our nags. My saddle-horse was dead immediately, the other three survived it but all had their hooves sheered off. I got off lightly with a minor wound when a stone hit me in the chest. My lead-rider had a gash in the forehead from shrapnel amd more gashes in a foot, the guard has his face and left arm peppered by shrapnel balls, the NCO with us applied a field dressing to the other driver, and then they shelled so abominably that we could not get away. We remained ninety minutes with the waggon, I went over to the horses several times, they were trying to stand up but

had no hooves. Once it fell quieter I went into St.Pierre-Division to fetch a rifle, when I came back the leading saddle-horse was also dead, and the NCO with us then shot the other two horses. Then we returned to Grandcourt where we reported to the Feldwebel at the pioneer park, who wrote out a report, our names, everything. We slept until about five in the accommodation room, then we two went to Miraumont where an ammunition waggon from our company brought us back. That happened about 1230. As I wrote before, the highway between Grandcourt and St Pierre-Division is dangerous because the British trenches can observe it and they fire star shell to light it up bright as day.

You should have seen their faces when we got back and told them how the other four-horse waggon which we had was no longer with us, and about the baggage waggon. The Feldwebel had been told that all four horses were dead and the drivers (therefore we two) wounded, which was true. I got a stone or splinter in the chest, a mere trifle, my lead-driver is wounded in the head and feet. I have no more horses and those were good. I have been to the front often enough, and nothing happened before, but you cannot win them all. Ahead of our front it is always hot, the name Pozières, lying before us on the Bapaume-Albert road, is mentioned almost daily in the Daily Report. The British offensive has brought them well forward, and now they can destroy all the villages behind the front, that is why we are so far back. Warlencourt, where we were first, had been reduced to ruins, and we were forced to evacuate Grévillers on 5th because they were shelling it. Other than that all I know is that there are so many flies in France that when it is hot by day there is nothing one can do to stop them eating you. Since I have been in the field it has almost never rained, the roads are so dusty that horse, man and waggon are covered in dust (. . .)

18 August 1916 (Favreuil)
(. . .) Driver Renz who fell last night will be buried tomorrow. His whole body is covered in balls of shrapnel. You must therefore not be anxious, if one gets hit, then in God's name.

27 August 1916 (Favreuil)
If you have a shirt which weighs less than one pound send me one. We all have lice and when we wash the old shirts they come apart. Occasionally we all get the shits which is bad. Otherwise I am well and in good spirits.

1 September 1916 (Favreuil)
The region where we are, all France, is very fruitful. Oats are abundant. One sees what it means to have the war on one's doorstep, the civilian prisoners are now all farm labourers. (. . .) I enjoy it so much better than in the garrison, in the field it is not so regimented. It remains lively though, enemy aircraft drop bombs in our neighbourhood daily, or one or two are shot down in aerial fighting with a German. My comrade Gottlieb is now also in the district but further south, he wrote me that it is a different kind of artillery bombardment here on the Somme than at Ypres, where he was before.

15 September 1916 Favreuil
The day before yesterday I was at the trenches, this time it was windy again. On the way out between Miraumont and Grandcourt a shrapnel bomb exploded directly above a waggon, I was hit by two shrapnel balls in the chest, not hurt, naturally I galloped away from this dangerous place. When we were driving later from Grandcourt to the front, towards Thiepval, the British fired gas shells. Despite my gas mask I got a mouthful. On the way home I had a headache from the inhaled gas and spent a long time vomiting (one says here 'threw up like a palace dog'). I soon got better and my appetite returned. Last Sunday 10th at 0130 we were awakened when an enemy aircraft used the fine moonlit night to bomb our village, and hit ammuniton waggons. Eight of these exploded with a terrible noise. Little damage was caused, two men were wounded, three horses and five cows killed.

**Karl Eiser, Sergeant, Reserve Feld-Art.Regt
29/Reserve.Div.28**

Source BA/MA Freiburg, PH 12 II/57

Report (Written in August 1916)

From my War Diary respecting the great fighting at the outbreak of the Battle of the Somme from 24 June to 4 July 1916, which I experienced as an artilleryman on the Staff of I Detachment, Reserve Field-Artillery Regiment 29!

The task is difficult, and I do not know if and to what extent I can do it: I will try to compose from my meagre notes what I remember of those days and what our battery, our I Abteilung, Reserve Field Artillery Regiment 29 achieved by almost super-human effort and offering up the last reserves of nervous energy.

We are in the Champagne region near the ruined village of Fontaine/Dormoise where we first understood correctly the full horror of the past days and for the first time could sketch an outline of our many experiences. Although the battle has already raged longer than a full month with the greatest possible consumption and use of enormous quantities of war materials and battlefield gases and the British have succeeded in breaking through our lines, their great planned breakout failed due to the iron will – after seven days bombardment and destructive artillery fire – of small fighting groups, lacking any reinforcements worth mentioning, who held off the powerful masses of enemy infantry and brought them to a temporary standstill. The great British Breakthrough Offensive of the Somme Battle failed!

'Battle of the Somme.' What a sad ring this phrase has when spoken by a German tongue: of inexpressible suffering, of unlimited readiness for sacrifice. There in northern France, our comrades of 28th Reserve-Div. went to their graves in their thousands. Most of them sons of our Baden homeland, many hundreds of them torn apart by shells, ploughed deeply under on heights and in valleys, while others rest in many war cemeteries, and finally the least number who receive their death honours and rest in the military cemeteries of the German homeland. In respect we bow our heads at the scale of the sacrifice. The name

Battle of the Somme is holy to all of the 28. Reserve.Div who survived.

It was the beginning of May 1916 when the British facing our sector became increasingly restless, and one operation followed another. In the earlier firing to unsettle us, our Staff MO at Pozières was killed, while Major Radeck and Oberleutnant Weissmann, previously active with our I.Abtg. were wounded. By then almost every battery had lost gunners and some spotters to enemy fire. The British became ever more active, but we had no idea what they were up to: nobody suspected what was in the wind. Hill 110 at Fricourt was often subjected to furious shelling, and the continuous trenches and long stretches of the main front were levelled.

Life at our Fricourt West observation post was often soured on excursions to collect food. For me today it remains an incomprehensible mystery what the purpose was of having our artillery spotters there, for it was certain that the main trench could not hold out against even a minor attack and we would all have to surrender or be wiped out. By mid-May nearly all communications trenches on Hill 110 had been bombarded and levelled. The forward part of the traverse trench leading to the Hill 110 trenches had been shelled beyond recognition. Usually around midday the British would fire large-calibre shells and heavy mortars at the trenches.

On 3 or 4 June we sent out patrols, and on 5 June the British did the same, with the objective of taking prisoners in order to assess the disposition of enemy forces. Increased alertness was required of our observers since, contrary to the usual practice, the enemy artillery fire did not diminish once his patrols returned, but often continued wildly for whole days and nights.

In mid-June it was quieter, the lull before the storm. From 20 May onwards there was great activity behind the British lines. From our observation point on the Contalmaison Tower we watched endless columns of lorries making the jouney between Bray-sur-Somme and Albert every day. These convoys often consisted of 100 lorries. We frequently saw great artillery convoys, so long that it would take three hours for each to pass a given point. A standard gauge railway track was laid by the British between Fricourt and Bécourt using German PoW labour. At the eighty-metre mark on the Bray-Albert road the British set up a large airfield. Their infantry activity was very noticeable by the number of patrols and armed reconnaissance sorties they made, and their many mortars. All our reports were fed by I.Abtg. to Division.

At 0300 on Friday 23 June a furious bombardment began, shells exploded along our entire divisional sector, on our trench lines, various lengths as well as the single ones, the whole defensive line at Fricourt, Lehmgruben (clay-mining) Hill to the Lehmsacke (clay bog) lay under heavy shellfire. Our landline to the Fricourt West observation post was cut, even though it had been buried one metre deep. At midday the heavy bombardment died away and quietened – Mars.

At 0130 on Saturday 24 June our whole line, in a semi-circle around us from the enemy side, was lit up as innumerable lightning flashes soared over, a hissing and howling, gasping, splintering and exploding – all this filled the air. I was on watch on the Contalmaison Tower, I shouted into the telephone, I could not hear myself, I had to assume they had understood in the mansion cellar. A few moments later Hauptmann Kipling, commander of 7.Howitzer Battery, stood beside me. It was a fine sight, this flashing and lightning of the enemy artillery. The British were pouring down heavy fire mainly on the territory to the rear, our artillery positions, so far as they knew them, and all known observation points, access roads and villages far enough back that until now they had been spared attention. The trenches received little fire. It was frightening, all that noise of exploding shells, an artillery bombardment involving all calibres and kinds of munitions, such as I had never known in two years of warfare, roared and hissed over and around us far and near. At sunrise at crossroads and on the access roads the little clouds of shrapnel balls came flying, in between the impact of heavy shells sprayed high into the air. The mansion received heavy fire from various calibres, several direct hits shook the building, a red cloud of disintegrating brickwork hindered visibility, the shells howled overhead, landing on the outskirts of Pozières village, hiding the whole locality in smoke and fumes. Almost at the same time huge explosions of heavy shells reduced to rubble the last standing ruins of the houses in our village.

The evening of 30 June brought no change: smoke, gas, foul fumes. The British continued shelling our village until late at night, also the outskirts where 911 platoon/1.Battalion was stationed, with shells armed with a delay fuse, in the dug-out one felt the tremendous jolt and tremor of the 'moling' shells with which they were showering the village. Heavy shells howled and wobbled high overhead into our *Etappe* right through the night. Over the entire rearward area, as we were now becoming used to it, the access roads were now being subjected to bombardment every night.

The morning of 1 July dawned. Towards 0330 I crawled out of our dug-out to orient the fall of enemy shelling. The depression between Contalmaison and Edinger village (position between Contalmaison and Fricourt) was shelled with a gas which smelled of bitter almonds, presumably prussic acid. A milky white, lazy wall drifted slowly towards our village. Inf. Res. Regt.111 reported from Fricourt that the British had filled their trenches, it smelt of prussic acid everywhere: we knew that our gas masks offered no potection against it. From Pozières to the Fricourt depression everything was hidden by a white veil of gas. At daybreak Res.Grenadier-Regt. 110 reported from La Boisselle that the enemy had filled the trenches there, and 109 reported the same from Mametz. We awaited events in high tension. What would the day bring? Perhaps we would not survive it – many thought this. As the first rays of the sun gleamed white, the vile gas rose up and soon we were immersed in it. Visibility was down to ten metres. The barking of the enemy guns increased every second, hell roared up: but only for a short time!

Since Thursday 29 June on Hill 110 we had seen only smoke, fire and exploding shells, on the eastern side a series of explosions. They must have hit the arsenal for our mortars. With deep sadness we think of our infantry comrades in the trench: how many of the company would still be alive? How many men would a battalion or infantry regiment still have who were fit to fight? We knew that on Hill 110, our artillery comrades, our own trench, were in the greatest danger: or were perhaps already dead? Hill 110 observation point, the stone quarry, the work platform and Fricourt West were on the forward trench line and short in numbers. I knew that the observation point here was in the hands of one of our best lieutenants, who was no coward and would rather die than surrender. He was Lt Mayer with two NCOs, Hittler and Viehoff, and two telephonists, Enderle and Baumann. A light wind began to disperse the swathes of gas a little. Observation point Hill 110 and Fricourt requested urgent covering fire: for this sector we had only two batteries, with only a few serviceable guns: these were 2. and 7.Battery with light field howitzers. They opened fire immediately. From Fricourt to Mametz, and as far as La Boisselle, urgent covering fire was being requested, 1. and 3. Batteries were under rapid fire. All heavy batteries in the wood at Mametz were out of action either from direct hits or the gas attack. II.Abtg. could not be contacted in the gully of shells! As all of our batteries were capable of being reached quickly, equipped partially with new guns but not all yet installed, the sector was under a barrage of fire. The hell that roared up is beyond my powers of description, the British artillery fire was a true hurricane, our own guns were inaudible. All our artillery fired for a full hour then gradually the iron mouths of the guns fell silent as hit after hit knocked them out. A wild slipping through of message runners began, coming and going to and from our Abtg. Platoon 911 at the village entrance also received a direct hit, my comrades, I knew them all, were seriously wounded: Schrempf, Kappenberger, little Noe dead. All at once the frenzy of enemy artillery fire ceased, although the heavy shells from the long distance batteries howled and twisted on their way to the *Etappe* villages. The decisive moment for attacker and defender had arrived.

The British had blown open a sector one company's breadth from Reserve Inf.Regt. 111 between the brickworks road at Fricourt and Bahngruben Hill. British assault troops followed up at once and poured into our trenches. At almost the same time the enemy broke through small parts of the infantry line along our whole divisional sector. Luckily the morning breeze had by now dispersed the major cloud of gas and the observation points had improved visibility. Before us lay Edinger village, not really a village but a well-fortified ready infantry emplacement. The main kitchen galleries of our infantry regiment, and pioneers, and all kinds of materials were there. The field railway ran here from Martinpuich and the Ganter Works. Between here and the ridge is the Totenwäldchen wood, a little north-west the Ferme Fricourt. About 500 metres to the west of our village beside the small wood and the known path through the depression was our 3.Battery Hauptmann Fröhlich, whose reckless spirit and black humour was well know to everybody: 200 metres to the south of him was a small artillery refuge called the *Völkerbereitschaft*. Our 1.Battery was strung out in three parts along the road from Contalmaison to Fricourt, two guns: platoon 911 on the outskirts of Contalmaison, one gun in the depression on the road to Fricourt and the other on the ridge, this was listed as a dummy gun but, in true fulfilment of duty to the last, by almost superhuman effort took part in the defence.

The morning breeze gradually swept the great swathes of gas from the foregoing terrain and our field of sight improved. Our divisional sector became noticeably quieter, almost frighteningly so. The British long-range guns alone continued firing on our rearward positions, the local British artillery had fallen silent.

It was 0800 on 1 July. In the Totenwäldchen Wood two MGs were hammering, a long drawn out fire began, a burst of fire clattered into our village. Finally we saw the British assault troops, wearing white recognition patches on their backs, appear on the Totenwäldchen and Ferme Fricourt: therefore they had made major inroads into our infantry line. They stormed No.1 gun, the dummy gun of 1.Battery, when it did not fire they ran for No.2 gun at the officers' dug-out in the depression on the road to Fricourt. The other two guns of 911 platoon were not ready to fire. Message runners and despatch riders circulated from our Abtg. to batteries in all directions with the order to fire. Our good comrade gunner Schölch had to run the order to 911 platoon but was hit by infantry fire and fell on the road from our village. I made my way to 3.Battery over the grim cratered field, leaping from one shell-hole to the next.

No 3.Battery was to fire immediately on the Totenwäldchen, the brickworks and Fricourt station, where the British were arriving in battalion strength on the Contalmaison highway. I met Hauptmann Fröhlich by his wrecked guns. He looked pale and bleary-eyed, gave me a message for Abtg. that he had no serviceable guns, all had been destroyed by direct hits. 3.Battery position looked awful. The British had come to within 200 metres of the battery. At that moment the *Völkerbereitschaft* came to life. The artillery refuge had the construction company composed of clothing store men and parts of Reserve-Grenadier Regt.110. This company was swiftly in action and opened a furious rapid fire from thirty to fifty metres range forcing the British back to the Totenwäldchen Wood.

Unteroffizier Kruger's dummy gun of 1.Battery, recaptured from the British, now opened fire on the retreating enemy, firing first numerous dummies and then at 100–200 metres range detonators into the British ranks, causing heavy losses. Finally No.2 gun in the depression began to fire, and Platoon 911's No.4 gun was repaired and readied. These three guns fired first on the Totenwäldchen, then the western end of Fricourt, the cemetery and station, where the British was present in large numbers. The two guns were fired over sights or by eye. Each round was a hit. Cornered like mice before the cat, the British left the Totenwäldchen and fell back on Fricourt. The detonators of No.1 Battery reaped an appalling harvest amongst the British infantry. Now they held only a small length of trench in the third infantry line. There was bitter fighting near Mametz where our Grenadier-Reserve 109 engaged in hand-to-hand fighting and fought for every inch of the trench line. We also saw all of Group Reserve 109 go into British captivity. Our infantry advanced along the road from Contalmaison to Fricourt, some companies even came up from the recruit depot. For us artillerists it was heart-breaking to have no guns or reinforcements worth mentioning, but at least our division had warded off the breakthrough for today. Our batteries in the shrapnel depression were lost, the enemy got to 7.Battery, the light howitzers on the edge of the wood at Mametz.

From La Boisselle on our right flank we heard unceasingly the explosions of many hand grenades, but on 1 July the enemy gained little ground. It was almost amazing, guns of various batteries kept up rapid fire for hours, firing mainly long-shell fuses without opposition. Fearfully we awaited a fresh attack almost all day, but the British did not risk the opportunity, preferring instead to consolidate and dig in along the sections of trench line they had taken. We did not receive enemy artillery fire because the enemy did not know the disposition of his own troops. In our battery positions the empty casings were stacked higher than a man, whole mountains of empty shell baskets lay scattered around, with a couple of smart companies the British could could have got right through to Bapaume in the *Etappe*.

This was the picture of 1 July: 'No significant reinforcements, no orders from above! Mametz and Montauban lost, held by British. Hill 110 near Fricourt likely to fall. Fricourt village still in German hands but surrounded. We have lost our right flank at La Boisselle. Our observation trench reports: Lt Mayer fell in the cratered field. Gunner Baumann fatally wounded, Unteroffizier Hittler and gunner Viethoff, telephonist Enderle captured.'

One shuddered to hear the words 'No reinforcements!' We were deeply disappointed: why had we been abandoned with no reinforcements or relief? Was that our reward for what we had given up and sacrificed? We could still hold the line with a little artillery reinforcement and a couple of fresh infantry regiments. Before us we had as good as no more infantry. The British rifle fire had now abated – were they exhausted or could we expect a new attack? We left the hour unused. In the *Etappe* the Staff drove off in their cars, overnight they shifted HQ and its complicated telephone system to the rear, the gentlemen fearing the breakthrough. That we learned, we who for eight days lay below death raging a thousand times around us. They left us alone. And why? On the late evening of 1 July a company of Landwehr Battalion fifty-five occupied our village (Contalmaison). Their officers had no maps and were clueless as to what was going on.

The three serviceable guns of 1.Battery was found on the night of 1 July and put behind the mansion gardens ready to fire from a half-built structure. That night many wounded of Reserve Inf.Regts.110 and 111 still able to drag themselves along came through on their way to the rear. They recounted the most appalling crimes committed by the British against their prisoners. We had to listen to the most terrible stories although we had no head for it. The British resumed their usual barrage to prevent traffic using the roads and access tracks, especially with sudden great bursts of firing. Our three guns behind the mansion had hardly fired a round before the British spotted their position and put them under heavy fire. On 2 July the British opened with rabid fire at our sector, but their fire was ragged . . . .

August Dänzer, President of Prince's Chamber, Freiburg im Breisgau

DIARY

5 July 1916
Reports by the French state that especially south of the Somme they have made further progress, taking Estrées and Belly, after earlier capturing Assevillers, Feuillères and Flaucourt, and the British La Boisselle. It seems we are involved in the greatest battle in the history of the world, in the most critical period of the whole war, and if God grants us victory this time, peace will dawn.

18 July 1916
In the afternoon, short walk with Sondger in the Sternwald. From a letter sent to him by his brother von Hanauer with Reserve.Inf.Regt.110, I infer that the regiment was involved in the fighting against the British at La Boisselle. These British are reported to have shot dead German prisoners with their hands raised. The Germans are then said to have retaliated and shot 1,200 British whom they had surrounded.

Whole companies of Reserve-Regt.110 were wiped out, and the regiment is now in the Champagne to reform and re-equip(. . .).

Hans Gareis, Vizefeldwebel, Bavarian Inf.Regt 16/Bavarian Inf.Div.10

Source: Kriegsarchiv Munich HS 2106

Report (Undated)
Experiences of the Somme Battle, 1916: Diary Notes

6 July 1916
Today I returned from leave to rejoin I Battalion/Inf.Regt.16. My battalion was on a ridge opposite Montauban. Towards

2200 I went up with the field kitchen: they handed out the rations on the Flers-Longueval road in a depression to the south of the village. Before we reached the location we came under shrapnel-shell fire. One horse of Field-Kitchen Company 1 was killed, one man was wounded. The running trench which we passed had been terribly shelled, the position looked as if it had been ploughed over, in the trenches only emergency galleries. The same night I took over my 1.Platoon/4.Company.

7 July 1916
The weather is dreadful, therefore lively enemy aircraft activity while we have no airplanes up. I lost another three men from my platoon today.

8 July 1916
Up to my ankles in water. On the road from Mametz towards Montauban and to the Mametz Wood with binoculars we saw British columns marching, preceded by their artillery. Our artillery did not fire. Twelve barrage balloons hung over the enemy trenches nearly all day. Towards evening we received heavy shellfire. A direct hit collapsed the right-side, heavily manned gallery entrance of the Company Commander's room housing the Battalion Staff. Lts Rosenthal and Auer, and Unteroffizier Bucher were wounded, nine men, some the best in the company, killed. My platoon is now twenty-five men and four group leaders. My people sat in the underground gallery and prayed. When darkness fell we started digging out the dead: the sight was ghastly, the most terrible thing I have seen since 1914.

9 July 1916
During the night terrible artillery fire. While fetching rations the company lost another five men, three dead, two wounded. In the morning the weather finally cleared and there was lively aerial activity. In the afternoon another terrible artillery barrage with heavy shells. Longueval burning fiercely.

10 July 1916
In the morning I had a group go to Longueval for ammunition,

Lille in 1914, (photograph by Georg David Bantlin)

German trench at Fransart, 1914.

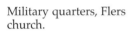

Military quarters, Flers church.

Divisional command post in the Somme Valley.

German guards with a variety of prisoners captured during the fighting at Frise.

Postcard from the pictorial volume *Der Krieg 1914/1915 in Postkarten, Abteilung: Frankreich, Inhalt: Umgebung von Sankt Quentin*, (published by Lehmanns Verlag).

Programme for a performance of Weber's opera *Der Freischütz* held at the German Theatre, Lille on 27 January 1916 to celebrate the birthday of the Kaiser.

French prisoners being paraded through Lille, 1914.

The Rulers of Lille at the Soldatenheim, 1916.

Ruins of the ammunition depot at Lille after the explosion of 11 January 1916.

A Lille street after the explosion of 11 January 1916.

Waiting for orders on the front at Cartigny, 13 July 1916.

3.Comp/Reserve-Infantry Regiment 29 in a trench at La Maisonette, 16 July 1916.

Sentry Raaf shouting 'Alarm!', La Maisonette trench, 19 July 1916.

Regimental band playing on the highway near Tertry, 22 July 1916.

Graves in the third trench line, La Maisonette, 19 July 1916. Péronne can be seen in the background.

Third trench line, La Maisonette, 19 July 1916.

German trench at Hattencourt, 1916.

German soldiers at Hattencourt, 1916.

'Operation Alberich', highway near Havrincourt, March 1917.

'Operation Alberich', felling their chimney of a sugar factory, February 1917.

'Operation Alberich', houses blown up at Roupy, February 1917.

'Operation Alberich', deportation of inhabitants at Metz-en-Couture, photographed by Georg David Bantlin, 18 February 1917.

Péronne town hall after the German withdrawal to the Siegfried Line, March 1917.

'Operation Alberich', the demolished castle.

British long-barrelled railway guns captured near Péronne, 1918.

Column of German artillery near Fontaine-lès-Clercs, March 1918.

Battlefield near Albert, 1918.

Albert church with its 'hanging Madonna', 1918.

Interior of the church at Péronne.

Aerial photograph of the village of La Vacquerie near Gouzeaucourt.

German soldier walking down the high street at Péronne.

Damaged tank on the banks of the Somme, March 1918.

German military cemetery in France, 1920s.

before they reached the depot it blew up. We have no mining frames for shoring up and no prospect of relief, one has to keep moving everything around in order not to become apathetic.

11 July 1916
In the morning fifty replacements came up with Lt Wagner, married men amongst them with no experience of fighting. At midday four men of my platoon were buried alive by a direct hit, two men of the morning's replacement were killed, one the father of four children. At night thank God we got the shoring-up frames.

12 July 1916
In the morning artillery fire as every day. In the afternoon the rear wall of the trench received a direct hit which collapsed the galleries. We were up to our knees in earth and had to struggle free. At night I got digging with everybody available. To protect the dug-outs at night we filled in the shell-holes above the galleries.

13 July 1916
Last night violent artillery barrage which went on all day. By evening the trench was a long series of shell-holes. In the early evening we received a report that the British are massing in the depression at Bazentin. The company sent a patrol to recon-noitre and they confirmed this.

14 July 1916
Towards 0300 we set up another mining frame in the gallery and I wanted to let my people rest, then came a rumour that 'The British are attacking.' In a trice the platoon was at the parapet, I distributed my people – not easy in the total darkness – the first flare rose and before us, barely 300 metres away, we saw the British advancing in large numbers towards our wire entanglements, steel helmet by steel helmet, an impressive sight. And now it started. A rage gripped us all, but also a feeling of joy to have the chance to avenge ourselves for what had gone before. I roared: Hurrah! and Fire! and knelt with the nearest people at the parapet to have a better field of fire. Others

followed my example. So we received the enemy with rifle and MG fire interspersed with shouts of Hurrah! The British artillery fire rained down on our position, luckily on the empty support trenches, but showering us with splinters. That all remained unnoticed in our lust for battle. Even our young replacents left nothing to be desired. I detailed a few people as munitions runners and to gather up the rifles of the dead and wounded to exchange for our hot-barrelled ones. I had three rifles, one in use, two cooling. In the light of the starshells we watched as the British line began to thin down. Dawn was coming.

A British aircraft arrived and with admirable skill replied to our rifles with MG fire. Ahead of our line the attack had petered out, they lay in heaps in the wire. A few who showed signs of life were dragged into our trench. Some took refuge in shell craters, then turned and ran for the British line, and were shot down. A few hundred metres away they set up mortars and fired on the sectors of our No.1 and No.2 Companies. Our sector was spared. I shared my last pack of cigarettes amongst my brave people, they wanted to hug me, so great was the jubilation. We believed we had the right to be pleased.

When the first starshell burst we saw the rows and rows of British marching towards our position, weakly defended by tired troops: we feared the worst, but not one British soldier had come over the parapet, and now their front rank hung dead or wounded in the wire entanglements. That it might be different to our right and left did not occur to us as we celebrated our victory. After this short pause we all went back to the parapet except for a few people attending to the dead and wounded.

From the Company Commander, I learned that the Company had lost thirty men, No.2 and No.3 platoons had fared worse than mine. We covered the dead with tarpaulins as an emergency measure, there being no time to bury them: then, with my two most senior corporals, I turned to face No Man's Land. We brought a British MG and numerous prisoners into the trench, including from No.2 platoon a wounded British colonel caught in the nearest barbed wire hedge, a smart man with a pleasant face. Soon it was completely light, and then I began to suspect the worst.

We could see without binoculars columns and columns of

British marching along the highway to Longueval and nobody fired at them. This meant they must have broken through the line here. For us the range was too great and in any case we had no ammunition. I hurried to the Company Commander to report and found the Battalion Staff there as well. Major Wölfel, Oberleutnant Marschall, Lt Sässenberger and a couple of orderly officers met me in a shell-hole in front of the battalion post in the forward trench. I listened to the reports. The enemy had broken through on the left at No.3 Company and now held the outskirts of Longueval. No.2 Group to the right reported the enemy at Bazentin. The Regimental Staff, including the commander, Bedall, had been captured. We were therefore adrift: if we did not receive reinforcements from the rear, or they failed to pull us back, we were lost, for the battalion had been so weakened that it could not withstand an attack, and we were out of ammunition: in my entire platoon sector we did not have a single hand grenade between us. The depression to our rear lay under a furious artillery barrage, and a retreat by day with the remainder of the battalion was rejected by Major Wölfel and the other officers . . . .

Gustav Krauss, Unteroffizier, later Leutnant, Reserve.Inf.Regt.29/Inf.Brigade 80.

In Civilian Life a Bank Clerk at Heidelberg

Report (Undated)
Source: BAMA PH II/502: Photographs BfZ I AH52.

12 July 1916
In the evening we moved into Cartigny where we were billeted in a fine mansion. The rooms had none of their former elegance, only two-tier bunk beds or wood in which we slept on shavings.

13 July 1916
The place has a fine old church which I looked over. We counted eighteen French barrage balloons while we have only three (a French aircraft shot down five in flames). The railway station was plastered continuously with thirty-eight-cm shells. At night

it is forbidden to show a light. There was a big artillery battle raging at the front which we watched from the roof of the mansion. It was a grandiose sight. Half left of the mansion was a twenty-one-cm mortar which the French were making efforts to wipe out. The firing continued throughout the night. We kept ourselves busy all the time and heard all kinds of rumours. We know we are not being invited to a party, but on the other hand we are hoping to be deployed soon so as to get away quicker. The worst is the waiting and uncertainty. In the evening we heard that it would begin during the night.

14 July 1916
Scarcely had we settled down for the night than we were awoken at 0100. Ahead we could hear the sounds of firing. We paraded, were issued with hand grenades and then marched down the wonderful highway towards Peronne, the night as black as pitch, only lit by the flares at the front. We turned off left to cross some fields. White strips of cloth on posts marked the route. On the way a comrade had a screaming fit. Soon we came to the banks of the Somme and crossed by means of a wooden bridge several hundred metres long erected by the pioneers and which is frequently fired upon – no casualties.

In a hamlet Chapelette we dug small holes for protection on a slope of the railway embankment near the station. The French had made a rapid advance to the river bank, driving the 25ers and 71ers back up the hill. The civilian population had had no time to evacuate in an orderly manner, everything was left intact, the same went for the controllers of the *Etappe* magazine of Inf.Div.121, who had abandoned the well-stocked dump at the station, and the rolling stock in the goods yard which could not be hauled out because the bridges had been blown. The tracks had been wrecked by numerous shell craters. In the magazine halls, which were under constant bombardment, we found enormous supplies of preserves: peas, beans, whole barrels of cauliflower, great stocks of bedding, and tents, lamps, stoves, sugar, tobacco, etc. Coffee stood ankle-high on the floor, we waded through it. Many drums of paraffin stood around. In one room there were lots of firemen's brass helmets saved from a museum collection. We set up some tarpaulins to shelter from the rain and cooked a good meal behind and below the goods waggons while the halls were being shelled, which cost us two dead and some wounded. One of the dead had been on leave with me.

In the afternoon the shooting hotted up, and it was really unpleasant in our rabbit holes. There was a terrible noise when a shell exploded in the halls. Despite the ban, several men went into the magazine repeatedly, especially when it became known that there was beer stored there. The following evening, to our great joy some beer was served officially. Towards 2000 the firing abated, and at 2145 we went off to the trenches. There were some aircraft overhead which we took for German because they wore a cross on the wings; they bombed us. We went through the village in groups under fire on the road to Biaches, which we crossed. More heavy fire forced us into a trench where we spent a half hour, we received fire there and a shell landed close by me. They were also firing gas shells. My NCO did not want to get down at first because somebody was out in the open. Finally he had no choice, and the Company Commander helped. Later we went to the reserve trenches where we dug until 0300. Ahead the sky was lit brightly by burning houses.

15 July 1916

Then we went back to Chapelette. After fifteen minutes there we were put on notice to leave for Péronne. We were to cross the river using a narrow improvised bridge balanced on barrels and under constant fire from a heavy battery. We were to run for it between salvoes which came at set intervals. A salvo of three arrived, two of which were duds, and we scampered to the river, arriving without loss. On the other side we entered the abandoned town through a fortress gate and soon found our cellar. Meanwhile it was day and we had to get under cover quickly because the town was in the enemy's sight and range. I gave a laggard a slap across the head to get him down the cellar, he did not take this the wrong way because he knew it was for his own good. The town had been evacuated suddenly by the population, and the houses had been left as though the owners would return shortly.

In the cellar in which the inhabitants had taken refuge when the shelling began, the food – with mould – was on the table, hats were hung on pegs etc. I had my breakfast drink out of a fine old decorated cup. We reviewed the house from roof to cellar. I moved into a bedroom with Imperial bed and quilt etc. which smelt wonderful. In an alcove were various perfumes etc. I washed using a large bottle of eau-de-cologne and then sprayed myself with perfume. In my filthy uniform and boots I then lay on the young maiden's bed and slept to 1130. Then I went on a search of neighbouring houses where the other groups were billeted.

In the conservatory I saw from the floor impeccably set tables, each with two plates, serviettes and wine glasses etc. Assuming this was for Staff I was about to withdraw when I discovered a comrade in the kitchen. In response to my enquiry he advised me that 'Gruppe Hussmann' dined here. He had all kinds of provisions, mainly preserves and tinned, but also rabbit and smoked meats. There were some well-stocked shops which had ladies' and children's shoes. At midday a wine and champagne store was found.

We had preserved meat, potatoes and peas. From 1500 our artillery was to calibrate and was expected to be put out of action by the French guns before nightfall, after which we were to attack. In the afternoon therefore we had to stay in the cellars. When our artillery fire began, the French response was much heavier, and our stay in the town now looked short. The town hall was burning and Lt Hofsummer salvaged the collection of Roman gold coins in a sandbag which he handed over to division. Wehrmann-König and Vohn caused great hilarity dressing up as a bridal pair, he in morning coat and top hat, the bride in white dress with veil, and insisted on making house calls, even on the officers and despite the shelling. Under the influence of the discovered alcohol stocks, the mood became even more high-spirited during the afternoon. A couple of individuals were well over the limit. When we marched out at 1830 we found a rifleman reported AWOL sleeping in the entrance to a cellar and cuddling a large doll. We then quick-marched across the market place towards the Flamicourt district.

At 0200 we advanced. Our Company Commander Lt Mersmann requested Vizefeldwebel Trieschmann to remain with him in the difficult situation. We hastened through the communications trench, stumbling forward over dead and wounded.

I still recall treading on something soft which whimpered and I saw that I was standing on the face of a wounded man. After a lot of manoeuvring hither and thither we found ourselves in a dreadful corner, men squashed against men in a two-metre deep trench unable to rest. Shells were flying overhead, the trench had no step-up for riflemen.

We lay here the whole day without food or water until late evening. There was no wire entanglement outside and the trench had no dug-outs. If an orderly officer wanted to pass through, two men had to lie down on their stomachs on top of one another so that passage was possible. Gradually we made scrape-holes in which we could at least shelter head and upper torso. The four men of my group to my left were wounded one after the other and disappeared. I sat in my little hole, abandoned to my fate, waiting for my turn to be wounded, but it never happened. Our Company Commander was mortally wounded by a shell splinter in the upper thigh. Reservist Kirchner and another wounded man making their way to the rear, carried the wounded Company Commander along in a tarpaulin. He was calling for his wife and children. A short while later all three took a direct hit. Mersmann had frequently had Kirchner on report for minor misdemeanours, but this did not prevent Kirchner from helping his officer as a comrade.

Towards 1800 the French started an attack which then faltered. I fired three rounds. At 2100 we were to storm the small wood opposite. The order was passed from hand to hand, the docket was signed, 'Ordered by God, Siebe.' When we were ready to go, the assault was called off. No.2 Company Commander Weller was informed by a reconnaissance patrol that our No.1 and No.4 Companies had retaken the wood from the French. So we were in luck. I had three rifles that day, two were damaged beyond repair, I narrowly escaped from being buried alive three times when the trench walls collapsed. When the Company count was made, of the 230 men who had come to the trench only 110 remained. During the night there was a downpour, I looked like a hippopotamus, yellow with mud, in the night we were relieved and returned as reserve to Chapelette where we were billeted in the cellars. When the kitchens arrived, our cook told me he had thought I would not survive out there.

17 July 1916
Our losses so far are nine dead and one hundred wounded. There are many black French troops lying around dead in the countryside. When we were fetching provisions towards 2300, we were put on alert and went forward. I had taken over 1.Platoon, 3.Platoon had three seriously wounded when moving up. We came to the left flank of the position directly facing the small wood at La Maisonette where the 21ers had fired too short. There were still some 10.Company dead lying around dreadfully mutilated, besides that flame-throwers and many armaments rooms.

18 July 1916
On the left flank was a trench with viewing slit. Through this slit one could see the French a few metres away through the viewing slit in their own trench. We had to keep awfully alert because they could almost jump across. During the day it was quieter and the artillery fire tolerable. Our twenty-one-cm shells roared into the French-held wood regularly. At dusk we gathered up the litter and found two cans of meat. We buried three corpses. Our people had just gone off to fetch the coffee and rations when their infantry began an intense fire, then the artillery joined in so that we had the same old story again. It lasted ninety minutes before dying down.

During the day there were numerous aircraft in the air and aerial fights in which three French machines were shot down. One of them hurtled to its fate nearby. Both wings had been shot off, and these twisted and turned in the air as the fuselage fell. The two occupants jumped out and thudded into the soft farmland not far from us. I will never forget the sound when they hit. It was as if somebody had tossed down two potato sacks.

19 July 1916
We had six men wounded. The little wood was peppered with twenty-one-cm shells. This evening we were supposed to be relieved. We were depressed when they failed to arrive, and that evening there was another long barrage which caused us more losses.

20 July 1916

The firing lasted all night, the whole front was up. We had worked on our trench and had protected it a bit against intrusion. In the paraffin-warmed hollows I had slept two hours when a violent canonade woke me. I got up, and we heard loud noises from the wood which we reported to the Company Commander. Meanwhile it had grown light and I quickly distributed the mail which had just arrived. Reservist Küpper with my platoon received his long-awaited letter and he handed it to me with a joyful smile. I had just started reading it when the barrage increased and the MGs began to rattle. I sprinted to my place at the centre of the platoon. I had just reached the gun rest when a shell blew up a tree and the whole works rebounded into the trench. My cleaner cried out loud, hit by splinters. When I looked back, reservist Küpper was dead in the trench. His skull had been ripped open and all his brains hung on the trench wall. The subsequent French attack did not reach the trench. Further right they were beaten off, three officers and forty-five men were captured. The weather was very fine. I took a nice photo of the moment when sentry Raaf gave the alarm.

21 July 1916

Towards 1800 it finally fell silent. We were all nervous wrecks. I was worried that the men could not hold out much longer. We had five dead and a lot of wounded, altogether ninety casualties. Yesterday (20th) evening we discovered we were being relieved, both a joy and a worry since we did not want a souvenir when leaving the position. We could not leave through the communications trench because the relief was coming that way, so we had to leave by the shell-cratered fields. A small fox terrier who had deserted the French during the night went with me.

21 July 1916

We sat in our emergency shelters in the road embankment and waited for our relief to arrive in the evening. The time passed very slowly. Concealed below a barrel I attempted to snap the great fountain of water thrown up by a twenty-eight-cm French shell as it hit the Somme river. The problem was to avoid the shell fragments while attempting to get the explosive column in the viewfinder. Finally I managed to get a photograph. Around our shelter were barrels, chairs, sofas, empty cartons etc. At midday a tremendous explosion shook the area like an earthquake. We heard it was a dynamite store at the brickworks. Many of the men in the trench were buried as the walls collapsed. A giant cloud of smoke lingered in the sky, the French began firing like crazy, obviously they suspected we were up to something. Some time later a house at Biaches was set ablaze by a shell. One thousand rounds were stored there. The dreadful chatter of the exploding munitions sounded just like an attack.

The waiting became ever more intolerable and nobody wanted to be transferred so close to being relieved. I still remember that moment when an officer's aide from the 111ers announced, in the familiar accent of my Pforzheimn home town, that he was the relief-leader and gave me the order to leave the area. Seldom was the Company ready so quickly and we crossed the Somme bridge at a fast trot.

22 July 1916
I was given my third platoon (as *Unteroffizier*) and a *Vizefeldwebel*, who had been ill, as my aide. We marched through Bouvincourt and Estrées to Tertry where we had a long rest and put our packs on waggons. The small dog stayed by my side. During our rest 2.Battalion regimental band, led by Major Krüger, passed us. I wrote in a letter this day: 'Tonight resting (1.Station) received fifteen parcels, my warmest thanks, we are on the march, suffocating atmosphere, heavy pack but heart light and mood happy, we cannot hear the firing any more! Hurrah! I am OK. Parcels everywhere properly stored, most still good.'

In the evening we reached Essigny-le-Grand via Vaux, and were billeted in barns.

23 July 1916
We had battalion parade and were addressed by Rittmeister Strahler. Our 1.Battalion was praised in regimental orders. For those who had held out at the front there was a reward of a bottle of wine and a bar of chocolate between every three men and a tin of sardines between every two. Personally I received a

bottle of wine, a bar of chocolate and a tin of sardines which tasted good. I was even happier at the recognition expressed by the Company Commander Lt Geditz and the recommendation he gave about me to Lt Sturm, who was now taking over the Company. Next day we entrained and reached the quiet position near Osly.

Georg David Bantlin (1879.1961) Stabsarzt, Inf.Div.26.

DIARY

4–26 August 1916 (Rocquigny)

Main dressing station set up in the church and nearby ruined schoolhouse for stomach operations and chest wounds. Forward a hellish noise, at night like a permanent drum roll with muzzle flashes and starshells an emotional experience: our brave men persevere in this inferno! One would not think it possible. What they have to suffer we see from the injuries, mostly artillery wounds of the worst kind, arms peppered, and how ghastly these look! And how long they take to heal! Wound care has to be more comprehensive than used to be the case with infantry wounds in order to avoid the need for operations.

So, we have plenty to do night and day, no night passes in which we do not have to perform one or two stomach operations and in which the church does not fill with wounded who are sent to the military hospital the next morning insofar their condition somehow makes travel possible.

We have fitted out the church gradually with beds and straw mattresses – rather a luxurious main dressing station now!

Luckily we are not coming under fire so that we can work in peace: bombs dropped on the hamlet by enemy aircraft always miss, even those aimed at my little house!

Letters to His Wife Hildegard Bantlin, Wyk-Föhr

6 August 1916 (Rocquigny)

Dearest Sweetheart!

It is a glorious Sunday morning – as I write this you are all probably around the coffee table making your Sunday arrangements. In my mind I pass around the breakfast table and kiss everybody on the forehead. So, good morning, dear Leutchen! And then we go together into the garden where the roses smell so sweet, to the hedge entwined with the Spanish peas, then I take your delightful photos to the beach, and so I am and remain all day with you, until at night I say goodnight to our beautiful little star! My warmest thanks for your letter of 1 August. It seems that my letters have been held back recently, at least it appears that you did not receive them for some days.

We are nicely settled in, although everything here is more primitive than we gradually got set up at Becelaere, but it will do. Dressing station is the church, very good during the summer. We were under canvas for a spell but now have quarters, and I even have a little room of my own. Our losses in the last few days have not been small, but at least not so big as we had feared. I wrote to Hermann saying that I am in his vicinity, but letters sent along the front take as long as they do to home and back, so I don't know if you will get to see him. He reported on 29th that he was well, that he writes to you little is understandable, it is not your turn until he has written to his new wife and us brothers.

A long leave for me is out of the question. On 1 August they recalled everyone in the Armeekorps who was on leave. When we will have leave again nobody knows, and as I mentioned there are two officers ahead of me for leave who have been waiting very long. The first of them made a journey with bride and parents at the begining of August and was called back. So do not cherish false hopes.

But perhaps peace will come soon. It is impossible to believe that this dreadful fighting can last much longer. In the end there will be nobody left. Yesterday I read the sad news about Robert Neumann, thus they fall one by one. How important is the work for peace when such gaps are drilled in the bloom of youth. The enemy should also consider that. May heaven protect you! Very affectionately.

A kiss.
Your D.

11 August 1916 (Rocquigny)

Dear Wife!

Today may I thank you for your Sunday letter of 6. and for the dear greetings of Erika which accompanied it. Our trip to Ostende was a nice ending to our Flemish experience. Here one has a lesser living standard, and villages are arranged much closer: the cleanliness in highly cultured France is more than questionable, but as the war goes on we are less demanding and have got used to filth so far as possible.

There is more firing here than previously, but the number of wounded has fallen over the last few days: unhappily because there is so much artillery there are many seriously wounded so that despite treatment many do not survive. Otherwise we are content, the situation is such that we have plentiful wine for those in our care. There are a large number of surgical operations to be performed but due to the long training period for the staff and our wide-ranging experience everything is going really well. I continue to be well, and I can achieve something. Yesterday we had refreshing rain, today it is fine again. Apparently it is warmer and more settled here than with you.

26 August 1916 (Rocquigny)

Dear Sweetheart!

My heartiest thanks for your short letter of 21st. In peacetime one begins to hardly dare think or hope for it. Hundreds, thousands fall daily, and we see no end to it. The first day of peace should be a national holiday and not a day to commemorate the fighting, nobody will give us back the people who have been taken. I am OK despite a lot of difficult work in the last few days.

Unfortunately I have not been able to see Hermann, apparently he could get no leave or our letters were delayed, mail in France is always rather uncertain. I would like to have shaken his hand and said something nice, for who knows if and when we will meet again: it is always bad for the infantry, at least where Hermann is it is relatively quiet, but that can change. I am very pleased that you are well.

My warmest greetings to the three of you.

Your D.

22 November 1916 (Avesnes-les-Aubert)
Dear Hilde!
A letter of 16th brought me yesterday your dearest greetings, my warmest thanks! Otherwise the post seems to be on strike for the moment. I am very glad to hear that Ischen's father is on the mend: another heavy stone lifted from the heart. We are still in the R&R quarter.

The musician with whom I am billeted and whose sick wife I am treating gives us much pleasure. He is a small, grey-haired Frenchman, talkative at all hours, never lost for a joke and the best is the mime with which he punctuates his long conversations and raises his nonsense to a delightful brand of humour. Yesterday was St Cecilia's Day, the Feast of the Musicians. Two of his small pupils – a girl as tall as Hilde and a Louis, brought presents and the boy read a wonderful speech of congratulation for the Day. After that choir-hour began in which the children sang the notes (do-re-mi-fa-so-la-ti-do) wonderfully for their age: finally coffee was served, in which I naturally took part, they also give me a cup of cocoa every evening which has to be consumed at the family sickbed. So you see it is not so bad for me. Otherwise it is really tedious. At midday we frequently go hunting: Pfister shoots and the rest of us do the driving with great strategic cunning, this being very important because the probably numerous partridge are very astute and rarely give the gunners a shooting chance: we caught a small hare and killed it at home.

30 November 1916 (Avesnes-les-Aubert)
Dear Wife!
We are still in R&R: it is a very lazy life and you may comfort yourself that it is an existence without danger which we are living. Nothing happens here at all, one is always glad to have the tiniest excuse for a trip out. Yesterday three of us went near Valenciennes on duty and made another excursion. I was very pleased to have the opportunity to revisit the city we saw fleetingly in October 1914, and view again the fine Rubens and Watteaus in the Museum, and remember the couple of fine churches and the Watteau memorial. This was our first encounter with culture in wartime then and therefore impressive

and held firm in memory: how many fine things since then we have seen and experienced in war and through war. For sure it has its good side and one must also tell oneself so in that connection – the effect of war on the people and the desire to do good deeds and to progress which are motivated by war will perhaps, so we hope, be valued by later generations more highly than the wounds it inflicts, if of course we also keep those in the foreground too.

It was difficult for me in Valenciennes to pass by the fine clothing shops: I should like to have bought you a fine morning jacket, but I remained resolute. For a few marks I had pleasure to buy you the enclosed butterfly brooch.

DIARY

3–12 December 1916 (Metz-en-Couture)
On 3 December with Stabsarzt Fritz as 'advance party' taken with twenty-four men of our Company and numerous 'advance parties' of other units by lorry to Villers-Plouich (between Cambrai and Gouzeaucourt): from there we marched in greasy dirt to Metz-en-Couture our new location.

Everything is confusion, the local *kommandant* has not got the business under control. We were put temporarily into a small house and enjoy the hospitality of the extremely beery and boozy medical company 235/222 Reserve-Div. whom we are relieving. As they have been shelling the place recently, a protective tunnel has been dug below the schoolhouse where the main dressing station is set up. Over the next few days we were active in visiting the outlying dressing stations of the medical company. That brought us to familiar terrain, which we found much changed: Rocquigny is a heap of rubble, church and everything collapsed, the roads ploughed up with craters from shells of every calibre, mud everywhere. This quagmire makes the road to the forward tunnels on the Le Transloy-Sailly highway, west of Rocquigny-Le Transloy road, which we often strolled in the evenings, no longer a pleasure, quite apart from the friendly greetings of the various calibres which come flying over.

The tunnel, hewn into the chalky subsoil, is a small relay post for a few-man medical company and a handful of wounded seeking protection here before being taken to the rear. Much larger is the chalk tunnel at Le Transloy, a large honeycomb in the limestone rock with numerous carved niches in which our own people and many soldiers have a place to rest. Further back in the Transloy 'farm' is the unloading bay, a cellar system protected as well as may be against artillery and to which in the morning hours the medical company's horse-drawn ambulances make their way, with great effort on the part of man and horse, over the steep churned-up terrain.

Le Transloy itself is the potential of destruction: ghostly remnants jut out here and there, beams or the remains of a roof in the rubble, showing that there was once here a blossoming village. Crater after crater, some so large that a horse standing upright could drown in them if they were filled with water: duds of all calibres litter the roads.

Also in Rocquigny itself and in the heavily damaged Bus, the medical people live their mole-like existence below ground: in the first are the front doctors, I took over Bus for some days when on 7th our Company finally moved in to relieve. Later the front troops will take over Bus since at Metz-en-Couture we have plenty to arrange for hygiene, surgery and service at the main dressing station.

On 12th, announcement of Kaiser's appeal for peace received by the men with interest but scepticism. The men at the front suffer very much, outside dreadful damp, no proper trenches so that they are always standing in water. When relieved they are half dead and covered in mud.

Letters to His Family at Wyk/Föhr

19 December 1916 (Metz-en-Couture)
Dear Wife and dear Ischen!

This will probably be the last letter from me to reach you before Christmas: it brings you warmest greetings and the certainty that I will be thinking of you daily: that is all I can do.

My mood is grimmer than grim, it was the same just before last Christmas, but to spend a third Christmas far from those one loves strikes hard at one's spirit: thus one becomes completely old and without energy in this war, while the years which should have been dedicated to consolidating pass us by. The misery of all people forces one under when one considers what is being destroyed with every day that the war goes on. What a wonderful Christmas gift it would have been if our Kaiser's noble offer of peace had been favourably received: but it never had a chance from the beginning, and the newspaper reports confirm that we have judged our enemies aright.[Tr.Note] One shudders to think how long this destruction will go on. The most recent failure at Verdun, which is not significant *in itself*, is being used by the French as such. There one must pray for patience and courage in the sure hope that despite the cruel energy of our enemies our people *must* remain undefeated, as they have always done previously(. . .)

Paul Kessler (1883–1978) Feldpostsekretär, Garde-Inf.Div.2

DIARY

27 August 1916 (Liéramont)
1000 hrs. March to Liéramont fourteen kilometres west, arrival 1200. The fighting in this sector had increased enormously in recent days. The outgoing troops whom we met on the way were often from companies reduced to twenty to twenty-five men, which left a very grim impression. The continuous enemy

Translator's Note:
In early December 1916 Kaiser Wilhelm II sent a note to the Vatican declaring his belief that the leaders of all Great European Powers secretly desired peace, but that each belligerent was reluctant to be the first to admit it openly. The German note stated that the war threatened to destroy the material and spiritual progress of the twentieth century. The Central Powers wished to call a halt to hostilities. If the Entente Powers would agree to immediate peace negotiations, the Central Powers would guarantee existence, honour and freedom of development, and would do everything possible to restore lasting peace for the nations then involved in the conflict. There was no reponse to this offer except that on 7 March 1917 Pope Benedict indicated that Britain and France would consider any attempt at mediation 'ill conceived.' Tr.

artillery barrage had demoralized them completely. This Liéramont is a dirty abandoned hamlet. Our service rooms in a farmhouse only meet our requirements to a limited extent.

The *Obersekretär* had taken over one room, in the neighbouring room Eichelbaum and I slept. Straw mattress filled with chaff! The worst thing is the swarms of flies even more than we had in Russia. As we are fairly close to the front – we are in range of the enemy artillery – the thunder of the guns is especially loud. Striking how many aerial battles we see. On 30 August two enemy aircraft were shot down overhead..

Letter to His Wife Elise Kessler at Lahr

29 August 1916 (Liéramont)
Now we are back in the filth, i.e. the same as last year, but at least this time one has a straw mattress and a room, if shared with one other. Worst of all are the swarms of flies almost as bad as in Russia. Even the High Staff are up to their ears in mud. We are fairly well forward on a windy corner [windy refers to enemy artillery.Tr], everybody billeted here has better things to do than make the quarters comfortable and leaves all the filth for the relief to clear up. When the fourteen days are up – usually it is never longer – everybody is glad to be out of it. How we would prefer a nice war like they have now in Rumania, more exciting and better than here under our rain of shells. It will not go well for the Rumanians, of that I am convinced, the fighting will be on their own soil, and what that means for a country they will soon find out: we know already. Rumania will be overrun. Strategically that may even mean an improvement for us. Down there Mackensen will have several hundred thousand men, he will soon show those vagabonds how Germans do things. As for the Italian declaration of war, it was merely symbolic and hardly changes anything. Yesterday evening we stood around in front of the house discussing whether the rumour about Rumania's declaration of war was true when a French aircraft flew over dropping thousands of leaflets. It looked like silver rain. I enclose one. We thanked him at once for the prompt confirmation with a few rounds, but he was too quick for us and disappeared into the clouds.

4 September 1916 (Liéramont)

My dear heart!

For the moment I would ask you to be patient, mail has been a complicated affair recently. From morning to late evening one works until one drops. After dusk we sit around a carbide lamp eating, an hour of chat and then we hit the sack.

Yes, all hell is let loose here, the inferno could not be worse and we are happy for our brave young boys when they leave here. It is very unlikely that the postal situation will improve significantly – Hindenburg! – a few weeks stoppage of mail in the interests of military security is OK with him. Is also quite right, much too much ink is being scribbled.

The weather is not very favourable for taking the cure, great shame, i.e. I am thinking of our present conditions here.

What are the little ruffians up to, have they got used to the food yet? Here we have to supplement our rations by buying food, in the difficult circumstances we get only the bare necessities. Therefore I have only sent you 300 marks. Did you get the money I paid you?

For today, cordial greetings and kisses,
Your true Paul.

Maximilian Jackowski (1893 – August 1918)
Volunteer, Motor-cycle Rider, Feldrekrutendepot I/Staff IX Reserve-Corps

In Civilian Life Food Company Employee, Hanover

Letters to Student Kurt Böhning at Dissen/Teutoburger Wald

6 September 1916

(Near Lens: Jockowski was on the Somme
until 25 August 1916)

(. . .) At the moment I am smoking a Homann cigar, which I find economical, and think about what is coming in world history. How will everything end? Courage and deeds will not fail us, nor will I if I am soon called forward to the trenches.

What must be must be. At the moment everything is going well for me. Our new area has many woods and hills which makes it rather tiring for the motor-cycle rider, but for that reason nature is also more revitalizing through change.

Lately I have had little mail, which is rather depressing seeing that there is little to talk about, therefore also today my torpitude in the letter.

The fighting here at the front is currently very cruel and murderous. People talk about treating prisoners well, but overcome by hate, cowardice and madness the captors kill or murder their prisoners: it often happens on our side too, but more sporadically. A prisoner is an unarmed person and he deserves mercy provided he is obedient and not devious. But where is humanity to be found today? Only greed, self-seeking, and destructiveness is to be found in society and not least amongst comrades. When peace breaks out there will be much unrest long afterwards. I ask: Where is God? And where do people seek God? Nowhere! Every person has almost become his own god, he loves only himself and whatever in the world makes him admired (. . .)

26 September 1916 (Lille)
(. . .) Somme, Somme! Yes, for us this word has in it something inexpressible. From here to Lille one hears this incessant activity, and if one reflects on it with somebody, he shakes his head, shrugs and says, 'Yes'. There is nothing more to be said. Whoever does his duty at the front, he has achieved something superhuman according to that. We should not speak any more of it. I prefer the heroic kind of battle rather than one against weapons which cannot be seen and against which one cannot fight heroically. It is a battle for the masses, for the individuals in the mass unrewarding.

6 October 1916 (Neuville/Bourjonval)
(. . .) We arrived here on 2nd, it was raining heavily. One had to exert oneself to the uttermost, and I know myself one keeps going even when one often thinks he cannot. The aerial activity here exceeds anything I have seen before. In the early hours one sees forty and more aircraft patrolling over the front according to

orders. The artillery fire here is incessant, often heavy, often light, *as we consider it*. One cannot properly describe it, the reader only gets a third of the picture. Our battlefront is Sailly (. . .)

12 November 1916
(. . .) I will gladly accede to your request for a description of the Somme front (. . .) It is now midnight, quiet to some degree. I will limit my account here to what I have seen personally, then other things will occur to me. Our quarters were in Neuville, a small village of only one hundred inhabitants. The area had been used in the past by the French military for manouevres. It is bare and hilly – only isolated patches of woodland, named after the nearest village, are to be seen. The French soldiery hated the area pre-war because on manouevres the people gave them short shrift and the Somme district is short of water. When we arrived the population was ordered out of the forward villages including Neuville. Next day the artillery big guns bombarded it. It was a beautiful morning into which I awoke early next day – I had slept poorly in my blanket and I heard the initial drum-roll of firing, frequently interspersed with the impact of twenty-eight to thirty-eight cm shells which were aimed at a village 1,500 metres from our own. The endless lorry traffic, ammunition convoys, provisions carts and individual troop units clattering through etc. made a major contribution to our sleep being only half-slumber and also quite light. Anyway, at 0500 as I lay dozing, meditating and listening I heard a peculiar noise which frightened me – something like ss-s-ssscht-bwuhm. Two shells hissed by leaking gas, deafening, tearing apart, killing. Ha – it went past – if the enemy barrel had been a centimetre shorter the shell would certainly have hit our house and then what would have become of me? Yes, all these thoughts they come to you without fail. If asleep one awakes at the whistling overhead, and when he awakes he is afraid, and though he may deny his fear and pretend to be brave – I say that man is a liar.

Today's war is more fearsome than when it started, when everybody was a romantic hero – today every man is a grave, strong man, almost one of the historic Germanen. What I describe here in excerpts, everybody experiences every day against a changing instrument of war, often ten, even one hundred times a day, torturing – until it has reached one and is not seldom welcome. Dear Curt, you will understand that to those, whom the horror has rattled their bones once or shall we say several times, to those no short rest is of use to win back quiet mastery of their nerves. Especially if one wants to unlock again experienced memories. At this time I feel unable to carry through my intention to fulfil your wish. Forgive me – another time perhaps when I am at home, I will be happy to tell you and then in more detail. We can then write it down for your memoirs.

Selmar Blass, Stabsarzt, Bavarian Inf.Regt.9/Bavarian Inf.Div.4

Bayrische Hauptstaatsarchiv/Kriegsarchiv Munich HS 2200

Report[21]

I was taken prisoner-of-war on 15 September 1916 by the New Zealanders at Flers. Shortly afterwards the lightly wounded and non-wounded were gesticulated to march in a certain direction. Although nobody disobeyed, the New Zealanders fired on individuals or groups of prisoners and wounded, either from confusion of some kind or the lust to murder, and killed many. Witnesses hereto were *inter alia* Hauptmann Biermer III Battalion/9.Inf Regt., Gefreiter Rügemeyer 9.Comp/9.Inf.Regt., both of whom were shot in the back, and Oberlt Golpert and Lt Wohlfahrt III/9 who barely escaped the same treatment.

My own wounded, medical teams and unwounded NCOs, and men who sought protection with me, were saved from the fate of their comrades by my successful intercession in which I insisted on an escort by a British squad.

Officers were frequently robbed after capture. Hauptmann Rubner from Bayreuth was deprived of his watch and money, Lt Bloch, 14.Inf.Regt. of his watch. A British officer did nothing and looked on while Feldunterarzt Wunsiedel was punched on the chin, causing him to pitch backwards into a shell crater. A stretcher bearer from 5.Inf.Regt, who after the fall of Flers emerged from the dressing station there with Stabsarzt Kliensberger to surrender was shot in the head despite the Red Cross armband he wore.

I did not witness the maltreatment of wounded prisoners, but most were relieved of their valuables under the pretext 'souvenir', a desire expressed as a command by officers and men alike.

British wounded were given priority in transportation from the battlefield. Despite the agreement of the British field-surgeon that German seriously wounded who needed an immediate operation would be allotted stretchers, and despite the fact that I had stretcher-bearers available, my people were forced to look after the British wounded first. This resulted in German wounded spending four days on the battlefield exposed to the weather and were then subjected to mutilating operations which would have been avoided by preventative treatment had they been brought in much sooner.

Each wounded man received a notebook similar to a cheque book, a sheet of paper without string with his name and type of wound was hung on a button of his uniform jacket. On the four cm broad block the surgeon made the same observations so that he had a simple and certain control without a patient's book. He was pleasant and professional throughout. He was practically the only British surgeon whose professional attitude merited unreserved recognition.

The field hospital consisted of tents well stocked with instruments and dressings but had no wards. There were three surgeons including Sikhs. A senior surgeon directed the ambulances. Medical treatment was on the whole satisfactory except for the obsessive tendency for mutilating surgery. There were insufficient surgeons and German help was called upon frequently. The nursing teams included a large number of Indian stretcher bearers. Auxiliary stretcher-bearers had the initials SB sewn on the upper sleeve.

The First Division camp was an open square surrounded by numerous barbed wire hedges. It was a real Hottentot corral without any protection against the weather except two square metres of roof per officer, but no protection at the sides. Few had greatcoats, there were no blankets or straw. Sleep was impossible because of the cold. Whoever fell asleep with exhaustion was half frozen next morning. Rations were ship's biscuit and tea on the first day, then two days of normal fare which was good and sufficient. No force was used during interrogations although the quest for 'souvenirs' was very lively. Stabsarzt Kliensberger was asked if he could not find 'an Iron Cross' for souvenir hunters. Incidentally the men were questioned cleverly by the use of a harmless conversational tone. The intelligence officer was anxious to know the effects on us of the new tanks used for the first time that day. When we told him that their existence did not come as a surprise he was scarcely able to hide his disappointment. The artillerymen, both officers and me, were treated less delicately, being subjected to heavy pressure, and every means possible being exerted to weaken their morale and so obtain details about artillery positions.

At Albert Camp we eleven officers were accommodated in a small round tent on white earth without blankets or straw. A persistent rainfall over two days soon had the improperly erected tent under water, and sleep was not possible in the cold and damp. Everybody gave Justinus who was sick whatever they could spare. The camp doctor, who allowed himself to be approached once, shrugged when we asked that Justinus be taken to the military hospital: 'The British wounded are no better off, they have to lie in the open all day waiting for the hospital train.' A memorable confirmation of the heavy British losses and pitiful standard of care available for the wounded.

A man whose bloodied stools undoubtedly indicated dysentry was forced to remain in the PoW camp even though he was very weak and should have been hospitalized. The inadequate medical care reflected the confusion behind the military front, so crass we had to smile at it. Our impression of the organization we knew was such that on the first day the exact work plan of the assault troops, tanks, the lorry park (over 50,000 vehicles was not unusual), the Indian cavalry at readiness (its horses near the guns presumably to accustom them to the firing): numerous light and heavy guns not dug-in but only surrounded by sandbags, their location being known to my precise recall: and finally the enormous stocks of ammunition.

Everywhere an uncoordinated nervous activity reigned and created nothing. Despite the surplus of labour, which included many blacks, the harvest was rotting in the field. The only people doing something useful were German PoWs formed up in work parties for road building. These highways, mostly three-lane, were very well constructed and led almost right up to the front line. Rails had been laid to the river Ancre. The Amiens-Rouen track had been widened by two new tracks but even so the transport difficulties caused them a tremendous headache. Between Mametz and Méaulte tent villages had been created for troops because the former towns at these localities had been demolished. These tent villages were disguised with trees against aerial reconnaissance, but at night showed lights without a thought to German aircraft.

The morale of the front-line troops was not good because of the terrible losses, but they put a brave face on it with their military bands. We were the object of much abuse: 'Hallo Fritz kaputt?'; once somebody shouted 'Captain Cöpernick.' Worse was prevented by our guards while the British officers tended to ignore it and looked on with a certain pleasure at our discomfiture. Discipline seemed very loose. Decorations worn very occasionally. A Prussian officer told me that the British officers did not dare to intervene to prevent wholesale looting by the Canadians. On the other hand morale amongst rearward troops was very high. This was noticed especially near Albert, where British troops exchanged insults with the French population . . . .

Inf.Regt.
Prinz Friedrich der Niederlande
(2.Westphalian) No.15.
I-No 4904 I/16 (Source BA/MA Freiburg PH 10 II/49)

Report:
26 September 1916
EXPERIENCES FIGHTING ON THE SOMME

A. General

The position taken over by the regiment, though badly damaged by shelling, conformed to basic trench warfare principles with running trenches, wire obstructions and fixed defences. 12 September brought a change in the tactical situation and objectives. The enemy breakthrough of the line at Marrière

Wood-Inf.Regt.55 transformed the fighting if only briefly into open-field battle. Determination and decisiveness, less necessary in trench warfare, was suddenly in demand, especially of the junior commanders. The commanders were equal to what was demanded of them. (. . .) The fact that on 12 September the enemy did not build on this penetration was a significant contributory factor to the success of the junior commanders. After the situation was restored and the line repaired, the objectives of trench warfare resumed.

B. Especially

I

The enemy artillery preparation for the attacks used almost exclusively heavy and the heaviest calibres. The ordnance and fire direction were first-class. The shell craters were laid in an accurate line successively in the immediate vicinity of the trenches. Only rarely in this 'preparatory artillery fire' was a so-called 'rogue' observed. Artillery spotting was apparently done from aircraft and barrage balloons. Apart from this cooperation with the artillery, the aircraft also engaged our infantry. At low level they machine-gunned the trenches and quarters causing casualties.

The effect here was greater against trenches than the cratered areas (or 'nests'9). The trenches could be simply blanketed by artillery while targeting the nests was much more difficult. Reserves and support troops moving up were repeatedly machine-gunned by aircraft.

Under the enormous expenditure of ammunition by the enemy to soften up the position, the trenches available were very soon collapsed and the subterranean rooms caved in. The remnants of the duty men and reinforcements used shell craters for accommodation and protection, and here their losses were far lower than in the trenches. The enemy lost the possibility of accurate fire, and the explosive effect of the shelling was diminished.

The enemy forces deployed for heavy artillery purposes and in aircraft was enormous and in the opinion of the regiment it no way corresponds to our own. Little plunging shellfire was observed. The following conclusions were drawn:

1.) During the softening up process before an attack, not too many people forward. Distribute the support troops (greater part of company) behind the position to be defended, so arranged that when enemy artillery fire ebbs can be pushed quickly into the forward line for possible counter-attack. The support troops can be accommodated in short lengths of trench or shell craters. Underground galleries are dangerous under heavy calibre shelling. There is no way they can be built to prevent their caving in. The galleries in this regiment's sector were almost all caved in. This caused the regiment heavy losses. The troops are safer in shell craters or open trenches.

2.) Set out the position so that as wherever possible it cannot be viewed from above, ahead or at the sides. Especially important for the support troops. The continuous line, very desirable for quiet circumstances and trench warfare, is not absolutely essential! Sudden fire from nests once the enemy believes he has exterminated the oppostion in the trenches will often disconcert him and ruin his attack. Small gaps in occupied trenches do not seem dangerous so long as they are defended to the sides and rear by machine-gun fire. On the contrary they invite the enemy to concentrate his fire on vacant areas of trench and so spare lives!

Camouflage all trenches and military nests against aircraft with tarpaulins and brushwood/vegetation. Avoid all unnecessary movement! Essential with widespread positioning of the men are energetic leaders who can control their people under all circumstances.

3.) Enemy aircraft have too little opposition to their activities. It is obvious that with the great expansion of our front and the large number of war theatres for which aircraft are needed, we are not able to provide the same amount of aerial forces at a particular place as can the British and French. Nevertheless we observed that only rarely were enemy machines shot down by our flak. Flak was therefore only available in *very* small numbers or was too far back. Especially important however is the use of flak and bombers during the attack while support troops are moving into the front line and reserves are being brought up. These will, even if they cannot paralyze enemy air reconnaissance because of lack of numbers, at least seriously hamper its activity. The enemy aircraft flew in an exemplary manner. Almost no movement of our support troops and reserves escaped their attention. Besides directing artillery fire they made low level machine-gun attacks on troops moving in rearwards terrain.

II

As with his softening-up process, the enemy's barrier fire was well organized. To coincide with his infantry attacks he laid a triple belt. Besides this the reserve trenches, so far as they were known to the enemy, the regimental command posts, the assumed transit channel for reserves, the roads and depressions to the rear were subjected to lively fire with shells of all calibres, shrapnel-shells and poison gas shells.

III

The enemy used few gas shells. Only seldom amongst the otherwise fierce artillery fire on depressions to the rear and the transit channel for troops did gas shells fall. The gas used was the same as at Verdun. Our gas masks provided excellent protection. As the regimental command posts were gassed several times, gas masks were worn there. In strong winds and where passage was possible the gas thinned and dispersed very rapidly. Health problems were only experienced by men who had not worn their gas mask or had removed it prematurely. They suffered sickness and dizzy spells quickly cured by fresh air.

IV

The enemy's infantry attacks proved enthusiastic leadership. The build-up of strong forces and movement of reserves forward was smart. Less smart and enthusiastic was the execution of the attack itself, where the morale of the individual infantryman was important. A large number of these were under the influence of alcohol. If the enemy infantry found our defences alert, or faced an MG, any initial enthusiasm soon waned and the waves of attackers flowed back. Prisoners were happy to be in captivity and to have survived the danger. It was noted however that all prisoners expressed certainty of their victory. They still believed that a decisive success on the Somme would eventually be theirs – *on se battra jusqu'au bout!* (We shall fight to the end!) one often heard. To the question what this aim or end was, they had no answer. The outward impression of officers and men was, according to the circumstances, not a bad one. There were some very old men amongst them.

VII Command Posts

Whereas it is desirable that senior commanders are close to their men, especially in such intensive fighting as on the Somme, where they can oversee the occasionally fast-changing situation and, depending on circumstances, become personally involved, never the less the location of the command post very close to the front line undoubtedly has its major drawbacks. This very often made itself felt with disruption to the secure distribution of orders and transmission of reports. Telephone communications both ahead and to the rear were almost permanently cut, especially since the regimental command post was in the second belt of artillery barrier fire, but several inter-post runners, a light-signal post crew, several despatch runners, linemen and two morse-lamp operators were also killed or wounded in performance of their duties. Additionally the barrier fire, which made personal observation at the critical moment almost impossible, was very disruptive. The lively traffic which could be seen by enemy air reconnaissance, receiving and distributing reports and orders in the open drew fire, especially on these posts.

VIII Signalling

1.) Morse traffic by lamp from the regimental post to a station near 26.Inf.Brigade performed excellently. Only once was it out of service, due to heavy fog. There can be no doubt, however, that the enemy was reading our telegrams retransmitted by the receiving station and that the use of cover words did not satisfactorily prevent this happening. The despatches had to be fully encoded.

2.) This required too much time when under pressure. A repeat of the message from the receiving station was necessary to confirm it had been taken down accurately.

3.) Morse lamp usage forwards was not possible because of the terrain. The connections had to be maintained by inter-post runners. These men carried out their duties with great bravery and ensured that contact was maintained even under the heaviest fire. One must be careful not to use for this task men unfit for front duty. They must be especially intelligent and physically able.

4.) [. . .]

5.) The regiment used carrier pigeons on only one occasion, to fly out two messages. It is not known if the birds arrived.

6.) A radio station would certainly have been useful.

7.) [. . .]

8.) Barrier and covering fire were requested from the front line by means of red and green tracer. Onc man was on constant watch for these light signals. They would then be repeated to the regimental command post. This method of signalling has never failed. A great deal of tracer ammunition is necessary in the front line. Keeping a reserve at the regimental post proved valuable. The urgent request from ahead could then be fulfilled quickly.

IX

The greatest demands were made of the medical teams in view of the high casualty rate. Several times every night stretcher-bearers had to make the run from the front to the medical post (1,800 metres) with wounded. This resulted in major losses in dead and wounded which could not immediately be made good. It is suggested for such emergencies to have a reserve of stretcher-bearers on standby behind the front to replace the losses. The medical company was fully engaged transporting the wounded from the medical post to the rear.

The measure proved the need to have at readiness at the medical post an energetic Front NCO to direct lightly wounded, sick and stragglers immediately to the front line. It is also rewarding to have energetic patrols frequently scour the rear area for stragglers.

The main cause of casualties was artillery fire. This resulted in 198 dead, 817 wounded, of whom 170 remained at their post, and 198 missing of whom most were buried alive and could not be dug free. Amongst the casualties are eight officers dead, twenty-two wounded, three missing.

The health situation was satisfactory even during days of fighting. There were some minor cases of neurosis due to days of high tension or as a result of cave-ins.

X Provisions

Food was plentiful and good. Coffee, tea, mineral water and alcohol were supplied to the front. Large quantities of tobacco goods were also available. The placing of a provisions warehouse at Allaines, continuously replenished by lorries from the rear, proved good. Corresponding to the circumstances only mainly cold fare, preserves, ham, bread, could generally be brought forward. It was occasionally possible however to provide hot coffee. The men liked mineral water.

The psychic impression of battle naturally rather thrust the need for food into the background, while thirst and the craving for tobacco were noticeable. Therefore sufficient liquids and tobacco must be made available. The availability of provisions was exemplary on the Somme.

XI

Rifles, MGs and ammunition were good. No major irregularities were reported. Equipping far more men with MGs to replace immediately men wounded by artillery fire or buried alive is required urgently. Little use was made of hand grenades under the present battle conditions.

XII

The front line made frequent bitter complaints against our own artillery which is alleged to have fired too short. Reports to the artillery and their command posts were unsuccessful. The difficulty for our artillery, which probably had insufficient information about the position of our front line following changes during fighting phases should be explained. It may also be that some flanking artillery fire came from La Maisonnette Ferme and that precise fire from these guns, often targeted by the enemy, was not possible.

That German artillery fired on German trenches is probably confirmed based on the direction from which fire came and by the observation that a particular battery fired initially on the enemy trenches correctly, but then suddenly one or both guns began to fire scattered rounds into our own trenches. The impression this made on the front line, which had already had enough to put up with from the heaviest enemy calibres, can naturally be imagined. Once during an enemy attack a request was made not to provide barrier fire and the decision was taken to defend with infantry only because front-line troops feared being fired on by German artillery. The men said after the attacks: 'Provided our own artillery does not fire we can handle the enemy infantry.' In any case it seems urgent to rectify this situation with all means possible since it is depressing for the men and they have no confidence in German artillery.

XIII Morale

The morale of the men was excellent from first day to last. The Westphalian man does not yield no matter how hard things may get. It is therefore not surprising that, after the men were from 8 to 16 September for the most part constantly under the heaviest artillery fire, without sleep, with little food, under great nervous tension and the greatest mental strain, remained at their posts and fought off numerous infantry attacks, they should go through an evident relaxation of body and mind. It changes nothing in the assessment of their conduct. It can be said generally that the impression of high morale was all the greater since they were exposed not only to very accurate heavy calibre shelling of their trenches but also inaccurate German artillery fire. The infantry attacks were a convalescence for the men. The attacks were greeted with relief and jubilation. It meant that they were thrown into hand-to-hand combat man against man and in that – as they knew – they were superior to the French. Pale and hollow-cheeked through lack of sleep and the nervous pressure, they came out of the trenches all in good heart. A certain reaction is now being perceived as the nervous situation subsides.

Signed: Riebensalm
Oberst and Regimental Commander, 26 September 1916

Hugo Frick (1894 – 12 May 1917)
Vizefeldwebel later Leutnant, Reserve-Inf.Regt.6/Reserve-Div.9

In Civilian Life a Law Student at Ellwangen
(Source: BfZ N97–1)

Letters to His Mother and Sister at Ellwangen

29 September 1916 (Somme Front)
And we made our Somme summer trip, whether I shall return from it I have no means of knowing. If not I shall die a hero for whom you need shed no tears. My things, diary etc. will then come home. Perhaps all worries are unnecessary and I shall escape from the mess safe and sound.

Leaving Champagne came all too quickly, mail was blocked, so that probably you have received no letter of mine for some time. I am lying in rain and mud in the bivouac. Tonight I have cold, damp earth to lie on, last night a nice soft bed. I look forward to seeing how it all turns out: we are north-east of Péronne near the greatest battlefield and cemetery in world history. As soon as it starts I will of course report to you as often as possible. But the mail stops for such large military operations. For Joseph, Father etc. I have a long letter which I could not post. It is still raining. Many people say it is not so bad here at

Verdun by a long chalk, so chin up. Today we go into battle as heroes. Therefore best wishes to all, parents, sister, relations, friends, sooner or later there will be an end to it.

Therefore warmest greetings. Your young Hugo TChr [abbreviation for the Tübingen Student Union Cherusker, to which Frick belonged.]

P.S. I should have been a Leutnant soon, but now nobody knows when our troops will leave the Somme.

3–4 October 1916

1 to 3 October, I never experienced anything like it, these seventy-two hours became an eternity, the seconds minutes. Believe me, my experience at the Vaux pales into insignificance against what I lived through north of Péronne. It is now 2100 on 3 October – my confirmation was ten years ago – a shell fell behind our hole. We have only shell craters etc. for protection – and it buried us in masses of earth several inches over our heads: I dug myself free, wriggled out and pulled out the other two, platoon leader Lt Völlger and the orderly officer.

None of us was hurt by splinters, escaped with understandable terrible shock, for what hours we had behind us, where one so systematically courts death. It mocks you, against this one cannot defend oneself, in the shape of exploding shells, whose ferocious splinters spray around, then mortar bombs which tear holes in the ground as deep as a house, myself in a one-metre deep hole in the ground, the whole three days long, seventy-two long, long hours: one might despair morally, run from it, get white hairs, three days in the forward trenches, then we were relieved 3 October evening and went into two (support) trenches where a moment ago giant twenty-eight cm shells lit everything up, yet we have, thank God, who can evaluate the word, a bombproof underground room for some time, but also the whole area ahead lies under French artillery fire. It is no longer war but mutual extermination with technology, what chance does the soft human body stand against that?

We have to stay here another twelve days, pray for me, I also have belief in, and comfort from, prayers in the hours of terror, just think, earlier if I spent half an hour in the rain I got sick, and now after thirty hours in the rain, sitting in the wet, afterwards no warm fireplace, no dry clothes, nothing happens. Tensing all one's strength stops one falling ill. Probably rheumatism will come later, now I am really well if you can call it that. I have received no post for ten days, have you been long without news from me? Well, let us hope to God that I survive this Somme (=summer) trip in one piece.

Warmest greetings and kisses, your young
Hugo Tchr!

9 October 1916 (Somme)

The strains and deadly fears we experience here are more than horrendous and defy description. We hope to be away soon, the losses are also considerable, mostly from artillery. On 29 September I went to the religious service: general absolution gave us the best preparation for everything which lay ahead. And you, dear little mother, are thankful in every letter that I am not at the Somme. It is a mutual war of extermination. Let us hope that Joseph also comes through well. With winter underwear I remain provisionally at peace still but since we are in the trenches I can carry nothing around. Also packed a large parcel with two shirts and underwear, chalk from Champagne and some other things, I do not know if I can get it to the Post. Once again my thanks for your four parcels! I am still rolling my own cigarettes. But you sent papers again, I had enough for 150, and when the tobacco is all used up I will still have 120 papers. The stamps are also all stuck together. At the moment I have no time to write letters to Africa and America.

Received hoey from Uncle Hugo, still in Champagne, still have had no time to thank him! I celebrated the Feast of the Rosary without being aware of it, with many rosaries, on 1 October one rosary, 2 October three rosaries, 3 October six rosaries. Was between Bouchavesnes and Moislins where the French are the most far forward. We will soon be relieved, probably Norbert will soon be taking part in the Somme playground, one is still astonished to think that soft, sensitive human bodies can still emerge sound from this hail of iron! It seems I am immune against colds. Over thirty hours under artillery fire, cowering in the rain in a small hole, water covering all members, and now after great nervous and physical tension, having been buried alive and caught nothing, not even a cough, that must be a miracle. I cannot explain it.

In Württemberg it is a Royal House anniversary, try to get a Jubilee thaler! Is it really the Queen's birthday and a Government anniversary? And since then daily one or two rosaries for consolation and strength. When I was smoking heavily it seemed as though I had something in the oppressive hours and days when I needed it most. I have now stopped the chalk work, I have no time for study and even less inclination! Fruit was good! The cigarette paper is gummed better.

Warmest greetings and kisses!
Your Hugo TChr.

10 October 1916 (Templeux-la-Fosse)

In commemoration of that wonderful day when Generalmajor von Glahn pinned the Iron Cross to the hero's breast and made me a knight – Also the birthday of Swabian Queen Charlotte. I had today the strangest stroke of luck: in enemy territory, in hard fighting on the greatest battlefield in world history, north of the Somme, north of Péronne, I have met my best friend, my bosom friend, for whom I would have gone through fire, and he for me! In Templeux-la-Fosse. That was really a wonderful day, 10 October 1916. True I am still in the dangerous Somme region and staying in a French private house from which the occupants were probably ejected suddenly, for many cherished things have been left behind, and those dear men in field-grey naturally use everything, and so we have a white tablecloth and cutlery at mealtimes. Many of them are fooling around dressed in women's clothing. Afterwards we sleep in the cellar, for at any moment a French shell can kill us all and bring the house tumbling down around our ears.

Well, we take that all into account, and today had quite a pleasant day. Today I tried out something new with alcohol. Coffee, tea, tea with rum. Cognac from Ellwangen and cognac from Jupp. One glass of beer, one bottle of wine and when I reported wearing my Iron Cross, which the general pinned on me himself, to my dear Company Commander Lt Steinbrecher (from Saxony), a very dear man whom I like, we celebrated with champagne. A few more cognacs but still alert despite that. With

God's help I will bring my Iron Cross home safe and sound. I look forward to meeting Joseph again perhaps tomorrow. Received today back-number newspapers of 12th, 14th and 16 September! Humbug. Also letter of 3 October (yesterday also of 5th), then a small package with socks. From father also received the watch.

Warmest greeting and kisses,
Your young Hugo TChr.

24 December 1916 (Sainte Emile)

Magic of Christmas! Today is Christmas Eve, the Feast of Joy and Love! We here in the tumult of war are slaves of war, of stone-hard hearts and rough appearance. Yet today a breath of Christmas pass through every heart! Therefore my dear ones! Only a single wish – Peace!

We have been here in Sainte Emile since 18 December, Joseph must know it well for he was here in October? We are here as divisional reserve, tomorrow we move out to Moislains, which was previously in the midst of the horror of the Somme cannonade, today somewhat quieter, and after a few days further on.

My losses in men here are from illness: whether I can hold out remains to be seen. We live the filthiest existence like animals of course. Today, Sunday and Christmas Eve we began with exercises. Then I rested and attended Christmas religious service for confessions at 0600 in a barn. Afterwards we sang carols around a Christmas tree, we are billeted in the big sugar factory. Otherwise we have no Christmas. Weakness is a stranger to me, though some would be happy to be taken prisoner as at Verdun. I gird myself against it and will defend the Fatherland to my last drop of blood.

Greetings and kisses,
Your Hugo TChr.

28 December 1916 (Somme Trench)

I wish you a happy New Year 1917: may this year at its birth bring us the ardently desired Peace on Earth for all people! Received yesterday the photograph with the four girls: many thanks! How I spent my Christmas: on Christmas Eve all warrant officers of the 8th were with the Company Commander: there was champagne and red wine, beer and various schnapps: towards 0200 on the shutter lamp. Then on 25th at midday we got ready to move out. Marched for hours with pack over tracks and fields, all covered in mud: some shelling greeted us, then this night at Moislains – was once a large village of 1,300 souls, today no house left in one piece, from the thousands of shell hits: additionally they fired at us at Christmas – had noticed our departure – especially heavy although nothing to compare with October. We sought a cellar: the one-metre high rubble of a house sheltered the cellar. A nice cat had remained loyal to the ruins and sat on my knees. From 26th I was with the 6th Company in a trench, but not the foremost one: colossal deep system. I never worked up a Christmas spirit with the carols, after the first verse I dried up.

My Christ child has arrived: ten marks for Maria, fifty to the savings bank.

Warmest greetings and kisses,
Happy New Year,
Your Hugo TChr.

31 December 1916 (Somme Battle)

New Year's Eve 2000 hours, last moments of the bloody year of war 1916. Oh, these are heavy hours, such portentous moments to live bound to a narrow dug-out with no merriment or punch, no freedom to move nor without the loved ones of home! I would love to be sitting with you on the sofa, singing, chatting and praying, afterwards burying myself in the pillows of my bed to sleep and sleep and never wake! How were the New Year's celebrations in the cathedral, I would love to have been there. The rosary is often my only comfort! We are not far from the British. Am near 6th Company and do not have my comrades of 8th, decorated a ten cm tall tree with lights and sang the first verses of several Christmas carols. I do not smoke very much. Anthon Withum wrote to me, he also wants to be an airman. If people have it good, they want to do better for themselves.

Warmest greetings and kisses,
Hugo TChr.

9 January 1917 (Somme Infantry Trench)

So, your Bua, your Boy has become a Prussian officer. But under what circumstances here have I become a lieutenant. This afternoon we trembled for our miserable lives despite all our phlegm. The French poured twenty-eight cm shells on our trench line – we are the fourth back – leaving nothing recognizable: many of the deep galleries were collapsed, and we were even scared in the deepest! When I describe how I look, that goes for us all. Covered in mud and filth! Same shirt and socks since 16 December 1916, therefore since last year chilled to the bone and then again breaking out in sweat. I have not frozen yet, and on 7 January I crawled out of my gallery and somebody came up to congratulate me, then my Company Commander – am still with 6th Company – but officially I still did not know. Two days went by, was with Company Commander and spoke by telephone to Battalion Commander Hauptmann Peschak who informed me that, according to an Order in Cabinet, I have been a lieutenant officially since 3 January.

Tonight 9/10 January 0400 we were relieved and will be resting at Sainte Emilie until 14th: I have not washed since Boxing Day, last time was at Moislains! Just now sewed shoulder straps with a safety needle on my old jacket – you know the one! I am surprised at my luck – if even the shells are not silent for officers – I became lieutenant as youngest of three 8th Company applicants and another two of 5th Company. God gives me no protection! Or does He? How are the trousers for which I was measured at Rindelbach? And have you enough material for a suit? If so, have it made, the tailor has the measurements! I will write then about my decoration. Therefore I hope to bring the lieutenant home safely.

Warmest greetings and kisses,
Your Hugo TChr.

17 February 1917 (Ancre Region)

Just received with gratitude the parcel with cheese and cigarettes from Würzburg. We have now arrived at the worst place on the whole Western Front, on the Ancre (part of the Somme Front) where the British attack several times a day every day, we live under a hail of iron. Whoever survives that has God's special protection. But you need have no unnecessary fears! Where Grandcourt was evacuated, near Miraumont, it is under fire from two sides. The earth trembles and shakes. The heaviest calibres do their work here, just the British and us. Therefore only a miracle can bring me out of this battleground, which puts Verdun and October on the Somme in the shade. All that is said to prepare you. If there is a delay in my letters it may be because of the postal system. If I am wounded you will hear soon enough. If I fall, I die a hero's death for the Fatherland. Am I assured for war in the policy? I hope you are all really well, and send the warmest greetings and kisses.

Your Hugo.

Fell in action, 12 May 1917

Sächsische Pionier (Mineur) Kompanie 323/Reserve-Div.23

Company Order
25 October 1916 (near Nurlu)

Point One   The fundamental principles of the German Army are discipline and order. Trench RII presents the contrary. We are responsible in every respect for Sector D. I therefore order: Upon arrival at RII trench, every sergeant must collect *at once* and *daily* from all living quarters all objects lying around. These include ammunition, hand grenades, dirty sandbags, rolls of barbed wire, stakes, entrenching tools, wire-cutters, miners' beams used as bridges, helmets, leather wear, gas masks, etc. He has at his disposal for the area of a single living quarters, a completion squad of ten, therefore thirty for three living quarters, who can clean out a small area of trench in a very short time.

Point Two   This morning a sergeant who had arrived at the position two hours earlier was unable to describe to me its dimensions. In future I will consider this attitude of disinterest as disobedience to my order of 24 October.

Point Three   The order that no more chalk trenches can be dug for lack of men does not mean that piles of chalk rubble should be deposited in the galleries. This abuse is to be countered energetically.

Point Four   I know that the demands on dutiful sergeants are great. The segeants are superior in authority under all circumstances to sergeants of the completion squads. These are to be used to assist.

Point Five   Our miners are preparatory workers and can deploy completion squads in any manner necessary at this location.

Signed Geissler

Hugo Natt (1881 – 1963) Stabsarzt, Inf.Regt 118/Reserve-Div.56

In Civilian Life a Physician from Frankfurt/Main

DIARY (Source: BfZ NO5.4)

8 November 1916 (St Quentin)

Not much to report. Remains tense awaiting next move to Somme. Thus no calm while working. General busy visit to the pension/restaurant on the market place. The first time with Carsten saw Prinz Eitel Friedrich with his Pour le Mérite. Later same place we saw Lt Althaus (airman) with same decoration. Airmen are the mainstay of the wine restaurant. Mostly good-looking figures, less lovely are the monocle-wearers and the amounts of champagne consumed. Ate together in the officers' mess at the Hotel de France. After that went back to pension where to my pleasant surprise met my colours-brother Ramsch, and agreed to see him later. A lot of drunkenness, as usual, before going to the front. Hauptmann Collmann, face florid, related in a loud voice so that all the adjoining tables could not avoid hearing of his exhausting contribution at Divisional Staff. Hauptmann Lüters was at his side, all interest and friendship: 'a pair of lovebirds, strangers to falsity' I quoted to Reuling, who was sitting near me and watching the theatre with equal enjoyment. The new regimental commander seated near them left because of the smoking. Next, orderly officer Klein was sent a glass of champagne. What a farce! This rivalry for the favour of superiors from the lower orders, who perhaps somehow, some time, might need some influence on the commander. Ramsch and I enjoyed a cordial bottle of wine. We talked of home and exchanged photographs in his flat at Rue d'Orleans 118. As he recovered only recently from diphtheria, I promised to call by early tomorrow to give him a check-up.

9 November 1916 (Fresnoy-le-Grand)
Visited Ramsch this morning. Regiment left 0900. Marched to Fresnoy-le-Grand where we spent the night. Good quarters in the pharmacy.

10 November 1916 (Walincourt)
Marched to Walincourt. Fairly large village. Mainly occupied by walking wounded from military hospital. On first stroll through locality immediately impressed by the women and girls who give you the eye more randy and brazen than anywhere before. My 'landlady' brings me her 'friend', a fat, tolerably pretty girl allegedly the bride of a German soldier. I gave her an icy reception. Next day I got another, much better and quieter lodging in the walking-wounded quarter. Great unrest, speculation on where we are being sent. Corresponding massive alcohol intake.

14 November 1916 (Marquion)
Left today for Marquion. The route led us through Cambrai, of which we saw little marching through the outskirts, arrived at destination late afternoon, worn out after twenty-five kilometres. All ate together. Oepen has been transferred to the field hospital, we have Graeff instead. We talked about the peace negotiations with Russia, of which much has been discussed in last few days. The talks are under way: in Berlin the Russian legation has been lit up and a double guard posted. Now it seems that the talks were broken off at the last moment after the Entente guaranteed Russia a big loan. Accommodation really cramped and unpleasant.

15 November 1916 (Favreuil)
Marched to Favreuil. Arrived late afternoon. Streets soft under-

foot. The entire Battalion Staff in a tiny room. We lay on stretchers. The companies in huts of corrugated iron, have window frames but no glass. The entire Battalion Staff in one similar barracks hut: the horses another, but no straw and the poor animals have to bed down in the mud. There are far too many people in the village. Heavy artillery fire can be heard from the front.

16 November 1916 (Miraumont)

This evening we went to the position, initially the so-called resting area *Felsenkeller* at Miraumont. The Battalion Staff marched together. Cloudless night. At Achiet-le-Grand I saw the medical team of Regt.120 whom we are relieving. Achiet is under fire and the patients are in the cellars. We became separated from Staff. We assumed they had gone on ahead. Near Achiet-le-Petit a couple of duds hissed by overhead. We waited ten minutes for them to explode. Unpleasant situation in the darkness, alone on the highway, not knowing roads, a lot of firing. We had just found out that we had to wait for the companies to arrive when Staff turned up. Hauptmann Lüters had waited fifteen minutes for us but we came along a parallel road and so missed him. The route was tolerable, single file. Now and then a shell-hole. The first to see it had to shout 'Shell-hole!' and everybody following then took up the cry. The roads got continually worse. Now and then an ammunition truck came roaring up, at the order 'Move aside right' we usually finished up in deep ditches alongside the highway. The trenching officer, the tall Lt Unterhorst, led us.

Next we followed a railway bridge and then, because this spot is under constant heavy fire, marched at quick tempo along a steep embankment up to the ridge where the Felsenkeller is found (a few metres above the embankment). Overall it took us three and a half hours. All terribly exhausted. 'What next?' Is the question repeated over and over. To our right, no more than a regiment's breadth away is where the British broke through. Apparently they had an artillery barrage for three days then attacked in fog without any softening-up, took five battalions prisoner including a regimental commander.

17 November 1916 (Miraumont)

Have a good spot in a niche in the rocks where a bed has been fitted. Graeff made himself comfortable on a stretcher. I surveyed our new surroundings. We are in an enormous chalky depression: walls, ceiling, everything white chalk. The walls are uneven with zig-zags and cracks, permeated everywhere by fissures running in parallel. The limestone is in layers and it is quite easy to peel away great blocks. In the candlelight the water trickles and glitters, less surface water than damp or from exhalations. In the depression is an entrance aperture about two metres high, three metres broad. A corridor about four metres wide and the same height, about eight metres long, leads slightly upwards. At its end it forks into two-metre high tunnels, one and a half metres wide, very narrow, into either side of the hill. The corridors are uneven and passage is very awkward over long stretches.

In an extension to the entrance corridor is an ante-room to the two main corridors, like a small hall built round a large column of rock. This is the dressing station. Between this room and the corridor there is a raised space like a grotto. Access to it is by a stairway of fallen rock: since its roof has deep fissures and cracks it is supported by thick beams. These are the living quarters for the medical team, and in the dim light the grotto looks like a thieves' kitchen, like the company in 'The Count of Monte Cristo' etc. I walked and climbed through most of the corridors. The conditions are awful. We have at the moment two battalions in the tunnels, apart from men of Regt.120 and pioneers, etc. Altogether about 3,000. There is only one exit: two small orifices so close to the exit that it amounts to only one way out. There is a single air vent. The air situation in the tunnels is so bad that men go naked because the heat is so intolerable. They lie together on the stone floors in the narrow tunnels. If a shell were to hit the air vent or exit I shudder to think of the disaster it would cause.

18 November 1916 (Miraumont)

Last evening Battalion Staff went to the position with Feldunterarzt Graeff. I did not get to bed until after midnight. Because of large fissures in rock – large blocks in roof seem to be hanging free – feeling of safety not great. Early today snow, deep mud. Heavy firing began early morning. After lunch we learned that the British had taken Grandcourt. Hauptmann von Beringe then came with the report that the British broke through Regt.106 to our right and had access to our trench from the side. Battalion 120 immediately ahead of us, whom we were supposed to relieve today, were taken prisoner. Our Company Commander at Battalion for briefing was also captured. We lost the three MGs. Lt Perron, Oberleutnant Becker and Lange are PoWs. I dressed a very complicated fracture of the upper thigh, then a wounded Regt.120 officer. This latter told me that the British approached the trenches with their hands raised in surrender, then suddenly hurled hand grenades. Orders came from II.Battalion to prepare. I Battalion was to take over trench of lost Battalion 120. Tremendous artillery barrage. Now and then heavy, thundering impact on the roof of rock bunker.

The British had Grandcourt bottled up. In general all down in the mouth. If the British wrap up Miraumont all of us in the rock-bunker mousetrap will go into the bag. At first we laughed about this then when we thought about it, it dominated all conversation. Graeff reported that the dressing station had been shifted back, also he was deafened in the right ear by explosion. A large number of wounded came streaming in. At 2100 suddenly: 'Gas alarm!' Earlier, when I smelled it, I could taste the gas. Rapidly donned mask. Some people searching around in desperation for their masks. Then it dispersed. Remove masks. Then it got stronger again. Outside the entrance we heard the repeated dull detonation of gas grenades. Feldunterarzt Binswanger arrived. More and more wounded. Wearing the gas mask, which continually steams up, it is really difficult to dress wounds. Meanwhile men excited, shouting, thought they had been gassed. It is exhausting to breathe through the mask for long periods. In the dimly-lit medical centre in the hollow, lit by a few candles, the wounded and sick-bay teams sat, lay or stood around, all wearing gas masks. Additionally outside heavy fire, the thunder of the hits against the rock-face, Ever more gas shells erupt before the entrance.

One conceals his fear behind the mask: fear of being blown up by a shell, crushed to death by collapsing masses of rock, slowly suffocated to death by gas or overrun by the British and killed. Hauptmann von Cappeln came to me seeking help: his eyes were bulging with the gas. I made him a borium compress: his valet Philipp brought him a bottle of wine to ease his distress. After midnight the gas shells stopped. Before going to sleep I tried to grab some fresh air: it was difficult to force a way through the men congregated around the entrance, especially since all were wearing gas masks. As I took a step outside a shell whizzed into the slope very close by. We saw the reflection of the explosion, everybody charged back into the hollow, sped on their way by a couple of shrapnel shells.

19 November 1916 (Miraumont)

Did not sleep well, probably as a result of breathing the gas. I got up at 0300 to receive wounded, found on the table a letter from home. Amongst the wounded was the Company Commander's cook Schmidt of the Staff Company. He was always a very brave man and Hauptmann Sauer, with whom he had been together earlier, thought a lot of him. I thought of St Gilles, where he had cooked for Hauptmann Sauer and Stabsarzt Zahn, and I admired his wonderful beef steaks. The poor devil was badly hurt, a splinter across the face, the left eye destroyed, the right also looked lost. Dressed him, also at his request the serum injection. After treating the wounded I tried to rest a little. At the foot end of my little camping space a large chunk of rock had broken away. I have a niche in the rock concealed behind tarpaulin and blankets. It is quite small, besides the bed a fairly narrow little table which rocks back and forth in a constant struggle to remain upright on the uneven floor, and two chairs. For reading matter I have Rohrbach: *Geschichte der Menschheit*, plus medical works, ear, nose and throat, and a book on viruses. For lighting I have candles. A Regt.99 wounded lieutenant arrived. Yesterday's report that Grandcourt had fallen was rumour: 500 British had been rounded up and pressed into service as stretcher-bearers. Two days later two carts full of seriously wounded came in, pulled by British. This cheered up our lancers (infantrymen) no end, and soon they were shouting 'Tommy, Tommy' from all sides.

23 November 1916 (Miraumont)

Early this morning I went forward with the orderly officer, Lt Klein. There had been a frost overnight and the ground was not so muddy as in recent days. At first to the railway bridge near Miraumont. Then along the embankment. Earlier this highway had received a lot of fire, therefore fast pace. The ground here was deep mud, and we had to wade up to our ankles.

To either side we saw the shelled ruins of the residences of Miraumont. Persistent artillery fire flew overhead towards the batteries. Clear, cold morning. Over a dozen British aircraft bustling in the sky. Everywhere deep shell craters, most filled to the brim with water. One skirts by them through mud. Then tree trunks, uprooted by the shelling, over which one has to clamber. Next a ghastly group of bodies, probably six, the torso in ribbons, covered in blood and mud. One has half its head missing, a bit further on a leg, and a pair of bodies so intertwined that the individual cadavers cannot be made out below their covering of mud. The single bodies. We went on at a fast pace, always with an eye on the aircraft circling overhead. Like poultry when a hawk circles. Lt Klein froze: a British aircraft above us banked sharply. We expected shellfire: suddenly there were a couple of explosions quite near: he had aimed two bombs at us. We ducked behind a heap of rubble.

Now we separated, I went to the medical post, Klein to the trenches. I passed through a deep morass in the depression, all churned up and ploughed over by shelling. To the left a battered tunnel entrance. I found Feldunterarzt Binswanger inside. A small room, primitively equipped. A couple of steps further on was the command post of Hauptmann von Cappeln who consulted me about his still thickly swollen eyes. After a short stay I went back as quickly as possible.

27 November 1916 (Favreuil)

Arrived back early yesterday in streaming rain. The mud was so deep that we decided to go along the embankment, but were then forced down, back into the filth. In places the mud is so deep that it slurps inside the boots or gaiters. Rain poured down incessantly. All the same we were in good humour, glad to be out of the cellar air. At Achiet-le-Grand the sick were brought into a cellar fairly near the railway. Schlüter told us that large calibres had bombarded the railway shortly before. I had the medical centre there evacuated to Favreuil.

Favreuil made a very poor impression with its roads of deep mud. I saw the provisions officers Lt Marchand and Lichtenberger, who supplied me to the best of their ability. Beautiful bright days, sunshine worth double.

14 December 1916 (Miraumont)

The stay at Favreuil was really unpleasant. I had bronchitis. Our quarters always overcrowded. I had a small alcove, stone floor, no stove. We ate together. Conversation low tone, mostly dull, miserable criticism of superior officers, especially Oberstlt Fabarius, then the active officers in general, then the divisional surgeon. Kept occupied with chess and a lot of skat. Yesterday they shelled Favreuil for the first time: one dead and a couple of wounded including a major in the pioneers. Great indignation. Lt Stein, who was a patient with us, and I were probably the least upset. At 2200 the order came from the district commandant to evacuate the civilian population immediately.

The little house was occupied by an eighty-year-old who could not bear to be parted from his small property despite having troops billeted on him. His forty-two-year-old daughter was also there. I often saw him entering his small room, modestly waving; a small, bent man with grey pointed beard. Like an old maid with a wooden face. The way the old man wept as he went through the rooms, and the daughter, with a bedroll full of clothing, all she could take from a trunk, plucked the heartstrings. Forced out into the night and fog with the certainty that upon their return there would be nothing left of their sticks of furniture and few possessions. Towards 2230 they left in silence. Scarcely were they through the door than the 'Inspection Teams' moved in, sorting through the cupboards for anything useful. There were four small hens outside, all dead within ten minutes. Lt Marchand, II.Battalion Provisions Officer, had given the order. He wanted to send two birds to his Battalion Staff, keeping two for the table. His devotion to the Staff was based on his fear of losing his comfortable post as Provisions Officer.

I found the scenes of looting so disgusting that I could hardly bring myself to speak to the gentlemen. I made my point of view absolutely clear but they were unable to understand my 'feelings.'

16 December 1916 (Miraumont)
Today with the ambulance to Irles via Bapaume and Grévillers. Bapaume seems to have been a small town similar to Roye: colossally bombarded. Enormous craters everywhere in the streets. The houses had great shell-holes, often more hole than wall. On the streets now in the early morning many troops, steel helmets and columns. Often the ambulance had to make a big detour, but in general one admired how quickly the cratered streets were repaired by the roadmakers. They keep at it. In Irles we stopped before the dressing and collection station of the medical company. Two days ago a big shell exploded here: four dead, five seriously wounded, six lightly wounded. We went through the ruins of Irles at the double. The whole village was a heap of rubble. Most of the roofs were on the ground or hanging down. We went safely along the Chaussee to Miraumont and the rock bunker.

Notes:
1 *Der Weltkrieg 1914–1918: Reichsarchiv*, Vol 10, Berlin 1936, p.348f (hereinafter 'WKW').
2 Historians mention more than twenty nations (as presently known) which fought on the Allied side on the Somme or whose citizens worked there as trench-diggers etc. These included: India, Pakistan, Barbados, Rhodesia, Burkina Faso, Ivory Coast, Guinea, Mali, Nigeria, Senegal, Vietnam, Madagascar, Algeria, Tunisia, Morocco, Russia, Italy and China.
3 Hermann von Kuhl (former Chief of General Staff, Army Group Kronprinz Rupprecht): Der Weltkrieg 1914–1918, Berlin 1929, p.488.
4 Hermann Stegemann: *Geschichte des Krieges*, Vol 4, Stuttgart/Berlin, 1921, p.117.
5 Major-General John Headlam: Notes on Artillery Material in the Battle of the Somme, 6 July 1916, p.10 in: *Battlefront Somme*, Keith Bartlett, Richmond 2002, Document 5.
6 See *Enzyklopädia Erster Weltkrieg* (hereinafter EEW), Hirschfeld, Krumeich and Renz, 2nd edition, Paderborn 2004 (Somme) p.851: also Hew Strachan: Der Erste Weltkrieg, Munich 2004, p.235.

7   EEW, p.853. German losses of 1 July were given as about 8,000, of which 2,200 were taken prisoner. See Martin Middlebrook: *The First Day on the Somme, 1 July 1916*, London 1971.
8   Robin Prior and Trevor Wilson: *The Somme*. New Haven, London 2005, p.115.
9   Maréchal Fayolle: *Carnets secrets de la Grande Guerre*, Henri Contamine, Paris 1963, p.169.
10   Kuhl, ibid, p.494.
11   And are counted several times here. WKW, Volume 10, p.384.
12   Ibid, p.349.
13   Diary entry, 23 November 1916 at Miraumont.
14   Stegemann, ibid, p.237.
15   Statistics from EEW, ibid p.855 and Strachan ibid, p.240. The official Army medical report 'Der Sanitäts-Bericht über das Deutsche Heer im Weltkrieg 1914/1918', Vol 3, p.51–54 gives the German losses as 335,688. British authorities speak of up to 650,000 (including lightly wounded): The estimated total losses at Verdun (February to December 1916) were about 500,000 as opposed to 1.1 million on the Somme (June to November 1916).
16   Prior/ Wilson, ibid, p.301.
17   WKW, Volume 11, p.105.
18   Ibid, p.108.
19   Robin Prior: *The Heroic Image of the Warrior in the First World War*: War and Society 23 (September 2005) p.43–51.
20   For Hugo Frick.
21   'Report of Military Surgeon Dr Blass on his Experiences in British Captivity, 1917.' On 7 December 1916 Blass was exchanged together with other prisoners.

Chapter Four

Retreat and Destruction

By Professor Michael Geyer,
Department of History, University of Chicago

The retreat of the German Army to the Siegfried Line in March 1917, and the massive destruction inflicted upon the evacuated region under the cover name *Alberich* has been rather marginalized by Great War historians. The pulling back of the Army has disappeared from the historical consciousness behind the politically hotly disputed, and militarily fatal option of unrestricted U-boat warfare which led to the United States entering the war. Both events were closely related. The withdrawal on the Western Front and the stepping-up of the U-boat War resulted from the crisis in German war policy following the great battles at Verdun and on the Somme in 1916. The effects of both decisions extended far beyond the Great War. With *Siegfried* and *Alberich*, the war with and against civilians was carried out knowingly and systematically by a modern Army and as a military necessity legitimized by defence.

Strategic Decisions and Operational Measures

The *Siegfried* movement was effected over the three days and nights between 16 and 19 March 1917. The disengagement from the enemy had begun towards the end of February in critical sectors such as the bend in the front line between Arras and Bapaume, in which attacks were expected or were imminent. The retreat itself was performed in a single large movement. It involved the southern wing of 6.Army at Arras, then 1. and

141

2.Armies on the Somme and the greater part of 7.Army north of Laon – in all no less than twenty-nine divisions together with all formations such as heavy artillery which had been present throughout the fighting on the Somme.

Whilst French units to the south were quick to advance, British troops in the northern area were more hesitant. The retreat was not disturbed, not even partially, anywhere however, nor were the destructive measures undertaken, only in the last phase of the withdrawal to preserve secrecy. The 'whole movement', as Ludendorff described it in his memoirs, was 'a brilliant achievement of the military leaders and men, and bore witness to the careful, forward-looking work of the German General Staff.'[1]

The Army Group *Kronprinz von Bayern* responsible for the planning and execution was no less eulogized.[2] The commander of Army Group *Kronprinz Rupprecht*, formed in the autumn of 1916 and coordinating the four armies, praised the military leaders and men not only for the 'smooth' transfer, the skilful and timely removal, and the deception of the enemy, but also for the 'fresh spirit of aggression' which the security units had shown during the retreat. He also drew attention to the major advantages of the new line – leaving behind the 'mud-filled craters' between Arras, Bapaume and Péronne and the crater landscape of the Somme, and emphasized the sparing of the German forces.

The *Siegfried* movement was actually extraordinarily successful. It improved substantially the German situation on the Western Front. The retreat therefore appeared in retrospect as a good chess move which deceived the Allies, even duped them, and left them in the dark. It demonstrated a masterly control of the battlefield, from great operational decisions to fighting a rearguard action, and proved the superiority of the German infantry in the movement. The Siegfried Line itself became the personification of a planned and skilfully erected defensive wall against which the enemy would hurl himself in vain. The subjective impression to be fully and completely master of the situation and to dictate the enemy's plans oneself, by a defensive sleight of hand, was still being savoured well into the post-war period. Siegfried Movement and Siegfried Line became the manifestation of the German ability to hold out in that time of crisis which developed in the train of the costly great battles before Verdun and on the Somme in 1916.

This positive experience of retreat was, however, neither expected nor prepared for. Most surprised of all was the military command at the Western Front, principally the OHL (Army Supreme Command) which had rather anticipated, as had the Army Group and the armies, the opposite impression.[3] What in retrospect was seen as the triumph of planned German General Staff work crystallized in reality into a tough struggle for the operational decision-making, which ultimately had to be extorted from OHL little by little.

In view of the critical military situation in the autumn of 1916, OHL lengthened the war to a certain extent both for German civilian society, and also in the social systems of the opposing Powers. What in 1916 was first seen as improvisation was actually a real reorientation and reorganization. The German military leadership was in deep crisis at the end of the two great battles of 1916, whose immediate consequence on the Western Front resulted in a turning back to defence. This operational defence had an offensive dimension in that it involved civilians both German and enemy. Less obvious is the circumstance that with the return to defence, the strategy at the front changed completely.

The officer corps with its 'cult of the offensive' and the military institutions, principally the General Staff, did not wish themselves to be remodelled without further consideration. Furthermore the thinking was offensive even though the situation was outright defensive: a state of affairs which for its fulfilment required the military planners to leap over their own shadows as it were. Thus 'strategic' decisions were easier to plan than the 'operational' measures were to implement. Major offensives in the East and South-East of Europe were cancelled, the well-advanced negotiation for an Austro-German offensive to relieve pressure on the (Italian) Isonzo Front abruptly terminated. In the West, however, ideas of attack were not rejected. Immediately after the first conference at Cambrai, Ludendorff had ordered the reconnaissance for, and at the end of September, the expansion of, rearwards trenches, but insisted that under no circumstances would this involve a retreat. On 29 January he wired the Army Group: 'A voluntary movement back to the Siegfried Line is not possible for political and military reasons.'[4] Retreat was the admission of a defeat and would undoubtedly give rise to a crisis of morale in the Army and Homeland – that was the general opinion.[5] To strike out from defence was necessary objectively, but this strategy was seen by front officers subjectively as absurd.

When Ludendorff finally changed his mind and took Hindenburg along with him, this had been brought about by the obstinacy of Army Group *Rupprecht*, responsible for the decisive sector of the Somme front, and so its role will not come as a surprise in the decision-making process. The hesitancy with which the Army group argued for the defensive is noteworthy, however. Kronprinz Rupprecht himself favoured recapturing the entire front facing his Army group from Armentières in the North to Laon/Soissons in the South,[6] but his proposal was not carried. In this case Corps Group North/1.Army[7], competent for coordination, protested that they saw no possibility of building a line of trenches in the forward Ancre corner south of Arras, which meant that the front sector was not capable of being defended,[8] while precisely here in the sector south of Arras a British major offensive was considered possible. In order to spare men and materials therefore, the only decision open was for 'an overall decision' – the retreat to the Siegfried Line. The Army Group had set down this interpretation in memoranda of 15 and 28 January respectively,[9] and its Chief of General Staff, Hermann von Kuhl, urged a decision in the matter in dramatic telephone conversations with Ludendorff, resulting finally in the order to retreat on 4 February. Two days later the Army Group issued the necessary orders.[10]

That did not conclude the debate. 1.Army, under General von Below objected, being unwilling to move under any circumstances from its territory of swamps.[11] 7.Army was planning a large offensive out of the retreat, while even the Army group was considering such plans.[12] Finally, Oberst Graf von der Schulenburg, Chief of the General Staff, Army Group *Deutscher Krronprinz*, swept the idea emphatically from the table: 'We lack the means for a decisive offensive.' Schulenburg required the released divisions as a reserve for the impending defensive fighting.[13] It was practically not until the last minute that the way was finally clear for a major orderly retreat, whose success was then naturally attributed to the perspicacious forward planning of OHL. The operation itself began on 9 February 1917 with the plan for evacuation and destruction (*Alberich*) which had been worked on down to the smallest detail for five weeks. Individual formations such as the previously mentioned Corps Staff North/1.Army drew back to the intermediate line from mid-February.

The tension was enormous. Nobody knew if the enemy was fooled and how he would react if he realized the German intention. All possible scenarios were examined, then rejected, but nothing happened, or at least nothing which compromised the retreat of the four armies. The respite was of short duration, for in the Battle of Arras (April-May 1917) British forces were prompt to attack the open right flank of the Siegfried Line which had not been fortified. A little later Canadian troops overran the German trenches at Vimy Ridge, where an archaic system of galleries similar to those at Verdun made the response from defence difficult. The retreat itself succeeded, and after the great tension of the previous year, resulted in a state of relieved euphoria. Nobody could quite believe how easily it had gone off.

The operational decision in favour of a coordinated orderly retreat succeeded against all expectations. The sensational gap between the (lower) German and (higher) Allied casualties in 1917 is explained by the reverse situation in which the Germans benefited from their failure at Verdun and the bloody stand-off on the Somme, while the French, in the Battle of Chemin des Dames, and the British in Flanders ate the bitter fruits of their victory and pushed their armies to the verge of collapse. The retreat successfully halted the beginning of the end for the German Army. In this reversal of the situation one finds also the beginning of that politically successful codification of war according to which the German military leadership, and later German society, accepted the proposition that warfare from the backfoot of defence, if only it could be prosecuted radically enough, might have made Germany invincible. The Siegfried

Line was at the same time a complex operational measure, the experience of a moment of invincibility and might over destiny.

The Building of the Siegfried Line

The Siegfried Line was probably the greatest construction project of the Great War. Between October 1916 and March 1917, no less than 510,000 tonnes of ballast, gravel and stones, 110,000 tonnes of cement, 20,000 tonnes of iron ingots, 8,200 tonnes of T-joints, boarding, wood panels, square timbers, round timbers, black plate, corrugated iron sheeting, cement pipes, ventilation tubes and so forth were worked with. Material to make obstructions such as three million iron and 1.5 million wooden stakes, 12,500 tonnes of barbed wire, smooth wire, wire mesh, mobile obstacles, mantraps, wire clamps and so forth found their applicaion. Additionally entrenching and other tools were needed such as spades, shovels, pickaxes, wire-cutters, cement mixers, welding apparatus, manual iron turning and cutting machines and so forth.[14]

Added to the building materials and equipment was naturally the total expense for rail installations and road-rail loading bays, field railway stations, engineer parks, warehouses, barracks – an expense which competed with trench construction itself. Only where the overall project was completed did the various departments involved obtain an impression of the unbelievable amounts of material that a modern military defensive system demanded – and despite the fact that 'only' a 150 kilometre long stretch was being built. The work itself was mainly carried out by PoWs and forced labour. The OHL made 65,000 men available altogether for the Siegfried work.[15] This number was reached in mid-November when the removal of soil began for the first trenches, and then fell back slightly over succeeding months. Of these 65,000 men – almost 70,000 with guards and support units – only 7,300 were drawn from the Army itself, and the majority of these came from the PoW Worker Battalions with the individual armies, so that initially the number of 'proper' soldiers was extremely small. It changed nothing that OHL sent an additional 13,300 Landwehr and pioneers (including 126 officers). The ratio only changed in February and March 1917 when the line had to be readied, and 1.Army detached another 60,000 soldiers to join the 15,000–18,000 workers.[16]

The principal labour force for the Siegfried Line was about 26,000 PoWs guarded by 3,800 Landsturm II soldiers and 9,000 forced labourers from Belgium and France also with their Landsturm II guards. Finally there were 6,000 'free' workers, initially mainly from Germany but towards the end increasingly from the occupied zone of France and from Belgium, recruited by civilian building firms.[17] For railway construction to the rear there were another 20,000 men, principally from the civilian-worker battalions and regular railway companies.[18] It should be added however that the construction of the connections to the rear could not have been guaranteed without forced labour.

In a building section of eighteen to twenty kilometres about 10,000 workers were used, all of whom had to be housed and fed. Up to seventy per cent of them were forced labourers needing to be brought every day from their quarters in guarded columns to the place of work. This kind of procedure was not unusual, for in the *Etappe* large numbers of PoWs had been employed previously in this way, although their numbers had built up gradually through 1915 and 1916. Nevertheless the large-scale use of PoWs and forced labour required forward planning.[19] Whereas the latter had been lodged previously in whatever was available, purpose-built camps were now created for them and new arrangements introduced and costed for their upkeep. Camps of barrack huts were laid out. Whole villages, factory complexes, hamlets – so-called 'Siegfried villages' – were evacuated by their inhabitants to be replaced by PoWs and forced labourers[20] identified in specific groups by an armband.[21]

In the framework of the erection of the Siegfried Line, within a short time there came into being a system of massed forced labour linked to work camps which were quickly perfected. Forced labour involved a totalization of the guard system and extensive restrictions on the freedom of movement. Nothing here was fundamentally new but a variety of individual measures, issued by subsidiary control offices, together with the regulations issued by the control and guard authorities in the rearward area contributed to a comprehensive regime of control and reinforcement.[22]

The Somme region overall was transformed into a giant camp which wriggled all the way from Arras to Laon. That it would extend beyond the Line itself was shown by the typical tensions within the forced system. The mixing together of PoWs, forced labourers and volunteer workers led to distrust and even strikes, despite the extensive militarization of the work. Civilian workers from Germany complained bitterly about the restrictions on their freedom of movement.[23] Belgian and French civilian workers were labelled traitors by the forced labourers, which resulted in the 'free' workers and PoWs performing the heavy manual labour while the forced labour battalions were ordered to work on individual tasks and in depots to the rear or on railway building.

The soldiers as a whole, but especially the fighting troops, looked down on this heterogenous collection of workers and considered the entire force as inferior and their work predominantly worthless.[24] Each group stood for itself and in the case of doubt competed against all others for small advantages and to maintain their liberties. The work was extraordinarily heavy and the guards, in general older men, tended towards brutality.[25] The main problem was inadequate clothing, lack of medical care and poor quality food – typical symptoms of work camps, especially these, which had suddenly taken root and were at the end of the supply chain.[26] The situation deteriorated in the cold winter months, and the numbers of sick, unfit for labour, and mortality rose drastically.[27] Those, such as German workers, able to give notice, left as soon as possible. By March 1917 very few German workers were still employed on building the Siegfried Line.

Although the practice was brutal and in many camps intolerable, one cannot say that it amounted to a concentration camp system, for irrespective of the purpose and practice no inhuman will was present, rather the contrary. Complaine was requested. 'Mean heartedness, indifference, ill treatment and excessive demands impair the building project.'[28] Here then was the typical paradox of all forced labour. Towards the predominantly 'good-willed and efficient' Russian PoWs, a kind of paternalism developed, though only after 'unruly elements' had been weeded out.[29] Although this paternalism still included the brutality, it allowed a certain relaxation in the work conditions.[30]

The relationship with the civilian forced labourers on the other hand was always tense because they remained uncooperative. It was believed generally that they would only work properly if enough supervisors and guards were on hand, but there was also a shortage of these. Excesses and rebellions were therefore common.[31] A situation arose with the arrival of two squads of Rumanian PoWs who were unfit for heavy work and the climate. After their physical collapse on a large scale they were 'removed on account of physial and mental inferiority as unemployable' which in this case meant that the survivors were returned to the PoW holding camp.[32] The high losses were due to physical weakness and debilitation of the PoWs, the cause of which was unknown. In any case the weaknesses were taken as an affront by officers and men alike who remained perplexed as to how such people should be handled. The idea that those unfit for work should be returned was on the borderline of tolerance. It was clear that this was not a matter of racial prejudice when another group of workers showed similar fatigue.

None of the fighting force had a good word for the German 'volunteer' workers and condemned them as 'workshy, weak, sickly, obstinate, immoral and undisciplined.'[33] It was noteworthy that rebellious French and Belgians were closely watched, rebellious Russians and unfit Rumanians were 'sent back' and work camps were wanted for German workers.[34] Thus the language of the concentration camp was present, but the practice of enforcement itself was in the hands of petit-bourgeois reserve officers with their own concept of work and order.

Precisely because the path to the future extermination camps was paved with the good intentions of ordinary people, the construction of the Siegfried Line provided an unplanned picture of what was looming. What developed in 1917 were doubtless elements of a totalitarian syndrome.

The original intention was that the entire system of fortification was to be performed by private German building firms using labour recruited from the occupied territories, or by forced labour in case of necessity.[35] Ultimately only 1,400 volunteers and four civilian worker battalions, with about 12,000 men, could be found to build the Siegfried Line. What remained was the conviction shared by all military centres that civilian firms and volunteer labour was not suitable for the front. Forced labour, on the other hand, worked, and even if it did not match up to the trenching achievements of the fighting troops it was far preferable to the private market. Therefore, so reasoned Ludendorff later, if only the right effort afforded by forced labour had been applied in the occupied territories in 1916, then there would have been not only a unified fortification system but also the lines to the rearward missing in 1918.[36]

The main lesson taken by OHL was that forced labour on a massive scale was an indispensable precondition for successful modern military planning. That these workers would come from the occupied territories went without saying because the German Reich was unable to call upon a colonial workforce. Ludendorff's logic was not abstruse, but it was already totalitarian.

Alberich

Alberich was the cover name for all preparations for the retreat in the framework of the Siegfried Movement – tactical clearance, destruction, inundation, deportation. The *Alberich* period was the five weeks in which the measures set down as an agenda were to be made ready and then executed between 9 February and 15 March 1917. It was no small matter to pull back no less than two armies (1. and 2.) and sections of two others (6. and 7.) with all weapons, equipment, installations and machinery, and destroy all weapons, trenches and whatever else remained. Yet *Alberich* has gone down in history for its scheduled evacuation of all civilian installations, all removable property and all inhabitants, and the systematic destruction of the evacuated region, its structures, farms and orchards together with the entire infrastructure.

Alberich produced *éspaces désertiques*, as a French contemporary aptly put it.[37] Clearance and destruction were almost perfectly completed when the Siegfried Movement concluded on 19 March. What had been done in the winter months was the planning and execution, therefore in the truest sense of the word the discovery, of the 'Scorched Earth Policy', a war of total destruction in at least a central aspect.

The starting point had been the instruction of the Chief of the Army General Staff to Army Group on 2 October 1916 in which Ludendorff ordered: 'The enemy must come across a land completely uprooted in which his freedom of movement has been made difficult to the greatest extreme.' Listed for 'complete destruction' were: 'roads, bridges, artificial waterways, locks, villages and all supplies and installations which we cannot remove but which might be of some use to the enemy.' The Army group interpreted the word 'clearance' to mean amongst other things the removal of the civilian population, and 'destruction' to include 'flooding, the burning of ground cover, destruction of permanent (electrical) cables (insofar as these cannot be removed).' Furthermore Army Group ordered that in the immediate ten to fifteen kilometres before the Siegfried Line destruction was 'to be carried out especially' and included 'accommodation in safe cellars, favourable observation spots, decorative structures' while in further-flung villages 'preparation for burning down and the destruction of plumbing installations (water pipes etc)' would suffice.[38]

The purpose of *Alberich* was summed up by 1.Army, which stated in its planning: 'Once the retreat is complete, the enemy will arrive to find a desert.'[39] Serious objections were articulated only by Kronprinz Rupprecht, C-in-C of the Army Group, but only in his private memoirs. It was not the first time that the Bavarian Kronprinz and OHL had differed on the treatment of the civilian population. In the spring of 1916 he had been beside himself with indignation when the (at that time 2nd) OHL was considering deporting the entire populations of occupied Belgium and France through the front line because of a threatened food shortage.[40] In October he reacted with consternation and declared: 'This instruction reminds me of the one that Louvois once issued to turn the Pfalz into a desert . . . it seems to me uncommonly harsh.' He did not wish to have his name associated with the measure. After a wild first year of warfare

Rupprecht had gained some of his consciousness of responsibility as a noble, but even so he committed the error of consoling himself 'that the instruction will prove impracticable on technical grounds.'[41]

Kronprinz Rupprecht's words of self-comfort were misplaced. 3.OHL did not countermand the instruction and built up the organization for the job, and in setting up a special, or *Sonder-Organisation* the way was found to do things which had hitherto lain beyond the wildest imaginings. The construction of the Siegfried Line and the destruction wrought in the framework of *Alberich* were so successful because for its planning and execution this S-Organisation was prepared by the General Staff, where all measures were coordinated and innovations created and then filtered down to individual company commanders.[42] When clearance and destruction was qualified and scheduled, the possible separated from the impossible and priorities set, the programme was feasible.

The systematic planning and work, and also the motivation to do everything militarily necessary, had its tradition in the Prussian General Staff, but the result was something new: an improvised framework to perfect the technique – the creation of a desert – which in its perfection exceeded itself.[43] In this way the instructions for the clearance and destruction were reworded into a document 'Memorandum for Alberich Demolitions' issued by 1.Army on 1 March 1917. In this edict the competent officers and pioneer commanders were obliged to supervise the fulfilment of the task 'in person', and 'to become involved on their own account and ensure that no effort be spared to complete the work of demolition most thoroughly and completely.' The pioneer units, security squads and the rearguard were reminded of the need to destroy all material, German and otherwise, which was to be left or could not be brought out: 'Nothing must be allowed to fall into the hands of the enemy which might be useful to him.'[44]

'Destruction' became a progressively larger catalogue of measures as the preliminary work proceeded. Objects for destruction had to be listed and reported, trial demolitions made, estimates as to material requirements submitted, the labour force and demolition squads distributed, underground galleries, chambers and stores destroyed, trees hacked down. The coordinating 'N-Group' earmarked to work in residential areas was advised: 'All villages must be burnt down, the remains of walls overturned, all underground places of safety, cellars, catacombs, all springs and water piping, streets and railways, all useful observation positions such as church towers, chimneys, high buildings and windmills must be destroyed, long rows of trees and park installations felled.'[45] How houses were to be satisfactorily flattened so as to offer no cover required special study.[46] Springs and sewage installations won special attention once it was realized (in the framework of the prioritization process) that large troop assemblies were impossible if there was no sewage and water. 1.Army came up with the idea of poisoning natural water sources, but this was eventually ruled out in favour of making reservoirs and stagnant waters 'unusable (do not poison!)' by chemicals.[47]

Blowing up springs caused a more persistent problem and in this case was probably more to the liking of the military mind. Precisely because the destruction was on the grand scale but planned down to the smallest detail and improved through constant reporting back was it so total. Towns and villages could be destroyed swiftly once the most efficient method was found: 'Thus the town of Bapaume was demolished in forty-five minutes (five simultaneous explosions in the centre, then the others, a few minutes later the town was burning in 400 places)' while the villages were much easier to wipe out and many 'disappeared completely.'[48] Seen as a whole the effort put into it – at every locality, every crossroads, every orchard of the entire gigantic region – was immense, but the destruction was so perfectly successful because the preparatory work had been so detailed and thorough. 'The pioneer service,' a pioneer officer summed up, 'is basically attention to detail (and) in the long run attention to detail can be decisive for success.'[49]

A major effort was also dedicated to destroying the transport infrastructure. This included the destruction of locks and damming waterways as part of the process to swamp areas along the front particularly in the sectors of 2. and 7.Armies with the aim of making whole regions impassable. Taking out electrical systems was found especially difficult and time-consuming but was eventually achieved by brute force. The systematic 'dismounting' of the remaining railway installations and sleeper beds required enormous application of labour.[50] Although it was generally held that the destruction of the highway network had been less successful, nevertheless judicious crater-making made roads at least temporarily unusable. What remained was, as N-Group noted in a memorandum attached to the 1.Army instruction, 'a complete desert.'

Before the final destruction all moveable property and possessions were cleared and the inhabitants moved out. The scale of this clearance is evident from the railway records alone: 11,711 waggon-loads were needed to ship out all the railway material: 7,522 vegetable waggon loads to remove the population to the rearward area,: 17,940 waggon-loads of moveable items.[51] A good proportion of the military equipment including Army and welfare installations was shifted by the Army itself. All cattle, provisions, feed and seed were moved out. All metals gathered up, all stores of clothing, furniture, house building and household equipment seized and shipped out.[52] The list of 'Supplies from the Land and Objects of All Kinds Useful for the Army' grew ever longer despite the shortage of transport.[53] Money was collected and exchanged, banks cleared, evacuated dwellings guarded. The land was literally denuded and nothing recognized as useful left behind.

'Useless objects' included almost 15,000 civilians unable to work – the elderly, the sick, mentally handicapped and children – who were transported to the clearance zone area under the control of 2.Army – to Noyon, Ham-Guisard and Nesle.[54] This group formed a small part of a mass re-settlement of 140,000 people of the native population able to work. If one includes the gradual transfer of the population from localities behind the front organized earlier by each district *kommandant*, who were then released for employment digging the Siegfried Line and in Army installations to the rear, then the number rises to about 150,000 displaced persons. These were all expelled in barely three weeks of *Alberich*, either on foot or in 'vegetable-waggons', as the railway adminstration described them, within the northern French *Etappe* zone behind the Siegfried Line or to occupied Belgium.[55]

The 'removal of the inhabitants' according to the internal report, 'was the most difficult clearance measure.'[56] The problems began when the proposed action was postponed to January.[57] Since no reason can be found for this, one assumes that the delay stemmed from an humanitarian impulse of Kronprinz Rupprecht, particularly since OHL had pushed ahead with the idea of deporting the population to the rear on foot because the railways lacked the capacity to transport all the passengers and material.[58] 1.Army refused on military grounds, 2.Army on humanitarian, and the Army Group added a rider to its retrospective memorandum to the effect that the transportation of inhabitants was in any case 'not feasible' without the railway 'within the parameters of the S-Organization.'[59] In practice this meant that the removal of the inhabitants had not been planned for even at the end.

The humanitarian strain evident in the thinking of 2.Army makes it all the more obvious how inhumane the act itself appeared. Thus 2.Army took great pains to ensure that especially the sick and elderly were conveyed in cars and ambulances with attendants on hand.[60] This does not alter the fact that the deportations were forced through abruptly, not least to prevent valuable materials which could have been confiscated by the Germans from being hidden or destroyed. Although villagers from individual localities were held in groups and great importance attached to not splitting families, nevertheless the elderly and the sick, the weak and children were (however one might like to explain it away) separated from the members of their families able to work. The 40,000 inhabitants of Saint Quentin were spirited away in a surprise raid because 2.Army considered their transportation to the rear as 'representing a danger to the secrecy of *Alberich*.' The deportation was admitted to be a 'harsh measure' but the practice was harsher than expected.[61]

It is clear from the foregoing that the deportations overstepped a critical mark. In itself this changed nothing, but hardly any German soldier felt comfortable about it. For this reason the argument of military necessity was finally hammered home with great frequency, but therein lay the rub, for if it had really been a military necessity it could only mean that the practices of war had been stood on their head. With the depopulation of the clearance region, from now on civilians on the Western Front had become the pawns of military planning.

What officers and men developed a talent for doing through *Alberich* was find a new way to get at the enemy in a critical war situation. *Alberich* was an enormous, creative act of destruction which, in that small area of the world forward of the Siegfried Line between Arras and Laon, completely expunged civilian presence and reduced an historical landscape to a wasteland.

Hugo Natt (1881–1963) Stabsarzt, Inf.Regt. 118/Inf.Div.56
DIARY

9 February 1917 (Péronne)
1530 we left in the ambulance . . . via Cartigny, Doingt to Péronne. Cloudless, bright day. Journey took about an hour. From Cartigny the usual picture of destruction. Doingt looks ravaged, houses all shelled to rubble, earth deeply churned. The torn-off branches and bark show traces of fire. A short distance from the highway the frozen Somme and swamp. From Péronne one sees at first large, shell-damaged walls, remains of former fort, with trenches and moat. Then one drives into the town centre down a fine, wide avenue. Houses both sides all holed, great heaps of dirt and rubble in front. At the town hall we got out, dressing station is in the cellar.

10 February 1917 (Péronne)
A cellar the size of a very large sitting room serves as the surgery. The walls are covered by fabric. Inside are two good beds, a piano, magnificent sofa with red velvet upholstery, on which in earlier times the gentlemen of the council would have disported themselves. Main decoration is two very large paintings in broad gold frames: *La Misère* by (Louis) Debras and *Daphne et Chloë* by Bonné. The first especially is captivatingly beautiful: a young mother, baby at the breast, tired from wandering, is seated on a rock. The pained expression in the fine, pale face, the beautiful wet eyes: the noble shape of the bare shoulders, the delicate hand, are masterly. Another corridor connects the surgery to the

operating theatre and room for the wounded, two cellar rooms, whose equipment leaves something to be desired.

The weather has changed and the bitter cold has gone. One enters the trenches by way of a wooden bridge over the very swampy Somme region here. At the moment it is frozen over. The bridge is good but one has to move smartly from one section to the next because it can be seen by the enemy. We were late leaving the line and had to take the detour back through the 'Paris suburb', a sorry-looking outlying district with very shell-damaged houses. The way over the bridge stages is very attractive, reed beds either side, between long stretches of open water. There are huge numbers of wild duck, which the men shoot at. With their service rifles! This shooting can be quite dangerous, for the bullets fly far in open country, and on some bridge crossings one takes his life in his hands. Then the *kommandant* introduced severe arrest penalties which resulted in the following. Two days ago I visited a private soldier under arrest who had just been sentenced to five days' harsher arrest. Today at midday the local *kommandant* sent for a doctor because the arrestee had gone wild. I went. The arrest cell was in a former prison. I was told: The arrestee had received good rations today. In the morning he had been given wood and an axe to chop firewood for himself. Then he went crazy, chopping up his cell and setting fire to the dry wood. As soon as anybody approached he attacked with an axe. Thick smoke was pouring from the cell. When I opened the small window and called to him, he raised the axe and went for me, then he threw small chips of wood through the doorway, screaming unintelligibly. As it was feared he would wreck the door and window and create more damage with the axe, there followed a conference on how to handle the situation. I advised we should wait. After two hours more we went back. There was smoke everywhere because he had started a fresh fire. To attempt to overpower him might have resulted in serious injury. I advised caution until he was overcome by the smoke. This took another hour, and then he was brought out. He kept shouting but finally explained: 'My poor parents. I have been in the Army five years, and all I ever got out of it was punishments. I wish I had fallen in battle.' I calmed him down, as did his sergeant.

20 February 1917 (Péronne)
From the street, apart from a large shell-hole in the wall, the decorated columns of the Town Hall façade do not suggest the terrible destruction within. The entire roof of the annexe on the corner of the market place has been destroyed, the dome with its pointed tower is a formless confusion of twisted metal framework towering above the roof. The house wall itself is protected by a porch supported by columns. Huge piles of wall rubble and all kinds of equipment are strewn in the street. The windows have no glass. If one crosses the market place over the rubble into the interior of the Town Hall,[62] one enters first into a large hall whose walls carry copies of Egyptian and Assyrian tapestries. Amongst the debris are painted fragments of a replica Egyptian altar. The wall paintings show Egyptian priestesses and artesans. These were copied from finds in Egypt. Adjacent is a small room with many glass showcases. There is said to have been a valuable coin collection here previously.[63]

Mixed in with the vast amounts of dirt and garbage covering the floor are fragments of plaster replicas, skeleton parts and all kinds of museum exhibits, e.g. old Roman handmills etc. Through a corridor one reaches the former council chamber. This looks particularly ruinous. In order to better protect the cellar honeycomb below against shelling, a layer of rubble one and a half metres thick has been spread over the floor. All kinds of old rubbish have been added, old bedframes etc. The junk contrasts strangely with the huge painted columns and the panelled ceiling. The building material used everywhere here is limestone. One proceeds to the first floor ascending a broad stairway maintained in excellent condition. Here used to be the library, now a picture of devastation. Books and files appear to have been deliberately strewn across the floor to provide protection against incoming shells. The books are badly damaged and lie in piles up to a metre high. The ceiling has been penetrated by shell hits in various places, allowing rain to enter. Amongst the books I found many old medical works of great antique value: Galon, etc.

In the next room are huge quantities of manuscripts, certainly also of high value. Here too are many volumes of official reports, and masses of official material. All for destruction. The stairway leads to the storeroom, totally destroyed, only the roof frames remain. Directly behind the steps from the street into the Town Hall is a room which served previously as an office. Also here metre-high rubble. So as not to spend all my life in the cellar I have arranged this room for myself. As it was impossible to remove the rubble, we levelled it and placed doors on the top to form a new floor. The actual door was useless because of the rubble and so we cut off the top part at the height of the rubble and placed some entry steps outside. It was difficult to get window panes and so I removed the glass front from a bookcase and nailed that in place. The remainder was covered by window remains from the neighbourhood. It was several days until my day room was ready, then I was able to spend a couple of hours each morning working there. At the moment I am working on an excerpt from Bandelier and Röpke's *Tuberculosis Clinic*.

25 February 1917 (Péronne)
Today I returned to Bernes for a conference with the divisional surgeon. On the way we passed through burning Cartigny. The inhabitants are long gone. At the moment they have started pulling down the usable houses, blowing up the water sources etc. We understand that a thirty kilometre wide strip of the entire Somme region is to be evacuated and everything in the strip razed to the ground. This includes Péronne. It has been ordered that all usable furniture is to be salvaged. The new trenches of the Siegfried and Wotan Lines mark the eastern edge of the evacuated region. Three Ottomans and a very fine sofa are being salvaged from our cellar furniture. Also the two great paintings (*Daphne et Chloë* and *Le Misère)* have been removed from their frames, rolled up and taken away. They will be returned to the town later.

26 February 1917 (Péronne)
Since 24th bad bronchitis with pain left side. This afternoon Oberstleutnant Fabarius invited me for a walk. I met him in a room of the Regimental Staff which has a really well protected home for itself in a small house along the old city wall. It has a deep gallery. The entire district from there to the Somme has suffered enormous destruction. Everywhere great heaps of

rubble block the streets. We went over the Bertha wooden bridge which passes for 500 metres through the rushes of the Somme. Wonderful clear day. The town of Péronne rose beautifully behind the Somme beaches, very picturesque. We discussed how Péronne had once been a rich town, garrison of a cavalry regiment, early in the war it was considered a rich military locality. Then we talked of home. Fairly heavy artillery fire which did not worry me, but very much the Oberstleutnant. Since we were coming towards the other end of the bridge near where the batteries were, which were attracting enemy fire, we turned back.

3 March 1917 (Péronne)
Bronchitis lasted three days, pain left side, especially when I move. Did not go to bed until after midnight. The many colds probably a consquence of lack of fresh air, particularly spending so much time in the warm cellar, where one sleeps clothed. After 0830 went to medical centre, which I have set up in basement of the school. There is not much light in the cellar rooms, and so I have made up three examination rooms in the utter ruin which is the basement. It required a lot of work before the centre had its beds etc. There are altogether seventy-two beds available, also tables and chairs. Lighting through enlarged cellar ports protected by glass from picture frames after the paintings had been removed. From there I crossed the Bertha bridge to look at the ice in the Somme. This evening it froze again hard. The water of the Somme is clear and green, and one can see that it is deep in places. Great areas are blocked off by iron railings, apparently there used to be a rich fishery here. Then I went along the bank for a short cut to the Town Hall. I arrived just in time to witness an explosion. They had drilled into the great wall of the Gendarmerie Nationale at six places and filled each with over forty-six kilos of explosive. A simple detonator fuse wire was used to set it off. The result was unsatisfactory. Great blocks of stone flew everywhere but it simply made the holes bigger: the building survived.

5 March 1917 (Péronne)
Early this morning all white: thick snow. Systematic destruction

in process for last two days. The remaining houses in reasonable condition are being pulled down or blown up. A couple of hand grenades primed against the door jamb and then house collapses. Yesterday some splinters from the houses opposite came through my lovely crystal panes. Opposite the town hall, the façades of the houses have been torn down exposing the wreckage inside. The roofs have either caved in or hang over the walls. There is rubble in the middle of the road. It is risky to pass by the houses as masonry and beams fall without warning.

11 March 1917 (Péronne)
Many places in town have been blown up. Several houses burn out. The fires have not been fully extinguished. This morning I walked over the Bertha wooden bridge again. A British aircraft flew very low overhead so close that we could see his black goggles, despite fierce MG fire from our infantry. In the afternoon it was not pleasant in the day room as in the last few days there has been a lot of shelling in the vicinity. Also today we had to shelter in the cellar because of sudden salvoes. For the first time clouds of shrapnel directly over the streets of the town. This afternoon I sketched with painter Weber.

12 March 1917 (Péronne)
This evening several places still ablaze. Spent a long time in front of the Town Hall watching the flames. Spellbinding, such great fires. The next morning they were still smoking well. Nearby an attempt had been made to destroy a house by explosives. Early today I noticed that the walls still stood, the floor was broken in. The cellar looked like the abyss to a ravine. The preparations for the retreat have been completed. We will have the first dressing station at Doingt. All preparations extremely secret. All orders regarding the retreat speak of it as Day X. The preceding days are known correspondingly as X–1, X–2. Today is X–1. With Feldunterarzt Graeff, I went to Doingt early in order to see the medical post. First through a suburb, then a long broad avenue, past trees felled by artillery, craters old and new, then into the ruins of Doingt. Our line runs upwards in front of the village. An old medical post is specified for it. Artillery emplacement to be used as battalion command post. The trenches have

no accommodations since the line will only be held for one day. Our principal protection is the many swamps of the Somme. We returned through the ruins of Flamicourt.

In the afternoon I went to regiment on account of the regulations for the medical service. The first companies have already left to occupy the reserve trenches. An extraordinary quiet reigns. No shelling for hours. Will there be an artillery barrage tomorrow morning? Tomorrow is Day X. The evening I spent alone. Despite the quiet everybody is very tense. Outside various places are burning. I sat before an oil lamp. The faithful Ofenloch has 'found' spirit lamps and covers.

13 March 1917 (Péronne)

Had a very bad night, woke at 0500. Felt a lot of heaviness when exhaling. The quietness is striking. Early this morning I took my usual walk over the Bertha bridge. Saw a few small cats in the meadows. No shelling anywhere. A 'breather in war.' I enjoyed the fine view towards the old fortress walls over the great swamps. The grey-green haulms of the reeds stand higher than a man. Went along the river bank, past the damaged Gendarmerie Nationale. Frightful street scenes. Many houses completely burnt out inside. Of others only a few low walls remain. The bricks and rubble block whole streets, an awful confusion of bits of beam, masonry, household articles, wires. The telephone people are just now taking out the last lines. It is a wonderful Sunday. The bright yellow-brown sandstone gleams happily so that even the ruins look pleasant. Especially fine is Brittany Gate (painter Weber did it for me as a water colour). Tonight the big retreat begins. This afternoon it was noticeably more empty in the depopulated town, over which a thick cloud of smoke hovers. Soon after lunch the ambulances set off, leaving me completely alone. I ordered a medical officer to the citadel to go back with the men. Myself I shall occupy the dressing station at Hancourt. To my delight another ambulance arrived with Chefarzt Kottenhahn. We returned in this together. In Hancourt I was given quarters in the same room I occupied upon my earlier arrival here with the Battalion Staff. The evening was quiet.

14 March 1917 (Hancourt)
Quiet night. Battalion Staff has arrived. We disengaged from the
enemy without a casualty. This morning what a benefit –
daylight through the window and fresh air after weeks of
breathing cellar air. Outside rain and gloom. The weather is
ideal for our retreat. The barrage balloons have no field of view
and the aircraft cannot get up.

15 March 1917 (Hancourt)
Still at Hancourt. I. Battalion moved out smoothly. III.Battalion
still in the line at Doingt. Two companies of II.Battalion remain
at Péronne. Moreover from I.Battalion, from each company one
officer with 1–2 squads and MGs to be set up at all places where
the enemy could penetrate. In the trenches traps have been set to
injure invading troops. So, for example, hand grenades have
been fixed to doors and will explode when the door is opened.
Landmines have been placed all along the wooden bridge and
will explode when trodden. I was told a lot about this kind of
thing but I do not have much confidence in its success since the
British are bound to exercise some caution upon entering a
German trench. In the afternoon I walked with Hauptmann
Lüters through the fields to Vraignes where there are more than
1,000 evacuees. On the way we met women collecting dande-
lions for a salad. The village has little damage. Unfortunately, as
in the entire evacuation region, all fruit trees have been cut
down. Even in the cemetery all trees have been felled.

17 March 1917 (Vendelles)
Still at Hancourt. Early today our forward patrols returned. So
far the British appear unaware of the retreat. In any case they
rained down shells on the trenches. Fine warm day. 2030 we left
for Vendelles. In the afternoon various barrack huts were set
afire. By evening the whole village was ablaze, an appalling sight
the equal of which I have only seen once before, in Belgium in
the opening days of the war. Huge flames licked out from every
house, above them giant clouds of smoke, especially black from
the uralite of the roofs. Meanwhile explosions and the chatter of
forgotten infantry ammunition, hand grenades, bursting bricks.
The horses were so restless at the sight of the flames that they

were difficult to control. Then we returned to Vendelles via Bernes. To all sides and behind us the flames of burning villages. At night we reached Vendelles. House No.8 was earmarked as the dressing station and spared. We have impeccable rooms, yet we slept poorly because of the constant explosions. The roads to the rear, which had been mined intensively in the past, were blown up by the pioneers. The small house trembled under the fury of the detonations. The window panes rattled endlessly and kept us all awake with fear.

18 March 1917 (Vendelles)
In the morning the same picture here as at Hancourt. The few remaining houses were destroyed by explosives until everything was a desolate heap of rubble. I.Battalion had the b-line, that is, the rearguard. The a-line was at Doingt, occupied by III.Battalion. The troops positioned at Péronne from I. and II. Battalions returned yesterday. Early morning today I and II Batallions are to march through here while we remain until evening awaiting relief by III.Div. The Division has already occupied the Siegfried Line, and our line is the fighting front. We left for the trench with Hauptmann Lüters. It is a simple trench of medium height. Despite the cold the men were all in good spirits. Marched off 2330, at first a stretch on foot. To the left and right of the street fire and smoke. Only a few houses are to be left standing, apart from these the village is a smoking ruin. The entire evacuation district looks the same: all fruit trees felled, together with all other large trees, all river crossings, railway lines, highways blown up, all houses destroyed. It is said that 500 villages have been obliterated. A massive measure: throughout the ravaged region the enemy will penetrate only slowly, finding no auxiliary assistance, and first of all has to lay streets and water supply. For example the water system has been systematically destroyed and polluted with faecal matter. The enemy's planned offensive has been rendered pointless by our retreat and the financial demands on enemy national reserves is enormous. Our troops until now in the occupied area have been released to other duties. The enemy has only been probing our patrols until this point. There are three squadrons of cavalry with MGs in the evacuated sector to cover our retreat and

unsettle the enemy. The night march was exhausting: thirty-one kilometres to Bohain – am very tired. About 0200 rations were given out. We sat by a roadside ditch: how good the thick noodle soup tasted. A cigar along the way helped. The road led from Vendelles to Bellenglise, Sequehart, Fresnoy-le-Grand, Bohain.

19 March 1917 (Bohain)
Arrived in Bohain 1000 hrs. Very tired, short of breath.

20 March 1917 (Wassigny)
Midday we marched twelve kms to Wassigny. Much swampy territory. Fairly long stop as lorry broke down. The road had to be cleared first by MG Company. Could not go round it as swamp and dense vegetation. The village is overcrowded. We stayed in a nice little house. I had a bed but no stove in the room.

21 March 1917 (Petit Fayt)
Sat together long while last evening as Feldwebel-Leutnant Lüthje was invited to dinner. Early this morning marched via Oisy to Le Petit Fayt. Very cold. Almost continuous snowfall, so that one was glad to dismount from the horse for stretches, hands and feet freezing. The road passed through hilly country. Clean, apparently well-to-do villages. Everywhere large orchards and pasture enclosed by thorn bushes. A joy for the eye to see a little green in the fields after so many ruins and piles of rubble. Clear skies in the evening.

22 March 1917 (Maubeuge)
In the evening another visit. A lieutenant from Inf.Regt.38 who was given quarters here. Was invited by Hauptmann Lüters in his hospitable way. Spoke about the coming offensive at Laon. Ourselves bound for Maubeuge. Where would we go after that? Early today everything blanketed by snow. Because of cold lots of socks. Fine hilly area. Very fine high up cathedral of St. Pierre (Dompierre). Many fine views from above down into valley. Large fine village so far untouched by horrors of war, people at the door. The women and our men shout to each other and make jokes just like on manoeuvres. Route today was twenty-

five kms. I rode on horseback the last half. Bitterly cold, as a sharp, biting easterly wind. Finally we went along the Maubeuge-Paris highway, one of the many roads built by Napoleon (cuts across country straight as a ruler, almost no bends) for strategic considerations (make fast troop movements). The last eight kms almost incessant heavy snow so that we look like snowmen. Good quarters on the outskirts of Maubeuge.

23 March 1917 (Maubeuge)

We ate in Maubeuge yesterday evening. Scheuerpflug came back today, told me about my dear wife and the two babes, that my dear little wife had a cold, that dear little Walter had bawled when he thought he had lost his little sweets. Was extraordinarily happy to receive this account. Lt Rönneberg also came by when the beer was served. He came from Péronne. Full of pride recounted the (to me very tasteless) surprise which they have left behind for the British. From the old command post they set up a table on the street with two plates of cooked rat and herrings, a glass of champagne and a note: 'Dear Tommy, enjoy your meal! Don't be annoyed, just admire!' There was additionally a pile of hand grenades, one primed in such a way as to explode if lifted.

Sebastian Hainlein, Medical Corps, Field Hospital 4/Inf.Div.56

In Civilian Life a Businessman at Reupelsdorf

DIARY (Source BfZ N04.3)

13 February 1917 (Berthenicourt)

Everything here is gradually being dismantled and carted off. Our Swiss barracks is broken up.

16 February 1917 (Berthenicourt)

The civilians have to leave little by little. The whole region from the front to St Quentin and further still is so to speak being prepared for dismantling. The streets are being mined, the springs of water filled in, the railway installations transported out. Arson squads are being formed who, at the appropriate time, will raze to the ground all villages and individual houses. A great retreat is under way on our front. A host of other measures are in hand of which we have no knowledge. It is even being talked of that we will relinquish St Quentin, because the main defence installations begin behind it in front of Neuville and to the side before Mézières. We heard firing all day, far and near, artillery getting the range.

20 February 1917 (Berthenicourt)
Yesterday in the house and porch, pioneers put something down in the cellar. Soon it will get serious. Explosive charge.

23 February 1917 (Berthenicourt)
0500 today all civilians deported. Yesterday there was the opportunity to buy beans.

24 February 1917 (Berthenicourt)
I sent one large and one small parcel home. Visited Fritz at St Quentin. All villages deserted except for soldiers.

26 February 1917 (Berthenicourt)
We had to form a tree-felling squad. All fruit, nut and decorative trees, and also all bushes are being cut down. The idea is to make the whole region so bare that the enemy can find no cover and our aircraft have a better of view of them.

27 February 1917 (Berthenicourt)
Today we left for Vermand. We took over a collection station for the wounded. I was detailed to transport on the rail line. Today the village of Maissdemy was blown up It was quite near and was very loud. The beams sprayed in the air. Everybody who could do so ran to the hill to watch. We unhitched from Berthenicourt at 1000 for Pontru, then left to Vandancourt, Bithécourt, Vermand. Our soldiers were at work in many places setting fire to houses and barns. Maissemy was burning.

28 February 1917 (Vermand)
Today the branch line was torn up as far as our transport section and taken off. At midday we put all the patients in the hospital train. Now it is abandoned here. Fresh casualties arriving.

2 March 1917 (Vermand)
Today we sent off more by hospital train. In the evening, fires in Vermand. The wind is set fair for departure.

7 March 1917 (Vermand)
Today the bath was taken out. I made a basket of potatoes rending for sending home. The explosive charges were laid today below the street behind our house. In the evening fires, but in Quentin.

15 March 1917 (Vermand)
We emptied the sacks of straw. The railway line on the bridge was blown up today. Today sections of the remaining tracks are being blown up. I mailed the second parcel of stuff. At midday our hospital has to be evacuated with the exception of the kitchen. It is to be blown up.

16 March 1917 (Vermand)
Today the railway line was blown up at various locations. In the evening we were ready to leave. The Chief was up in arms at the number of packs the inspector was sending (. . .)

17 March 1917 (Bohain)
We marched out at 0400. Awful roads. We gave the main front line a miss, both there and at Bellenglise. It runs through various villages. We are now seeing some civilians again. Quarters in Bohain. We have to stow all carts in the hotel coach house. Twenty-seven kms.

Georg David Bantlin, Stabsarzt, Inf.Div.26
DIARY (continued)

18 February 1917 (Metz-en-Couture)
What has long been discussed, the pulling back of the front to the Siegfried Line, is in preparation. Today all inhabitants of the village of Metz are to be evacuated. A desolate sight, these roughly 500 people, women, children and old folk with few bits of possessions (only twenty-five kilos per person may be taken with them), gathered together on the market square on a rainy Sunday morning, stowing their few things on waggons, handcarts and children's perambulators. The young and fit have to walk to Gouzeaucourt, the others ride on a vehicle. How miserable it must be to leave house and property to head for an uncertain future! Nearly all are completely resigned to it though some of the young are optimistic, perhaps they are hoping to get to the Golden Freedom of France. I only hope they will not be disappointed! We made a wide detour to avoid the market square.

19 February 1917 (Metz-en-Couture)
We have retaken Beuffen (a trench near Lechelle). Everything was well prepared, relatively light but sad losses. The three officers who led the assault were either killed or seriously wounded. In these events the officers have to throw themselves into the fray if the thing is to succeed. The British prisoners relate horrific tales about the flame-throwers. It is an appalling weapon. What next will they dream up to cause death and destruction?

20 February 1917 (Metz-en-Couture)
Our most recent success has given the line its old stability, but Bernhard's grave is now out of reach. We would very much have liked to re-bury him in the local cemetery, which unfortunately is getting ever bigger. Under my direction it was gradually developing from a modest installation of improvised military cemeteries into a pleasant place of burial. The venerable trees of the neglected old part of the civilian cemetery provide a good background.

22 February 1917 (Metz-en-Couture)

The abandoned houses have a desolate look about them. Passing by, one misses the blond head of a child at play, the loud shouting of wild kids of the backstreets, the everyday silhouette of women and girls, who despite war and few chances of elegance seize them (carrying indispensable water). From the roofs the straw soon disappears, here and there a window frame or beam is missing, used to feed the stove. Soon there will be nothing left but rubble. Our soldiers are fabulous at demolition. Explosive charges have been set in all the cellars of the houses we occupy. 'Achtung! Charges ready!' is the sad warning posted outside many houses. All the same we sleep deeply and well on the powder keg. Every day explosions as water mains and military accommodations are destroyed. The church bells have been taken down, even the bell from the roof of the 'Cock', later to be used as a trophy to adorn the pioneer's barracks at Ulm. The British will find some pretty bare little quarters!

26–27 February 1917 (Metz-en-Couture)

Since the dressing station at Le Transloy, handed over by our Division to its neighbour, is to be reoccupied by the front medical officer of Inf.Regt.121, we are alternating for two days in the dressing tunnel at Rocquigny. What a difference to the summer of 1916! When one leaves the tunnel at night and hears the firing, one hears a symphony of overpowering anger: a continual roll of thunder in which shells of all calibres erupt near and far, and are combined with the hammer blows of our own artillery, a strong mix of heavy instruments, while MGs tack-tack and the less symmetrical, less regular chatter of rifle fire takes on the role of the lighter instruments in the orchestral presentation.

In silent complaint, walls and the skeletal structure of ruined houses point fantastically to the skies and build the foreground to the scene, sharp silhouettes against the unquiet, terrible yellow-red light inflaming the horizon. In between rear up dull red fires of bursting shells, ghostly sudden bursts of white light from rocket flares and, as if mocking the devil's work, red and green pyrotechnic columns from the signal lamps.

The stage is deserted despite the thousands and thousands

who lie between in suffering and death. With a cold shudder, the spectator senses the grim reaper's smile above the destruction and misery (. . .)

6 March 1917 (Metz-en-Couture)
At the main dressing station we still have a number of seriously wounded of whom some are recovering, we kept them back to spare them onward transport so that the necessary operations will be possible for those who by quick intervention can still be saved. The majority of cases we have here are stomach wounds and we operate if the circumstances allow (Stabsarzt Dr Weil) as we have long been convinced that the self-healing of stomach wounds earlier than thought possible scarcely ever occurs.

Thanks to the comfortable transport conditions for the trenches we have tolerable conditions for our wounded, good feather beds and mattresses, white jackets etc. – for a medical company a previously undreamed of luxury. Also more is being done now for science. (. . .) Recently I had to set up a legal section after a British prisoner stabbed to death an infantryman who was escorting him. The two had set out in high spirits and had been drinking schnapps. The Englishman was a publican from a London suburb, the German was of good reputation and had never been known to be drunk before. During the course of the drinking session the stabbing occurred. The accused defended himself skilfully at his military trial but was convicted on the basis of the medical evidence (the manner in which the wounds were inflicted indicated the intention to kill), sentenced to death and shot.

The dismantling and transport out of valuable materials is proceeding at a fast rate. The retreat has begun from the Ancre – apparently all went off smoothly and cost the surprised British great losses. Here we will also spoil their designs.

15 March 1917 (Metz-en-Couture)
Yesterday I was at Rocquigny: not without a feeling of slight regret one reflects on how all this hotly fought-for territory, littered with the bones of so many brave fighters, will be yielded to the enemy – voluntarily certainly, we do not turn back as the

defeated, but to prepare for the British a warmer reception from a better situated spot. And they will have to overcome a lot to get there. The many strong trenches which lie between the Siegfried Line and the present front will demand a lot of them.

We are moving out tomorrow night: all the details have been worked out. The foremost line will remain occupied at first by officer patrol, who will deceive the enemy into believing the trench fully occupied. They will not leave until 17/18th when fresh troops will move into the vanguard trenches on the Villers-Trecout Height etc.

Our Division is to march through the Siegfried Line on the night of 17 March to rest: at that point the rearguard will hold R–3 trenches east of Bus behind the advanced patrols. It is hoped that if all goes to plan the British will be taken by surprise. At Metz-en-Couture meanwhile the work of destruction had proceeded: my little room was almost blown up by an explosive charge on the water main, and only the alertness of my valet, who quickly opened the windows, left the panes intact and so ensured our little room remains warm at night.

All the time in the neighbourhood we hear houses dynamited and collapsing, and close by the occupied houses a friendly departing neighbour, who set fire to his barn as a token of farewell, amused the men during their work of tearing and burning down. There is still a lot of the robber and savage in people. Such a retreat carried out with such ferocious energy does not elevate the spirit of Man. The British will now certainly accuse us in all the world's languages of barbarity, and they will not lack for evidence when they take over this tract of earth: there is no water spring which has not been blown up and made unserviceable by artifical contamination, no cellar and no house left standing by the demolition squads. All cross-roads have been caved in and mined. At important places the trees along the main highways have been three-quarters felled and require only two blows from an axe to pitch them across the road. It will be almost impossible in the foreseeable future to get this territory fit to house attack troops. In these days of destruction, dark humour makes itself valid. Our poet Stabsarzt Fritz has written the British a friendly note of welcome on a toilet cubicle door:

'You cry Poor little Belgium
Poor Ireland you don't care
Protecting Culture, God and Law
You brought the niggers there.
I know you're always hypocrites
Now hear, what I you tell,
Our Germany will go ahead
But you, will go to hell!
With every good wish for a Happy Xmas
And bright New Year at Metz-en-Couture.

Yours truly,
Hermann'

Tomorrow we are moving to Gouzeaucourt to set up an un-protected main dressing station again. I was notified on 17th that I should report for a medical course at Charleville in Nouzon.

16 March 1917 (Gouzeaucourt)
At Gouzeaucourt it is the same as at Metz-en-Couture: burning and dynamited houses, soldiers going about the work as if on a morning stroll. The railway track to Cambrai has been dismantled, we are receiving almost no wounded. Apparently the British are not taking us on.

17 March 1917
In the automobile in order to reach the railway at Caudry, I drove through the interesting trench systems of the Siegfried Line with their broad wire entanglements at Le Pavé. Long stay at Busigny, where an old mansion is being furbished for the General Command with the furniture and artwork from another mansion further forward. First day of spring!

Paul Kessler, Feldpostsekretär, Garde-Inf.Div.2

DIARY (continued)

19 February–17 March 1917 (Hervilly)
As it happens the accommodations were all very fine, both for

the service post as for private quarters. This time I have a very nice room with Eichelbaum such as we have seldom seen before. A few times we took an evening stroll to Roisel two and a half kms away where a start has been made to blow up or burn down, as the case may be, the houses, because the German Line is being pulled back to the Siegfried Line and the vacated territory subjected to the 'Scorched Earth' policy to deprive the enemy of any accommodation. The houses are also being brought down in Hervilly: even in our own quarters the explosive charges are in place, on the day we left – 17 March – only three houses were still standing including our post office. These will be destroyed by the rearguard. At 0530 on 17 March we moved out, on foot, destination St Souplet (near Le Cateau).

Notes:

1   Erich Ludendorff: *Meine Kriegserinnerungen* 1914–1918, Berlin 1919, p.323.
2   *Der Weltkrieg 1914–1918* (hereinafter 'WKW'), Vol 12, Berlin 1939, p.145
3   WKW, Vol 12, p.61. See also AOK 1, 1a Nr.1858, 7 December 1916, also of the other armies: Bayrisches Hauptstaatsarchiv (BayHSTA)/Abt.IV, Army Group *Rupprecht*, 107.
4   Telegram Ia2079, 29 January 1917: BayHSTA/Abt IV, Army Group *Rupprecht* 108.
5   See also 6th AOK 1a Nr.430 dated 10 December 1916 expected 'major disadvantages of political nature and morale in the armies as in the Homeland would be difficult to bear': BayHSTA/Abt.IV.Army Group *Rupprecht*, 107.
6   See the unpublished diary entries of 15 and 26 September 1916, BayHSTA/Abt.III, N1 *Kronprinz Rupprecht*, 704.
7   Group N was formed at the end of 1916 from the Genkdo. XIV Reserve-Korps and formed the right flank of 1.Army.
8   WKW, Vol 11, p.510f.
9   Army Group *Kronprinz von Bayern*, Obkdo 1a Nr 2026, 15 January 1917, 'Suggestion for Operations in the French Theatre in the Spring of 1917': Army Group *Kronprinz von Bayern*, Oberkdo, 1ad, Nr 2104, 28 January 1917, BayHSTA/Abt.III N1 *Kronprinz Rupprecht*, 586.
10   Army Group Kronprinz von Bayern, Ia Nr 2177, Army Order 4 December 1916: BayHSTA/Abt.III N1 *Kronprinz Rupprecht* 586. Army Group *Kronprinz von Bayern*, I ad, Nr 2200, 6 December 1916, BayHSTA/Abt IV, Army Group *Rupprecht* 106.

11 AOK 1, Ia Nr 1858, 7 December 1916, BayHSTA/Abt.III N1 *Kronprinz Rupprecht* 107: Nr 2150 dated 1 February 1917, *Kronprinz Rupprecht* 108.

12 Army Group *Kronprinz von Rupprecht*, Oberkdo Ia Nr 2344, 21 February 1917, 'Outlook for Attack Operations at Alberich-Siegfried', BayHSTA/Abt.III N1 *Kronprinz Rupprecht* 586.

13 WKW, Vol 12, p.72.

14 Army Group *Kronzprinz Ruuprecht*, Id Nr. 2271 geh., April 1917, Siegfried-Alberich Memorandum, Part 1: Development of Siegfried Line, here Appendix 5; BayHSTA/Abt.III, NI *Kronprinz Rupprecht*, 564.

15 See additionally the files under Siegfried-Allgemein III; BayHSTA/Abt.III, NI *Kronprinz Rupprecht* 564.

16 Army Group *Kronprinz von Bayern*, Id Nr 4023, 16 November 1916, BayHSTA/Abt.III, NI *Kronprinz Rupprecht*, 585.

17 Ibid.

18 Chef des Feldeisenbahnwesens, IVa Nr.4435g/5732 geh., Memorandum 'The Siegfried-Alberich Railways', War Diary, Annexe 15h; BayHSTA/Abt.IV, Rekodeis, Vol 6.

19 On the question of this employment see the lively exchange of telegrams between the Army Group and OHL at the beginning of October; BayHSTA/Abt.IV, Army Group *Rupprecht*, 106.

20 Siegfried-Alberich Memorandum, Part p.22f.

21 GQM, IIc Nr 33866, 2 November 1916 and Nr 40462, 2 January 1917, BayHSTA/Abt.IV., Hgr. Rupprecht 106.

22 Hgr. Kronpr. Rupprecht, Id Nr 643 geh. (N.O. Nr 97), 29 September 1916: BayHSTA/Abt.IV, Hgr. Rupprecht 107.

23 Siegfried-Alberich Memorandum, Part 1, p. 40–42.

24 Additionally: Bauleitung 69 Abt I (tech.) Nr. 449, 24 March 1917: BayHSTA/Abt.IV, Hgr.Rupprecht, 108.

25 See war diary entries 1 July 1916–12 December 1916 for Württembergisch Guard Company, PoW Work Battalion 88: HSTA Stuttgart M 420, batch 37.

26 Also see the files re the care of PoWs, the civilian workers' battalions and the free workers in the records of 27.Württembergisch Inf.Div: HSTA Stuttgart, M 39, Vol 30. GQM IIc re Accommodation and Employment of the civilian workers' battalions: BayHSTA/Abt.IV Hgr.Rupprecht, 106.

27 7.Armee, AOK Id 138 Siegfried, 9 December 1916: Bay HSTA/Abt.IV, Hgr.Rupprecht 106. See also the scattered lists on arrivals

and departures in the civilian workers' battalions towards the end of the volume.

28 Siegfried-Alberich Memorandum, Part I, p.42.
29 See telex, Hgr. Rupprecht to OHL, 1 October 1916 regarding a group of 600 Russian PoWs from the Beverloo camp who initially refused work building trenches: BayHSTA/Abt.IV, Hgr.Rupprecht 106.
30 Report on the Construction of the Siegfried Line by Hauptmann Schinnerer: Bay HSTA/Abt.V, HS 2695.
31 Siegfried-Alberich Memorandum, Part 1, p.41. AOK 7, Id 488, geh., 24 March 1917: 'Free Belgians in general good: less so the non-volunteers': BayHSTA/Abt.IV, Hgr.Rupprecht, 108.
32 Siegfried-Alberich Memorandum, Part 1, p.41.
33 AOK 7.Armee, Iva N. 23290/3536, 25 December 1916: 'Sickliness, moral inferiority, political unreliability': BayHSTA/Abt.IV, Hgr. Rupprecht 106.
34 AOK7, Id 488 geh., 24 March 1917: 'If necessary it must be possible to coerce German civilian workers and apply military discipline. Resignations and strikes must be outlawed.' BayHSTA/ Abt.IV. Hgr.Rupprecht, 108.
35 Pioneer-Regt.30B, Nr.70/16, 4 October 1916, Nr.138/16, 11 October 1916, re-volunteer applications in Belgium: Hgr. Kronpr. von Bayern Oberkmmdo Id/Pi R30 N. 1103 geh. 20 October 1916, BayHSTA/Abt IV, Hgr. Rupprecht, 106/107.
36 Ludendorff: *Kriegserinnerungen*, p.324.
37 *Les espaces désertiques: impressions d'un combattante*: in 'L'Information', 26 November 1917.
38 Chief of Army General Staff Ia Nr. 281 geh.op: BayHSTA/Abt IV, Hgr.Rupprecht 107.
39 AOK1, Ia Nr.1304/Appdx.A: BayHSTA/Abt.IV, Hgr.Rupprecht 107.
40 Report by Krafft von Delmensingen to the Bavarian President, 2 February 1916: 'HRH gave vent to his indignation in the strongest terms at the cruelty of the planned measures and declared that he would have no part in it': BayHSTA, MA 944.
41 Diary entry 1 Ocotber 1916: Bay HSTA/Abt.III, N1 Kronpr. Rupprecht, 705.
42 Ibid.
43 For perfection in practice see Memorandum 'Erfahrungen über Zerstörung im Vorgelände' (Experiences regarding Destruction in Forward Territory) (June 1917): Bay HSTA/Abt.IV, Hgr Rupprecht, 106.
44 Gruppe N/Ia/Bod. General Staff Officer Nr. 723, geh., 1 March 1917, HSTA Stuttgart, M 200, bundle 43.

45 ibid.
46 AOK2, Ia/Is 173/apr/560 geh., 11 April 1917, Annexe 2, 'Destruction of Buildings': BayHSTA/Abt.IV, Hgr.Rupprecht 108.
47 Siegfried-Alberich Memorandum, Part 2, p.81. Hgr.Kronpr. von Bayern, Oberkommando Id Nr. 1496 geh., 2 November 1916, BayHSTA/Abt.IV, Hgr.Rupprecht 107.
48 ibid.
49 Submissions to the Siegfried-Alberich Memorandum, 25 March 1917, BayHSTA/Avt.IV, Hgr.Rupprecht 108.
50 Bavarian Regimental Commander of Railway Troops (special purposes) (Rekodeis) Nr. 1, Appendix 15g: Alberich Memorandum, April 1917: Bay HSTA/Abt.IV, Rekodeis 1, Vol.6.
51 Memorandum: Die Eisenbahnen bei Siegfried-Alberich, p.29f('The Railways in Siegfried-Alberich').
52 GQM IIb Nr. 2068 geh., 5 January 1917 on the question whether households were to be cleared in addition to warehouses and businesses, in this case in Saint Quentin. The answer was negative, but the practice looked otherwise. BayHSTA/Abt.IV, Hgr.Rupprecht, 106.
53 AOK 2, Is Nr. 523 geh., 18 October 1916 (Appendix 1 to Alberich Memorandum): ibid.
54 Additionally Hgr. Kronpr. von Bayern Oberkommando Id. Nr 1454 geh., 7 November 1916 and Id 30 November 1916: BayHSTA/Abt III, Nl Kronpr. Rupprecht 586. See also the OHL instruction, Id. Nr 1695, 30 November 1916 which excludes the inhabitants of Saint Quentin, including those incapable of work: Bay HSTA/Abt.IV, Hgr.Rupprecht 107.
55 The true figures differ from those compiled from the lists of names. In their turn these do not coincide with the published figures. The Railway Administration reckoned on 149,000 persons in 5,688 coaches, but transported eventually 135, 530 in 341 trains with 7,522 coaches. 1.Armee had many more (32,000), 2.Armee somewhat less (14,100 backwards, 19,150 forwards , 36,180 from Saint Quentin) and 7.Armee very many less persons (23,700 instead of 49,000) than reckoned. Plenipotentiary General Staff Officer, Field-Railway at Oberkommando, Hgr. Kronpr. Rupprecht, Memorandum, 9.April 1917: BayHSTA/Abt IV., Hgr. Rupprecht 108: Memorandum 'Die Eisenbahnen bei Siegfreid-Alberich.'
56 Siegfried-Alberich Memorandum, Part II, p.89.
57 The question of removing the inhabitants was not resolved until the GQM ordered it on 21 January 1917. Hgr. Kronpr. von Bayern Oberkmmdo. Id Nr.1469 geh., 2 November 1916: 'Abschub der Zivilbevölkerung unterbleibt' ('Removal of Civilian Population Remains to be Done'): BayHSTA/Abt.IV, Hgr. Rupprecht, 107.

58 At the end of January 1917 AOK2 was still not in agreement with a deportation on foot because the distance was over 80 kilometres: AOK2, Is Nr 357 geh., 30 January 1917: BNay HSTA/Abt.IV, Hgr Rupprecht, 107.
59 Siegfried-Alberich Memorandum, Part 2, p.89.
60 AOK 2, Ia/Is Nr 173/apr/560, geh. 11 April 1917; BayHSTA/ Abt.IV, Army Group Rupprecht 108.
61 AOK 2, Is Nr. 117 geh., 3 December 1916, pressure for an early evacuation of the town. AOK 2 Is Nr. 472, 12 February 1917; BayHSTA/Abt. IV, Army Group Rupprecht 107: Siegfried-Alberich Memorandum, Part 2, p.91.
62 The Art and Antiques Collection *Musée Alfred Danicourt* was housed in the Péronne council offices.
63 See additional report by Gustav Krauss, 15 July 1916.

Chapter Five

Return to the Somme 1918

Markus Pöhlmann,
Lecturer, Historical Seminar,
Ludwig Maximilian University, Munich

The story of the German operations on the Somme in the spring and summer of 1918 is the story of a return. German troops returned to many places and regions in the course of the First World War: to the Upper Rhine, East Prussia, Poland, Galicia, Chemin des Dames, the Marne and the Kemmelberg. From scarcely any return was a decisive effect upon the war expected as that from the Spring Offensive beginning on 21 March 1918 on the Western Front aimed at regaining Picardy across the battlefields of 1914–1917.

How did the landscape appear after four years of destruction, and what effect did it have on the troops? The area which German forces abandoned at the beginning of September 1918 had been transformed from a geographical region, an administratively defined region and a sector of the front, into a war landscape. The Somme was a war zone and a region of remembrance simultaneously.

From 'Michael' to Amiens

A decisive offensive on the Western Front was first considered by OHL (Army Supreme Command) in the autumn of 1917 after the failure of unrestricted U-boat warfare.[1] Following the failure of the British offensive in Flanders, the British had been hard pressed and were planing for a defensive posture for the spring of 1918. The outbreak of the Russian Revolution made it possible for Germany to release forces from that front for the Western Front. Time was pressing for the German military leaders, who expected the arrival of US forces in the European theatre of war during 1918.

From this analysis of the situation in November 1917, the question arose as to where and how the planned attack was to be made. The competent Army Groups suggested attacks in the Lys (Pas-de-Calais) and Somme regions against the British, and in the Verdun pocket against the French. The preference for Picardy and the subsequent operational intentions were fixed by Hindenburg and Ludendorff on 11 November 1917 at Mons.

A memorandum from Army Group *Kronprinz Rupprecht von Bayern* proposed an attack plan under the code-name *Michael*. The attack was to take place at the seam between the French and British armies. The southern flank against the French would be covered by the natural obstruction of the Somme while German 2. and 17.Armies would break out to the west and then wheel north-west. This would threaten the rear of the BEF and force it to fall back on the Channel ports. Operation *Michael* was at first only a preference and not a final decision. In the meantime the Army Group received instructions to prepare other operational plans for their areas. OHL made its decision at the end of January 1918. It involved a reformation of the units on the Western Front, 17., 2. and 18.Armies being envisaged for the attack. This meant that the three armies would be controlled by both Army Group *Kronprinz Rupprecht* (2. and 17.) and *Deutscher Kronprinz* (18.) The basis for this decision was probably the desire of OHL to maintain a tight rein by recourse to the policy of divide and rule. On 10 March the order for *Michael* was issued, the prospective date for the attack being the 21st of the month.

During the winter the troops had been reinforced, re-equipped and further trained. The preparation for the Spring Offensive was a model for military lesson-taking which extended from the lowest to the highest ranks: learning from the Battle of Flanders, from the British attack at Cambrai and its German counter-offensive, but also from the 12th Isonzo Battle in Upper Italy, both in the late autumn of 1917 (the latter two being included in the memoranda at the urging of the fighting troops, and turned into new standing instructions).

The military preparations were accompanied by a 'political offensive' in which the anti-war lobby was to be quietly drawn into the plot with the German public for one last great effort. Whilst the amateurish German overseas propaganda arm collapsed all along the line, the political leadership succeeded in reviving morale in Germany itself – despite the dreadful losses and miserable food situation. The 8th War Loan of March 1918 was launched under the slogan *Der Letzte Hieb* – the Final Push.

The morning of 21 March 1918 dawned foggy, the ground softened by recent rainfall. There had been none of the usual days of preparatory shelling, which as a rule put the defenders on alert for an offensive. At 0440 the artillery fired on the British lines between Arras and La Fère. Gas was used at the outset against the British 5th Army artillery (General Gough). The command posts and communication tracks received fire from 6,608 guns and 3,534 mortars, after that the trenches. At 0945 the first of the German infantry went over the top. The Germans had thrown 76 divisions into the attack – about 1.4 million men.

The attack orders to 2.Army (General von der Marwitz) whose route was through the Somme region read:

2.Army will attack west from the line Villers-Guislain-Bellenglise. 2.and 17.Armies will be responsible immediately for cutting off the standing British forces in the Cambrai pocket. Operationally that will be achieved by 2.Army if the centre of XVIII Reserve-Korps and XIV Army-Korps pushes ahead as far west as possible against the line Manancourt-Péronne without stopping, cooperating tactically with the inner wings of 17. and 2.Armies at Ytres (XI Army Korps) and Equancourt (XIII Army Corps). The aims must be achieved in an uninterrupted attack movement, a schedule has therefore not been prepared. The quicker the aim is achieved, the greater will be the initial success: the wiping out of substantial British forces and the overrunning of the enemy trench systems.[2]

The factor of surprise and the fog favoured the initial penetration of the first British trenches, but the fog also limited
German air support. In the poor conditions of visibility in many
places the infantry was not able to follow its own advance fire.
The German troops also suffered from their own gas after the
wind changed direction and drifted it over the German lines.
Contact to the Staffs was soon lost so that within forty-eight
hours the infantry had to fight its way through the first and
second British lines mostly without artillery or air support. Here
they came up against scattered instances of dogged resistance
from the surprised British. On 23 March the first German troops
reached Péronne and the banks of the Somme.

The same day a new order specified the operational goals of
2.Army, which would now not push westwards along the north
bank of the Somme river and then wheel north-west to cut off
the British, but cross the Somme and head south-west instead so
as to attack the French. What had brought this about?

During the fighting all three armies had made gains of territory, the most advantageous of which was that by 18.Army in
the south, which had initially had only the task of protecting the
flank of the main operation. In the centre and north on the other
hand the mobile wings of 2. and 17.Armies had run into stiff
resistance. Ludendorff had reacted to this situation and decided
to reinforce the successful attack in the south. The consequence
was that the attack changed from a comprehensive encircling
movement into an eccentric operation.

On the morning of 24 March, 2.Army reached 'The desert of
the Somme', the area which the Germans had so thoroughly
obliterated during Alberich. Beyond it to the west lay the old
battlefield of 1916 whose trackless crater-land now obstructed
the bringing forward of German artillery and supplies. The
attackers fought here around places which recalled the bloody
fighting of 1916, long since existing only as names on a map: Le
Transloy, Lesbouefs, Morval, Cobles, Ginchy, Longueval,
Guillemont, Hardecourt. On 25 March the resistance stiffened
and the strength of the attack ebbed markedly. The commander-
in-chief 2.Army, General von der Marwitz recorded:

'Yesterday's journey through fighting area of Somme-Battle the most sad thing seen until now: villages difficult to find, anonymous region of craters covered with sparse dead grass strewn here and there with small British crosses. It is the same for hours and hours, often over tracks made from wooden planks. That is northern France.'[3]

On 26 March the Army finally came free of the Somme desert and now attempted to force a crossing of the Ancre. Albert was taken after fierce hand-to-hand fighting. Rumours circulated about exhausted German troops refusing to continue after coming across British depots of alcohol and food. The resistance had also begun to take shape: Allied air superiority had started to make itself felt, the Army reporting that half its losses were attributable to air attacks.[4]

For the continuation of the attack over the Avre towards Amiens, ordered by OHL on 26 March, neither troops nor ammunition were now available. After an attack to consolidate either side of the Scarpe on 28 March ('Mars') had been warded off, on 5 April OHL finally abandoned *Michael*. The same day Kronzprinz Rupprecht noted in his diary:

'It strikes one that in all OHL instructions no actual inten-tion can ever be recognized, but only sectors of territory are spoken of as being necessary to reach, and I have the impression that OHL has a hand-to-mouth existence so to speak without laying down definite operational goals.'[5]

The German total losses were around 230,000 men, the enemy forces lost 212,000. 2.Army had pushed forward about forty-five kilometres, 18.Army sixty kilometres – distances hardly imaginable in the fighting of 1915–1917. What seemed to be at first a great success, and was postulated as such by propa-ganda, lost its significance when one considered what the originals goals of the operation had been. Even in the view of the official military historians, the Germans had 'not even come decisively nearer'[6] their aim of dividing the French and British armies and either encircling, or at least forcing, the British back to the Channel coast. Insufficient forces, the fog, the adverse conditions in the Somme desert, faltering supplies and not least the enemy's stubborn resistance led to the failure of *Michael*. In the operational respect, however, the decision of OHL may have weighed heavily when, following the first holding up of the attack on the right flank, the focus was transferred to the left, converting the encircling operation directed against the British into an eccentric operation against the British and the French jointly.

2.Army turned to defence in the new line. It was no longer involved in continuing the closing-up offensives to consolidate in Flanders, at Chemin des Dames and in the Champagne region, known as 'The Great Battle of France.' Picardy returned to being a minor sideshow. There could be no talk of real quiet in the 2.Army region: what played out in the months April to July 1918 was an outwardly unspectacular but final burning out of the Army. A battalion commander wrote:[7]

> 'But in watching the men I have often said to myself: They look like ghosts. Colourless, starving, dressed in tattered uniforms, lousy, dragging themselves from here to there, many almost bearing no similarity to human beings.'

Repeated British and French attacks concentrated against restricted localities, and unsettling artillery bombardments of long duration which pointed to the increasing material superiority of the enemy, sapped morale and fighting ability. Additionally troops were transferred out to the heart of the fighting. The reserves arriving from Germany were almost untrained and in poor physical condition due to lack of food. Additionally, in June and July the Spanish influenza epidemic affected 8,100 men in 2.Armee alone. The weekly reports on fighting strengths for the period between March and August 1918 give a clear picture: on 13 April the Army had twenty-eight divisions (twelve operational, sixteen resting). On 3 August the Army had seventeen divisions[8] operational, seven resting). On 13 April, of the twenty-eight divisions only four were at full fighting strength, however: twenty-one needed further training and two were only suitable for the trenches. By 3 August 1918 the number of fully battleworthy divisions had fallen to two.

Eleven divisions needed rest and training while five were now only suitable for the trenches. The deterioration was obvious by observations such as 'standard of infantry training poor': 'high losses in officers': 'artillery at the moment almost immobile as large proportion of the horses have mange': 'desperately in need of relief' or simply: 'non-operational.'[9]

On the morning of 8 August 1918 this shadow army faced a well-prepared Anglo-French offensive concentrated initially east of Villers-Bretonneux between the Somme and Luce-Bach to the south. In the course of the fighting the penetration of the German front extended to the Oise below Noyon. As with the German offensive before it, the Allied attack came as a complete surprise, being without any artillery preparation and favoured by thick fog. Contrary to the German experience in March, however, this attack was supported by 546 tanks. In a massed advance the armour enabled a swift breach of the German front. When the mist cleared, Allied bomber aircraft attacked the retreating defenders. Next day the Germans were forced to evacuate the hard-fought town of Montdidier, their few reserves being hurled into the fray as they arrived, to be soon overwhelmed.

The dramatic nature of the breakthrough is shown by the order of 2.AOK to the German artillery to engage the armour 'directly from the open or the trench positions.'[10] Once the attackers reached the difficult terrain of the 1916 battle, the attack faltered and halted on 12 August. North of the Somme, the Allied spearheads rested near Bray and to the south near Chaulnes. The operational success, considered soberly and in comparison to the German attack in March, was average, but the moral advantage enormous. What shocked the German military leaders was the speed of the attack, the success of the new tank arm used massively and operated with great tactical skill, and the apparent crisis in the fighting ability of German troops, shown above all in the large number of them taken prisoner. Although the British and French had had to stop after four days to reorganize and bring up reserves, unlike the Germans in the spring offensive they were not spent. Rather in the coming weeks they began a series of attacks which finally drove the Germans out of the Somme altogether. The attack of

8 August thus initiated the prelude to the great retreat of the German armies in the West, which would end in the Armistice of 11 November 1918.

The Somme Warrior of 1918

Against this background one may ask whether the two models of soldierly mythology, Langemarck (1914) and Verdun (1916) by Bernd Hüppauf might not be complemented into a trio with the addition of the Somme (1918) variant.[11] According to Hüppauf, whereas the earlier two types were distinguished primarily by traditional heroism and readiness for self-sacrifice, the Somme Warrior fought not from nationalistic principles or for the sake of fighting: he fought on from obedience, and primarily because it had become his way of life to keep fighting, and for his concerns for the fighting force. Above all he fought on in the knowledge of the inferiority in numbers and materials of his own side and thus knew that the cause was hopeless. One of the most prominent representatives of the elite front-warrior, Ernst Jünger,[12] wrote of the exhaustion and expectation of defeat as being the true underlying tendency. Looking over the reconquered war landscape near Puisieux in the summer of 1918 he observed 'a weariness in word and attitude which extended even to the style of dying.' The Somme Warrior of 1918 was therefore a stoic rather than a herioc figure.[13] Over the war years, veterans returned repeatedly to the Somme as campaign succeeded campaign. This does not appear to have been so stressful in 1918 as it was during the course of the fighting in 1916, for it had become 'a homecoming' to somewhere familiar. Jünger describes in *Feuer und Blut* his return to Quéant immediately before the beginning of Operation *Michael*:

' . . . How this large village has changed since last I saw it! In the winter of 1915 we had a pleasant time here. On the left over there by the road where you can see that 30-cm shell-hole was more or less where the little house stood that day when we threw a great breakfast for the brand-new shoulder straps on our greatcoats. It lasted from morning until well past midnight, myself and little Schultz, who now lies cold and silent on the Vraucourt-Mory highway. How many others I have seen fall, with whom I was close.'[14]

The war landscape awakens memories of a familiar place ('little house'), of a carefree time ('breakfast'), of careers and promotions and the loss of comrades. For General von der Marwitz it was the memory of 'my little town Péronne', which he let slip in a letter dated 3 September 1918 on the occasion of the final German retreat while reminiscing on his recent past:

' . . . I love this town. It has always been the hub of my military career around which the so variable path of war turned.'[15] Some even went so far as to say that the friendly warscape of the Somme should be reclaimed as 'old German soil.' This was implied by a divisional field-priest on the grounds that the Germanic Franks of Clovis had driven the Romans from the region around the year 500. This cultural tie accordingly had a long term effect:

' . . . The many blond heads with blue eyes playing in the child-rich northern French villages, in streets and on farms, and who have become good friends with us German soldiers, tell of the old German racial inheritance.'[16]

Naturally one also finds in the post-war accounts a similar kind of reminiscence. By then the Somme had already become 'a half-forgotten saga.' According to author Veit Rosskopf earlier:

' . . . The peasant blood of Lower Bavaria feels strangely attracted by the earth of Flanders [he meant Picardy – author]. Many would like to be able to stay here until the end of the war on this homely, good farming land, light and flat, where one feels for the first time what it is like to live in peace.'[17] 'Homely' feelings were expressed in regimental records, as when one met again enemy units known from previous encounters, although this had no effect on military tactics.[18] To the chronicler of 5.Bavarian Infantry Regiment which had fought at Bapaume in 1916 the Alberich region was 'barely recognizable'[19] in mid-August 1918, while the Grenadier Regiment 123 historian described the return of his unit during the 1918 spring offensive as a 'homecoming':

> ' . . . Now we were back in familiar territory: we had come this way often in 1916 and 1917. Heudicourt, Sorel, Fins – who would ever have thought that we would have to recapture these villages which before the Hindenburg retreat had been destroyed and cleared by us, never to be seen again? Changeable fortunes of war, for us as for the enemy now having to pay the price for all his battles in the Somme and at Cambrai! We have the feeling of being at home . . .'[20]

The visualization of the Somme as the 'German Soldier's Homeland' has something disturbing about it, since the allegation was free of any irony. It is understandable from the specific nature of trench warfare and the long period that the military social group existed. The war landscape was a place where great effort had been invested, where one had lost trusted friends and had to bury them. Despite all the intervening destruction, in 1918 one often came across old graves from the 1914–1917 period. In quiet phases the warscape was cultivated. In the same way that trench systems might be named after German towns or prominent personalities, in the rear areas staff and welfare establishments had hedges, flower borders and an apt motto above the lintels of the doorway: farm animals were kept and agriculture practised. German soldiers had thus begun to build on the Somme, the Homeland they had left. In many private photographs this curious and charming land seizure is important for propaganda as proof of German 'cultural achievement.'[21] The experience of 'Home on the Somme' was a pleasant relief for the German soldier, made even easier by the lack of protest from the French population, absentee landlords since the beginning of 1917. The concept of the Somme as Homeland developed in the course of the war and not as a literary or ideological idea created afterwards. With the return of the troops to Germany and their reintegration into civilian society, the tie to the Somme soon died out and was lost, whereas it endured until recent times amongst British veterans, for example.
    An interesting mutual interest developed between the

Germans and the French over the Somme and Verdun. The unique dominance of Verdun in the modern German collective memory never existed before the end of the Second World War. The Somme had demanded at least equally high tribute, and unlike Verdun the Germans had been there defending it for several years, fertile ground for the creation of military myths of sacrifice. The significance of the Somme was not to be under-estimated, for this front sector had been for a long period, and until the late summer of 1918, of decisive significance for the war. The memory of the fighting there could not be over-shadowed. The later dominance of Verdun as a place of remembrance has no military basis, and was not of the same dimensions in death and destruction as the Somme had been, although both were of course apocalyptic. What was required after the Second World War was a warscape around which French-German reconciliation could be sealed. The international battlefield of the Somme was hardly suitable whereas Verdun, fought between Frenchman and German, served the cause perfectly. Thus the Somme Warrior as a figure for German remembrance faded away, and with him also disappeared the memory of the Homeland on the Somme.

Order To Attack[22]

10 March 1918
His Majesty orders:
1. The Michael-Attack will begin on 21 March. Entry into first enemy trenches at 0940 hrs.
2. As its first tactical objective, Army Group Kronprinz Rupprecht will cut off the British in the Cambrai Bend and advance north of the Omignon river to its confluence in the Somme, holding the line Croiselles – Bapaume – Péronne – Omignon River. If the attack by the right wing of 17.Armee advances favourably, it is to continue beyond Croisilles. Further task of Army Group is to thrust ahead in Arras-Albert direction, hold the Somme at Péronne with the left wing, and with the strongpoint on the right wing destabilize

the British line in front of 6.Armee, thus freeing other German forces from the trenches for the advance. In this case all divisions behind 4. and 6.Armee are to be brought up without delay.

3. Army Group *Deutscher Kronprinz* will take the Somme south of the Omignon River and the Crozat Canal. In a swift advance 18.Armee will engage enemy forces to seize the Somme and Canal crossings. In connection hereto, 18.Armee will wait in readiness to extend its right flank as far as Péronne. Army Group will give consideration to strengthening the left wing of 18.Armee by divisions from 7., 1. and 3. Armeen.

4. OHL (Army High Command) will operate 2.Garde Inf.Div., 26.Württembergische Inf.Div. and 12.Inf.Div.

5. Regarding *Mars* and *Erzengel*, OHL reserves to itself a decision depending on state of operations. Preparations are to proceed continuously.

6. Other Armee will operate per General Staff Ia Nr 6925 geh.op.Mob. of 4 March 1918 (a diversion-Author). Army Group *Kronprinz Rupprecht* will cover the right wing of the *Mars/Michael* Operation against British counter-attack. Army Group *Deutscher Kronprinz* will avoid a French counter-attack against 7.(excluding *Erzengel* front), 1. and 3.Armee according to plan. OHL reserves its decision re Army groups *Gallwitz* and *Herzog Albrecht* respecting operational measures to be taken in the event of a French counter-attack or the further removal of divisions from the battlefield.

General Georg von der Marwitz, C-in-C., 2.Armee

Letters to his wife Helene von der Marwitz, and Notes.

24 March 1918 (Le Cateau)
A quiet quarter of an hour for this letter. Therefore it really is a victory over the British, perhaps not yet decisive, but we calculate we have forced back thirty of his divisions. After the first penetration succeeded almost everywhere on 21st, at first

progress was slow but on the afternoon of 22nd everything began to flow. Yesterday we made good strides forward despite the British bringing up tanks, basically they are no longer the terror they were, people just report now: 'There was a counter-attack including the use of tanks, it was beaten off, X number of tanks destroyed.'

North of the Somme my foremost infantry have gone beyond my 1916 position at Péronne. I should like to have visited Péronne again, but had no time for it. It is too wonderful, who would have thought it? Today I went forward for a Supreme Command meeting into the region destroyed by us in 1917, and stayed with a division where the report reached me that the Kaiser was on his way to Le Cateau. I retraced my steps only to find that he was going via Cambrai. We detoured but I caught up with him at Gouzeaucourt, where I found him eating his packed breakfast. I was given a bowl of soup and – the Komtur-Cross of the Hohenzollern Order with Star. I protested: 'But Your Majesty, the battle is not yet concluded.' He replied, 'The first part of the great Battle *is* concluded.' Well, at that I accepted it. Then he opened the greatcoat at Father Hindenburg's chest and, pointing to the Star there said, 'What about that for a medal?' I saw that it was the Blücher Star which I had read about in Blücher's letters and had seen recently in the museum. 'Yes,' the Kaiser said, 'Blücher got it for his victory *with* the British, Hindenburg for doing the same *against* them.' Father Hindenburg said nothing, but stood like a wall. I congratulated him, after which he enquired about the situation, but not much. We were near a British military cemetery and the Kaiser read every inscription, picking up a small metal plate which had fallen off, taking it with him. As His Majesty was leaving I requested permission to return to my command. It was high time, for I had to see to the orders. Yes, it is a great time for us, the Lord will help us through, it seems to me as if that is His intention. How glorious that would be (. . .)

26 March 1918 (Le Cateau)

Today is a day of changes: our offensive has progressed so far forward that a quarter turn is essential, but to where? Well, before us was the destroyed zone of 1917, all villages turned into rubble, and so we went into a large British barrack dressing station at Tincourt near the gates of Péronne. I was there today, the rooms are nice and bright, not much furniture but it will do. The Supreme Command which I am now visiting was in a similar state, but most were worse off. It is really a peculiar coincidence that – I especially – defended Péronne and district with everything we had in 1916, after becoming C-in-C at the same spot I vacated it voluntarily in 1917, only to return in 1918 with the strongest forces to recapture it. There was very heavy fighting for the Maissonette Farm near Cléry where I crossed the Somme in 1914 as cavalry-leader, forty British guns have been totally destroyed. What changes the land has had to undergo, now it is a desert, ghastly to see, mournful in the grey of the endless dust which covers everything from the treeless avenues. Many tanks, Britain's great hope, stand around: they held up our troops occasionally but they cannot be decisive.

Now from this greatly comfortable life we are striking out in the field. I leave Le Cateau unwillingly, in every respect things have gone well for me here and I would be ungrateful if I did not recognize that. The motivation is glorious: press ahead to victory! What difficulties my army has yet to overcome I cannot say since the greater part of it had to cross the region of the earlier Somme battle. The crater landscape permits movement only around the crater ruins, which makes it extremely difficult for vehicles: now they are through, however, for they took Albert on the Ancre. Behind it is Hallue where General August von Goeben defeated the French in 1871, they will probably resist there again.

29 March 1918 (Péronne)

I can say nothing about our battles, the region in which we are engaged is appalling. It is the area of the earlier Somme Battle and is a giant desert. Villages are scarcely recognizable as such and topography resembles upland covered with brush and thicket. Our front lines reach to the edge of the *undestroyed* region, but it is not pretty there either, for the British have wasted no time in devastating everything. How they will ever make this land inhabitable again is anybody's guess.

12 August 1918 (Péronne)
The enemy has not attacked since yesterday. We have to keep a lynx-like watch, however. The enemy's entire success was due to his tanks. After the Battle of Cambrai I saw the tank as over-rated, I had become convinced that the things were too slow and the view out from them too limited. Often they go forward into total darkness, get stuck and are wiped out. I emphasized then, on the other hand, that the idea of caterpillar tracks for cross-country travel was brilliant and absolutely had to be used in the design of armoured guns. In my opinion that will be the artillery weapon of the future. Our enemies have beaten us to it, they already have guns like that, and in very large numbers. They travel much faster than before, about as fast as a lorry on a good road.

On 8 August there was thick fog and our guns could not shoot. Tanks were everywhere but naturally immobile and thus non-operational, and then they had tank [probably means gun-Tr] batteries whose horses had to be held nearby despite enemy fire. But before these could be harnessed up, naturally a while went by, and even when that was done and the guns were positioned to fire, teamed-up batteries could only fire once the horses were unharnessed again, and before they got that far they were wiped out. In short, in fog it is an evil weapon. Now, if one had armoured batteries they would be ready, immediately, as with an automobile to set off by turning on the motor, and they can fire when on the road or straight away after stoping. These batteries would therefore be brilliant escort artillery for our infantry. In the trenches, as I have just described it, and in mobile warfare as batteries, which remain close to the infantry and can support it. We shall see whether our technology will also develop along those lines, and I would consider it correct.

In there recent fighting our enemies have had to take heavy losses to their tanks and I would like to take advantage of the peace and quiet we have had since yesterday to arrange things. In some places, very many tanks have been destroyed by our artillery . . .

3 September (Gouzeaucourt)
I drove yesterday up to the high ground east of Péronne, I know

the view from there well, have often been up there on horseback and rode back down the slope past Doingt, often with General major Bolko von Oheimb. While there I could distinctly see our infantry lying in front of the town, the brave heaps which warded off the attacks from the town on the second day. Of the town and its once imposing cathedral there is little to be seen, one has to actually know that there is a town there to recognize it as such with the binoculars.

I love this town, it has always been the hub of my military career, around which the so-variable paths of war turned. This thought haunted me during the ride back: wonderful, some middling enemy nuisance fire with shrapnel, we went through it quietly and came to no harm.

When I passed through Moislains-Bouchavesnes in 1914, I saw the town for the first time on my left, partially hidden behind the former fortifications which were then distinctly recognizable as such. I knew that IV.Korps was striving to get there, while I was with II.Korps which I had joined from the north the previous day. I was sure that I would not be able to cross the Péronne bottleneck and so went down to Cléry to attempt the crossing of the river farther down but I failed, the swampy river valley was too broad and my guns did not have the range. I met General Alexander von Linsingen, leader of II.Armeekorps and suggested he could help me across with his heavy artillery. At first he was against it, since he did not want to cross the river with his Korps, but was finally persuaded and after a brief artillery preparation the advance guard got over. I left our town to the left, therefore to the east, and set off for Paris in satisfied mood. I was certain I would not be seeing Péronne again very soon, but as Generalfeldmarschall Hermann von Eichhorn used to say: 'First it turns out different', and secondly 'Than you thought.' We lost the Battle of the Marne, with great effort the cavalry plugged the gap which had opened between 1. and 2. Armee when the former bore away, and hurried via Soissons in the Laon area to be relieved by 7.Armee under Generaloberst Josias von Heeringen, C-in-C Coastal defences.

It was now essential, on the outermost wing of the Armee, to detach and operate against the enemy flank. A nice idea but every time I got into a position to break loose the Korps would say: 'I am partially surrounded by the enemy, you will have to remain on my wing and fight, otherwise I shall not be able to hold out.' Thus at Noyon, Nesle and also on the day when I wanted to pass behind Bavarian I Korps through Péronne, the Commanding General informed me he was at the front tied up with all his forces, and was being closed down in the Somme bend at Bray, and I should protect his flank. I did this and fought there for one whole day, preventing the wing being surrounded, for which I was awarded the Bavarian service Order later. Next day I left the Schmettow Division and headed with 2.Cavalry Division (Thumb) for Péronne.

On Mont St Quentin, which I visited today probably for the last time, we raced to get to the wing of XIV Reserve Korps (Stein-War Minister) and so onwards for the coast(. . .)

The great Spring Offensive of 1918 also had Péronne as its goal, and my Armee marched with the central section. The attack exceeded expectations and it was still March when I re-entered Péronne. The town was even more ruinous than before, slogans in English and French on the cathedral and town hall stated that the rubble would remain where it was until peace. Well, we cleared up what we could and began to restore the best houses.

On 8 August the big tank attack began in fog along the front in the Villers-Bretonneux area which I had long previously identified as very threatened. That same morning I realized that the attack was too far east to be intercepted, and that the installations at Péronne could not be held. The fighting led to progressive surrender of the territory of the Somme, the battle-field came ever closer to the town until it had to be abandoned. The East and South held out although surrounded. That gave me the motivation to take a last look at the place which had been so significant so often for me and my troops. Will this be the last look or shall I see it again? God alone knows. I shall accept what He sends and will not complain.

Feldunterarzt Walther Vogt (1888–1941) Inf.Div.35 (BfZ N97–8)

Letters to his Parents at Marburg/Lahn

27 March 1918 (8 kilometres from Albert)
My last letter was a letter-card dated 22nd from Lesdain, south of Cambrai, since then no possibility of posting mail. All are pushing forward, no connections to the rear. The only thing they can think of is ever forwards, and the Homeland can wait. As to what I have to tell you, I hardly know where to begin. The scenes everywhere are overwhelming. Our division did not reach the village before Albert until 26 March, took Albert yesterday and is now about three kilometres beyond it. There was a reserve division ahead of them, the one with Stabsarzt Wurm in the medical company, an old friend from Inf.Div.61, whom I have met repeatedly. I got about the initial fighting from him. The first goal was Epehy – we passed through there on 24th and were amazed at the confusion of trenches, wire obstructions, flanking installations, underground shelters, large fortified positions – all earthworks though, no concrete. *How* we managed to capture this main base is beyond me, and our losses were by no means heavy. After the five-hour artillery preparation with a lot of gas the attack began at 0940, thick fog so that the shock troops went forward in a line and had reached the first enemy trenches without a shot being fired.

28 March 1918
Cannot write at length, only short passages: we followed well behind the fighting in slow and difficult march via Nurlu (night of 24th in British officers' barrack hut, where I found a nice, useful short coat with fur), Manancourt (nights from 25th to 27th under canvas, frost and north wind), very unpleasant night-long aerial attacks which caused many losses in the Army camp. Yesterday marched here through the ghastly dead terrain of the Somme battle, through Sailly-Saillisel, Combles, Guillemont, Longueval to Bazentin-le-Petit, here comfortable in heated corrugated-iron hut. A blessing that I kept my field bed from when I was in Poland. The land is devastated, graves, lack of

water – I got really depressed going through it. Today apparently an attack through Albert. An officer has been detached to handle the mail.

12 May 1918 (Lesbouefs)

Our surroundings are more pleasant and lively than before except that the weather is so cold and damp. If we did not have the big stove in the tent it would be unbearable. Today beautifully sunny. We three younger men are now living in the ruins of what once was a 'room', many holes in the ceiling, despite much repair work dust, plaster and chalk still drizzles down. Sandbags are stacked wall to ceiling, the walls are all cracked, some of the floral wallpaper has survived in patches, complete with original German and English graffiti, but in most places all adornment has come off in great ribbons; the door is missing, we have bricked up a second door and the fireplace, the large window has no glass, canvas has been stretched across the ceiling recently to catch the flakes. The boys have fashioned tables, chairs, washstands in a competition for a prize, and so it has become a very original stay although its romance will enchant the visitor more than the inhabitant. But all the same – four walls for the first time in six weeks – that is worth a lot. I have found out that the ruin itself is the only building left standing in Lesbouefs and all the surrounding villages: because the roof was a Sword of Damocles nobody had dared to move in, obviously it looked worse at the beginning, having to climb over a mountain of rubble to get in.

In the main room – the 'business room' – there remain only bits of wall and ceiling – a gigantic hole gapes – a heavy calibre hit which went throught to the cellar. Our room was reduced to rubble when a wall of sandbags collapsed. What really cheers me up is the garden in which a few dwarf fruit trees are pushing outwards again, and a damaged lilac bush has begun to bloom white. Gooseberry and currant bushes, rosebushes, are forcing through the swathes of tall grass, even the garden hedge is recognizable so that we are settled in our own house and grounds so to speak.

Well, you yourself will soon be able to admire the unique beauty of the dreamed-of mansion in fine photographs. The whole region here looks more alive because even the craterland is covered in green, prolifically overgrown by advancing pasture and meadow. At the foremost bivouacs it could easily be November there, so brown and bare is the desert terrain. When will we get to see again real trees and gardens? I believe it cannot be too long, we must go forwards, it is not like they whisper it in the pitiful Reichstag, that the offensive has stuck fast – no, on the line where we stand we have been ordered to halt with divisions still fresh. We stop for the gigantic problem of supply, and the repair to streets, railways, bridges: to fill depots with ammunition, engineering equipment, food, water installations, whole camps of barrack huts and tents – what has been brought about in a short period of time is beyond description.

A campaign in the West does not proceed as it does in the East, an army one million strong is so held back by the masses of slow-moving supplies that pauses *have to* occur, all relationships are thrown to the wind, a pause in the fighting – in the East on a major advance eight to ten days is here many weeks. Eckart's story of the life of horseflesh in a rich, formerly opulent region proves how quickly the land's produce is devoured by the thousands, and it is the same with ammunition. Therefore – our trench war is in a battle pause, we content ourselves with that and wait full of confidence to strike the next great blow (. . .)

Fähnrich Paul Knoch (1898–1982) (BfZ N.Knoch)
Letter to his parents at Hanover-Waldhausen

7 April 1918
I am sitting on watch again, but see nothing but ridges occupied by ourselves and so there is no shooting, today we are only reserve. I am sitting in the sun under a blossoming bilberry. What that means after four days of rain, always marching through mud ankle-deep, through porridge and sauce, at night only sleeping on and off, tottering from one hole in the road to the next, stumbling against stones, and always little sleep, outside in the tent everything wet, covered in mud, all on a half-spoonful of jam daily. If you have not seen it, you can hardly imagine it. The 5th was the worst, we marched all night on 3rd

and 4th, even ran a bit on 4th so that on the 5th we were utterly done for. We had to go on though because it rained all day. I used my English rubber cape which keeps all the water out, and packed away my muddy greatcoat. I was wet below the knees but I did not care, I was dry everywhere else and was not hampered by the heavy greatcoat unlike almost everybody else. That evening we put up our tents in a wood in streaming rain. Had a good sleep, because I have a lot of capes. I laid my rubber cape on the wet ground, then a Gderman (canvas) one doubled on top of it, then I lay myself down, wrapped in three blankets and greatcoat.

I have just eaten and had the first good wash in days. Wonderful feeling. The rain did not upset me much. Many of them have got apathetic. My comrade Müller for example, he started saying if only I could be at home now. What's the point? I keep thinking it could be worse. Things are going well. Besides, it must get better, and the main thing is our offensive is progressing forwards. In the past I used to envy the men who got a wound and had to be sent home, but those were fleeting thoughts, I do not let myself get depressed (. . .)

In the region of the 1916 Somme battle, Péronne etc., everything looks totally devastated. Crater after crater, many villages, for example Bouchavesnes, no more than a one-metre high heap of masonry, of trees only splintered stumps remain. In the streets everywhere dead horses, bodies of Germans, British and French, bits of equipment, guns, ammunition, here and there a wrecked or abandoned British artillery piece. One gets completely used to the picture. One does not want to reflect on it. Now we are in a civilized region once more, brown ploughland, green fields of sproutlings, and villages (. . .)

Notes:

1 Der Weltkrieg 1914–1918 (hereinafter 'WKW') Vol.14, Berlin 1944 (reprint 1956).
2 WKW Vol 14, p.117
3 Georg von der Marwitz Weltkriegsbriefe, publ. Tschischwitz, Berlin 1940, p.286
4 WKW Vol 14, p.221. Also Tschischwitz, p.299 and 304.
5 Kronprinz Rupprecht von Bayern: Mein Kriegstagebuch, publ. Eugen von Frauenholz, 3 volumes, Munich 1929, Vol 2, p.372.

6   WKW Vol 14, p.255–258. Despite its Ludendorff apologists, there was no lack of distinct criticism in the appraisal of the High Command. Thus the plan to strike at both opponents simultaneously was 'attributable to a serious overestimation of what had been achieved to that point' (p.257) and the fighting lacked 'a clear strong-point build up' (p.258).

7   Report of Officer Commanding II Battalion/Inf.Regt.48, Major Würtz, from: Thilo von Bose: Die Katastrophe des 8 August 1918, Oldenburg/Berlin 1930, p.30 (Schlachten des Weltkriegs, Vol. 6). Contains other impressive examples for the breakdown in fighting strength.

8   Bayrisches Hauptstaatsarchiv, Abt. Kriegsarchiv (Munich): Collection Army Group *Kronprinz Rupprecht* Nr 80: Weekly Report 'Fighting Value of the Divisions in the Army Group Sector' (secret) 1918. The difficulties in the statistics arose from divisions being on the move and treated in a non-uniform manner in the preparation of statistics.

9   WKW Vol 14, p.561

10   Bernd Hüppauf: Schlachtenmythen und die Konstruktion des 'Neuen Menschen' in: Hirschfeld, Krumeich & Renz: Keiner fühlt sich hier mehr als Mensch, Essen 1993, p.43–84.

11   Ernst Jünger: Das Wäldchen 125, from Jünger: Collected Works, Section 1, Vol 1, Stuttgart 1978, p.301–438, here p.305 (first edition 1925).

12   See selection of contributing authors, not free of heroic pathos, in Wolfgang Förster & Helmuth Greiner: Wir Kämpfer im Weltkrieg, from Reich archive material, 1929, p.440–504, clear also in the concluding part of Remarque: *All Quiet on the Western Front*, although silent as to the actual location.

13   Ernst Jünger: Feuer und Blut, from *Collected Works*, Section 1, Vol 1, Stuttgart 1978, p.439–538 (first edition 1925).

14   Marwitz, *ibid*, p.310.

15   *Zwei Jahre an der Westfront*, 323 pictures from Artois, Picardy and French Lorraine, published by 'a German infantry division', Munich 1917, p.9–10.

16   Veit Rosskopf: Ein Tag in einer Artilleriestellung, in: *Jünger, Das Antlitz des Weltkrieges, Berlin 1930*, p.112–139.

17   Thus the author of a regimental history described the British division they were facing in the summer of 1918 as 'the old lady friend': Richard Bechtle: Die Ulmer Grenadiere an der Westfront: 5.Württ., Nr 123 in: WKW, 1914–1918, Stuttgart 1920, p.140.

18   War Diary, 5.Inf.Regt *Grossherzog Ernst Ludwig von Hessen*, Munich 1929, p.122.

19   Bechtle, *ibid*, p.130

20   *Between Arras and Péronne*, pictorial record of trench warfare, publ. a German Reserve-Corps, Bapaums, 1916.

21 WKW, Volume 14, Berlin 1944, p.85.
22 General von der Marwitz: Weltkriegsbriefe, Tschischwitz, Berlin, 1940.

Chapter Six

The German Memory
of the Somme

Professor Gerd Krumeich,
Heinrich-Heine Universität, Düsseldorf

After the lost war and the 'war guilt' provocation of the
Versailles treaty, it was not only German politicians, especially
of the Right, who made sustained efforts to justify the war: the
majority of the German people sought some expression of
legitimization. One and a half million dead German soldiers and
– according to the officials statistics of the German Army
medical bulletin – more than 4.8 million wounded, called out for
the war to be placed in an historical context with some reasonable basis for it. The central place in this search for rationality
and the creation of a tradition was divided by memories of the
enormously costly battle at Verdun in 1916 on the one hand,
and on the other the retreat to the Siegfried Line in February and
March 1917 and finally – though less prominent – the Great
Battle of France in the spring and summer of 1918, during which
the German armies returned to sections of the original Somme
battle front.

Even during the war most Germans had already begun to
draw a clear distinction between the military events on the
Somme and at Verdun. The principal difference between the two
was that at Verdun the Germans were obviously the attackers,
while on the Somme they defended. Today we may find this
differentiation academic, for both the Somme and Verdun were

French territory and the Germans were present there as invaders. Understanding this line of reasoning is important, however. At the Somme the Germans held the 'Watch on the Somme' as it were, a kind of 'Watch on the Rhine' extended westwards, and it was no coincidence that the 1.Army soldiers' newspaper from the autumn of 1914 should have the title 'Die Somme-Wacht.'[1]

Here the fortified positions were like 'a wall of iron and fire.'[2] Even the troops – and here the propaganda functioned only as an echo – were totally convinced that it was precisely this wall 'in the midst of enemy land' which had saved the German people from the horrors of war, from death and destruction. What the soldiers had achieved as defenders of the Homeland appeared to be unarguable fact when seen against the cruelty of the war suffered daily elsewhere. Moreover the Germans were not only determined defenders of the Home Front in France, they were also witnesses to events on the Somme – eyewitnesses above all to the destruction which the British and even the French in their own land had wrought by their ruthless military planning. In thousands of photographs, in letters and newspaper articles 'from the field' this accusation was repeated endlessly: not we Germans are responsible for the enormous destruction in the Somme region, but the French themselves, and the British, and finally also the Americans. From 1917 onwards there appeared pictorial documentation in book form which served this kind of propaganda. Best known was *Zwischen Arras und Péronne* which appeared in numerous reprints.[3]

The contention that the Germans had only defended at the Somme made irrelevant to them the destruction which German forces had inflicted during their retreat to the Siegfried Line in 1917. Neither the war damage resulting as a consequence of the advance during the *Michael* offensive of 1918, nor the dreadful destruction during the last German retreat in the autumn of 1918 brought into question the image already forming in 1916. The entire Somme-discourse in the Weimar Republic post-war was dominated by the twin themes of how they defended at the Somme and tried to preserve the French cultural heritage. To the degree that after the war the victors (especially the French) accused the Germans of war crimes against property, this solidified the conscious and raucous German defensive strategy, and culminated in the assertion that selfless and untiring German soldiers had had their hands full coping with the task of saving French cultural treasures from being wrecked by British and French shelling.

The basis for the argument and its justification were formed during the war and made systematic after it. As is well known, the 'war guilt clause' in the Treaty of Versailles was received with great indignation by most Germans and led to an immense outpouring of literature in repudiation of the clause during the 1920s. Less well known is that Article 231 of the Treaty laying the war guilt at Germany's door, with the resulting reparations and costs, was directly related to the damage done especially on the Somme and in Northern France. As 'the perpetrator', Germany had to pay for all the damage 'which the Allied and associated Governments and their citizens had suffered in the war forced upon them as the result of the attack by Germany and its allies.'[4] This meant all and any damage whatsoever and howsoever caused was a consequence of the war for which Germany was responsible. The Germans were, or remained, overwhelmingly of the opinion – narrow-mindedly but perhaps understandably – that this demand was totally unjust, being adamant that they themselves had not inflicted most of the damage. It was pointed out again and again that the Allies had destroyed towns, villages and cultural treasures.

To the forefront in the polemic literature was the rebuttal published in August and December 1922 in the leading revisionist journal *Süddeutsche Monatsheften* by former officer Joachim von Stülpnagel. His argument and exhaustive documentation was aimed principally at exposing the lie of 'wilful destruction', a term which, though it did not occur in the Treaty itself, was often heard in statements by foreign politicians and statesmen in their attempts to morally justify the Allied claim for reparations. In the Treaty draft, French Prime Minister Clemenceau accused Germany of responsibility not only for starting the war, but also for its subsequent brutalization. During the negotiations in London in the spring of 1921 to set the level of reparations, British Prime Minister Lloyd George also mentioned the 'wilful destruction' of Belgian and French localities by the Germans. French President Poincaré, who at the opening of the Versailles

Congress had accused the Germans of 'the worst crimes in human history', strung this together with a host of other accusations the following year respecting the wilful and barbaric destruction of Northern France and Belgium.

Relying on a large number of German military documents, Stülpnagel set out to prove that 'the German share in this destruction of French and Belgian regions was much smaller than that of the Allies.'[5] Above all, the Germans had been forced to stand by and watch massive destruction by the Allies while all destruction by the Germans, especially during the retreat to the Siegfried Line in 1917 and the final retreat in the late autumn of 1918, had been a 'military necessity and was therefore a completely lawful measure in international law.'[6] Similar arguments were heard by the Parliamentary Committee of Enquiry (the so-called Third Sub-Committee) in 1919 set up by the National Assembly which was investigating alleged breaches of international law in the Great War. Besides other questions – the deportations of Belgian forced labourers to Germany, the Allied naval blockade, gas warfare etc. – 'the destruction in Northern France occasioned during the retreats of the German Army in 1917 and 1918' were also on the Commission's agenda.[7] The committee took evidence from a series of witnesses including General von Kuhl, former Chief of Staff of Army Group *Kronprinz Rupprecht von Bayern*. General Kuhl explained the efforts made by those responsible to ensure the most humane possible 'removal' of the inhabitants from the 'area of destruction.' With direct reference to the documents presented by Stülpnagel amongst others, Kuhl argued that 'the destruction undertaken was limited to what was necessary militarily. It must be established that not merely in the retreat to the Siegfried Line, but in the war as a whole, very much destruction had been committed not only by the Germans but also by the enemy side.'[8]

The sub-committee accepted this line of reasoning without further debate. Kuhl's assertion appears almost verbatim in the Conclusions of the Third Sub-Committee of 29 September 1923: the German measures were fully within the 1907 Hague Convention on Land Warfare. Moreover it 'had to be pointed out that towns such as Cambrai, Douai, Denain and

Valenciennes, despite the efforts of the German Army leadership to spare them a bombardment, were destroyed by Allied artillery.'[9] Obviously this would be hard to swallow for those Frenchmen who, returning home, gazed nonplussed on the rubble of their villages, the hacked-down orchards, the flooded mine workings and the poisoned springs. Nevertheless much destruction wrought by the Allies in Northern French towns was (and to some extent still is) wrongly attributed to the brutality of the German occupying force.

An example here is the case of Saint Quentin, a town which plays a leading role in Stülpnagel's documentation, since he could show by reference to the 18.Armeekommando war records show how between April and October 1917 the Germans had watched 'the enemy artillery' batter down, in successive stages, the famous cathedral which dated from the Middle Ages. In the French wartime and post-war propaganda, this destruction is blamed universally on German barbarism. The same goes for other onslaughts against Northern French towns when facts and propaganda, both during and after the war, became hopelessly interwoven. While the Germans attempted to prove that it had been British artillery alone which reduced Cambrai to ash and rubble, the British military and Press emphasized that whatever the facts of the matter, the destruction had been exclusively a consequence of German war policy.[10] Such polemic and mutual recriminations were to be expected in the wake of the war experience but ultimately served little useful purpose.

The fact that remembrance of the war dead after 1919 frequently assumed strong political overtones and remained a constant area of controversy was prejudicial to any rapprochement on the Somme. At first German war graves there were tended almost solely by the *Volksbund Deutsche Kriegsgräberfürsorge e.V.* which at the time never – contrary to the present case – worked together with the British and French across the national divide. The French hatred of the Germans was so firmly entrenched that there could be no place for a common remembrance, and at international talks the vengeful attitude and intentions of the French were striking. No effort was spared to keep the Germans out of French military cemeteries. The Germans remained bitter for a long period at having to paint their wooden grave markers black while the French ones were white. There is still no explanation for this today, but many Germans considered it a deliberate insult to their dead. During the recultivation of the region after 1919 there occurred a general upheaval of German memorials and cemeteries in which local inhabitants would uproot gravestones and toss them on rubbish heaps. The French Government would not allow the Germans to put up new memorials honouring their dead as they permitted their Allies to do across the Somme in the period up to the Second World War, and as may be found today everywhere in eastern Picardy, but at least they did guarantee that new German military cemeteries could by formed by amalgamations and be properly maintained.

What remains a mystery to the present day is why, despite the granting of passage across the frontier to German cemetery visitors from 1924, and the 'social excursions' to France organized by the Volksbund from 1927, the total of German visitors to the Somme fell far short of the stream of British visitors.[11] Given that the journey was made extremely tiresome by passport formalities and having to declare in advance the exact time and place of border crossings there and back, nevertheless according to the Volksbund, in the years 1920–1930 only three per cent of the relatives of the German Fallen on the Somme went to the graveside. This absenteeism was perhaps based on a rejection of the mass-cemetery innovation which tended to emphasize the dehumanization of the individual soldier and made the paying of respects to that person 'in that place' difficult or impossible.

An analysis based on the files of the Somme Département showed that for the period to 1933 only a few large group excursions of battlefield visitors to the thirteen German military cemeteries were registered.[12] Of note here was the excursion of fifty persons from Aachen travelling in September 1933 to the Rancourt cemetery near Péronne for the consecration of the new memorial. In order to avoid any possibility of giving offence, the local prefecture was consulted on whether anybody would mind if the group sang the Dead German Soldier's song *Ich hatt'einen Kameraden* at the ceremony.

Notes:

1. Die Somme-Wacht, newspaper of 1.Armee, Nr 1–5 (1917).
2. War Correspondent at the Front Georg Wegener: *Der Wall von Eisen und Feuer*, 3 Vols., Leipzig 1915–1920.
3. *Zwischen Arras und Péronne: Reserve-Korps-Verlagsbuch-handlung, Bapaume, 1916*: a pictorial record with 311 photographs recalling the period of trench warfare and the struggle to repel the British offensive.
4. The Treaty of Versailles together with concluding Protocol and the Rhineland Statute, Berlin 1925. The words 'German aggression' in the original are translated as 'German attack' in the German translation.
5. Otto von Stülpnagel: Die Zerstörung Nordfrankreichs und Belgiens (361 photographs) in: *Süddeutsche Monatshefte, 20th year* (1922/1923) December 1922, p.117–157. Also: Die Wahrheit über die deutsche Kriegsverbrechen, Berlin 1920.
6. Raymond Poincaré: Messages, discourse, allocutions, lettres et télégrammes, 3 Vols, Paris 1919–1922.
7. Stülpnagel: die Zerstörung, p.124.
8. Ibid, p.127.
9. Völkerrecht im Weltkrieg, 4 Vols, Berlin 1927, here Vol I, p.55–154.
10. Ibid, p.76f.
11. See Susanne Brandt: *Vom Kriegsschauplatz zum Gedächtnisraum – die Westfront 1914–1940*. Baden-Baden 2000, p.160ff.
12. Claudia Figge: *Das visualisierte Gedenken an den Massentod des ersten Weltkrieges*, Magister-arbeit, Univ. Freiburg, 1994.

Chapter Seven

Museums and First World War Memorials on the Somme

Frédérick Hadley, Reseacher,
Museum des Historial de la Grande Guerre, Péronne, Somme.

By 1917, 'battlefield tourism' had begun in the liberated areas of the Western Front: family members of British and French dead, and many curiosity seekers, wandered the 1914–1916 battle-fields and visited the regions from which the Germans had withdrawn. The British vistors included a number of writers and historians from the recently founded Imperial War Museum in London, and the latter proved the inspiration for the creation of places of remembrance in those localities where British soldiers had fought and died.

In November 1920, the French Chamber of Deputies agreed a Bill declaring World War remnants 'historical monuments', and a year later the Chamber identified a total of 236 monuments (infantry trenches, MG posts, forts, craters, etc.) as being places along the former Western Front which had been of decisive importance to France for the outcome of the war. These were to be preserved unconditionally. At the same time the military cemeteries laid down during the war, and which were of varying sizes, were to be reorganized and their numbers reduced substantially by amalgamation. In 1925 there were throughout France 174 French, 165 German and seventy-six mixed-nationality cemeteries.[1]

After the war the Somme region experienced a record influx

of visitors, particularly people who had been left at home during the fighting, and British and French battlefield tourists. After the mid–1920s numbers of Germans travelled to the Somme to visit the graves of fallen family members, mostly under the auspices of the Volksbund Deutsche Kriegsgräberfürsorge e.V. founded in 1919. Nowadays about 300,000 visitors come annually to visit the Great War military cemeteries and places of remembrance on the Somme, including 100,000 from abroad, primarily Britain.

German military cemeteries on the Somme are easily recognized by the black crosses in metal or stone, often in the centre of a park: the French by a simple white cross and the flagpole with the French tricolour. The gravestones bear, if known, the name of the fallen soldier, his rank and as a rule the date of death. The French headstones have the inscription *Died for France* next to the military unit. The British cemeteries are very numerous in the area since there was little option to bury their fallen comrades where they lay. British cemeteries are marked by a 'Cross of Sacrifice' where there are more than forty dead, and with a 'Stone of Remembrance' for more than 1,000 dead. Remembrance tablets carry frequently the biblical inscription *Their Name Liveth for Ever More*: the headstones bear the name, date of death and the regiment of other unit. On the gravestones of the unidentified fallen is found the simple quotation *A Soldier Known Unto God* from Rudyard Kipling.

Today the Commonwealth War Graves Commission maintains in the entire Somme region about 410 cemeteries containing 130,000 graves of the fallen from Great Britain, the former dominions including Australia, Canada and South Africa, and the former colonies. The French Defence Ministry cares for the twenty national military cemeteries on the Somme, while the Volksbund Deutsche Kriegsgräberfürsorge e.V. is responsible for the maintenance and care of thirteen cemeteries with German dead. There are twenty-two, 632 German fallen alone in the amalgamated Vermandovillers cemetery set down in 1920.

The Historial de la Grande Guerre at Peronne

A museum with annexed research centre dedicated to the Great War was initiated in 1986 by the General Council of the Département of the Somme. The project was realized with the help of French and international historians and Great War experts, and the Historial de la Grande Guerre was opened in the Péronne fortress on 16 July 1992. The building, in white reinforced concrete, and designed by the French architect Henri-Edouard Ciriani in the Le Corbusiers tradition, is immediately alongside the old fortress ruin (a brick structure) through which visitors pass to access the actual museum.

The tri-lingual (English, French and German) museum is neither a place of remembrance nor a war museum but is oriented towards understanding the social and psychological effect the war had on the populations and fighting men of the nations involved. The 'trenches' set into the white marble floor symbolizing the chalky soil of the Somme are intended to make trench life comprehensible. Uniforms spread across the floor are adorned with all kinds of personal and military memorabilia. Above the replica trenches is an exhibition of trench art by soldiers of the time. This reflects the conditions of military life, the mood before an attack, the sorrow at the loss of a comrade, also hygiene, the food, humour, leave at the front, etc., in a war increasingly mechanized and anonymous.

The glass walls of the exhibition hall are devoted to the civilian populations. Each theme is spread across three storeys (Germany upper floor, France middle, Britian the ground floor). This allows a systematic comparison of the similarities and differences in the pre-war and wartime cultures of the great nations fighting on the Western Front. In four great exhibition halls the immediate history and causes of the Great War are explained. Everyday life in wartime and the increasing totalization of warfare by technology and industry: the political and cultural consequences for European society in the remainder of the twentieth century are also considered. The unique Historial collection of commercial and everyday objects includes artwork. The brutal transformation and contradictions which the war engendered are well portrayed by the *Der Krieg* series of paintings from the German artist Otto Dix. These are found in the entrance hall. Dix, a volunteer at the Somme front, spent six years after the war completing his work which bears witness to the trauma of industrialized warfare.

A curious example of soldierly morale is the giant wooden board with the insciption *Nicht ärgern nur wundern* (Don't be angry, just admire) which the Germans fixed on the heavily damaged council house at Péronne in 1917. The edifice had been severely damaged by British artillery. Shortly afterwards the Germans pulled back to the Siegfried Line leaving their own trail of total devastation.

Contemporary film material from the Great War shown at fifty video posts throughout the museum highlights the importance of photography and film technology in the war for official propaganda and personal memories. The Historial regularly exhibits to various themes: outstanding personalities in politics and literature, religion and religiousness, the everyday life of the peoples in occupied regions, children in war, the Treaty of Versailles in the perception of the Germans, the architecture of the reconstructed Somme after 1919, the contradictory works of contemporary artists. Coverage of the Battle of the Somme of 1916, and the final battle in Picardy in the spring of 1918, are included in the Historial exhibition in order to provide the visitor with a better understanding of the regional war events.

The Remembrance Circuit

The Historial has set up a special 'Remembrance Circuit' for visitors to the military cemeteries and memorials. The route is marked by the red poppy insignia on local signposts. There is also an audio trail compiled from the writings of many authors who fought on the Somme.

I – The Historial de la Grande Guerre is in the Péronne town centre. In the Great War Péronne was a strategic hub for the German armies and therefore an important goal of the 1916 Allied offensive. This offensive stopped short of the gates of the badly damaged town. Like most towns and villages in the area, Péronne has been almost completely rebuilt in the brick style characteristic of the region. At the Rue Saint Denis-Avenue MacOrlan crossroads there is a post-war temporary building. MacOrlan was a writer from Péronne who fought close to his native town. The monument with the inscription *Picardy curses War* and the despairing mother with raised clenched fist is the work of sculptor Paul Auban.

2 – At Flaucourt towards Biaches is one of the few German memorials from the Great War still standing. Most of the others were destroyed during the war or shortly after. In a field above the street are the remains of a small cemetery. A plaque on a brick wall reads *Zur Ehre der für Kaiser und reich gefallenen Söhne Deutschlands* – In honour of the sons of Germany fallen for Kaiser and Reich.

3 – At Frise overlooking the bend in the river there is a fine panorama of the whole Somme valley. One can find here the remains of French and German trenches from 1915. In the summer of 1916 the seam between the British and French armies ran through Maricourt, north of the Somme.

4 – At Mametz a memorial to the 38th Welsh Division dedicated in 1987 recalls the bitter fighting for the neighbouring wood. The locality was taken by British forces on 1 July, but the Germans held the wood itself until 12th. The memorial with the red dragon is reached along the Welsh Road in the village.

5 – Fricourt, which fell on 2 July 1916, was a heavily fortified village in one of the advanced front sections held by the Germans. In the German cemetery to the north of the village the 'Red Baron', fighter ace Manfred von Richthofen, was interred after he was shot down over the Somme in April 1918. His remains were re-interred at Wiesbaden subsequently.

6 – Albert is even today a place bound up with much emotion for many British. During the autumn of 1914 it was repeatedly shelled by German artillery. In January 1915 a shell hit the bell of the neo-Byzantine basilica. The gold-plated statue of the Virgin Mary, which towered over the edifice, remained at a horizontal angle until the spring of 1918. This gave rise to the legend of the 'Hanging Madonna of Albert': on the day when the statue fell, the war would be over. When the Germans besieged the town during their 1918 offensive, the British destroyed the church to prevent its use for orientation purposes. Albert, totally devastated in the war, owes its reconstruction to the city of Birmingham. Beside the basilica is a small, fairly conventional war museum 'Somme 1916.' The imposing town hall underlines the significance accorded after 1919 to rebuilding the area.

7 – In the village of **La Boisselle** is the Lochnagar crater where every 1 July at 0730 – marking the beginning of the great Somme battle in 1916 – a simple but moving service of remembrance is held. The crater has a diameter of 100 metres and is thirty metres deep. It was created by detonating twenty-seven tonnes of ammoniac explosive. Dust and rubble were ejected up to 1,000 metres. The subsequent attack by Irish and Scots regiments came to nothing, and the greatest crater of the Great War became an icon for the Battle of the Somme. Lochnagar is owned by Englishman Richard Dunning, who ensures that it remains accessible to the public. The unevenness of the ground in the vicinity recalls the heavy shelling common in the region from October 1914. Every year about fifty tonnes of war material comes to the surface in the Somme region. The signposts on the road from Albert to Bapaume (D–929) show the various stages of the slow British advance.

8 – In the village of **Pozieres** situated on an elevation, only the foundations remain of 'Gibraltar', a command post called 'Das Blockhaus' by the Germans. The 1916 battle can be accurately followed with the aid of the orientation table. The command post 'Die Windmühle' (named after a seventeenth century windmill on the site) in the German second line of trenches no longer exists. A metal plaque on the spot recalls the 2nd Australian Division which suffered heavy losses in the fighting for Pozieres. Facing the elevation, directly on the highway, is a memorial with four miniature tanks recalling the first British tank attack in September 1916.

9 – The elevation of the (disappeared) village **Thiepval** was the axis of the German defence in the north of the Somme. Thiepval became the place where the British sustained their greatest losses in the period from 1 July to 26 September (the day when it fell). At this location so important for British war memories, a memorial was dedicated in 1932 in memory of the British and South Africans missing in the Somme fighting. There are more than 73,000 names on the sixteen columns of the imposing monument which is visible for miles. The Ulster Tower at Thiepval, built in 1921, is the replica of a tower in Belfast, and remembers the soldiers of the province who fought on the Somme.

10 – Beaumont-Hamel is the official place of remembrance for Newfoundland, a British colony of the time. The Newfoundland Park of Remembrance dedicated in 1925, the work of landscape architect Rudolph Cochius, is sixteen hectares in extent. A number of trenches have been preserved. Of the 801 Newfoundlanders who took part in the attack of 1 July 1916, only sixty-eight survived. The Hill (Caribou Hill) with the bronze sculpture of a reindeer, allows a good view over this bitterly fought battlefield. The German front line ran only 100 metres from here to the rear of the present parkland. A memorial in the form of a kilted Scots soldier marks the capture of German positions on 13 November 1916 by the 51st Highland Division. A new information centre supplies interesting details about the Battle of the Somme and a chronicle of the fighting in this region.

11 – Courcelette is the official place of remembrance for the Canadians, who from September to November 1916 had two divisions fighting on the Somme. The total Canadian losses are estimated at 24,000. In 1964 at Martinpuich, where in mid-September tanks were used in warfare for the first time, German veterans laid a plaque at the foot of the local memorial.

12 – Longueval is the place of remembrance for the South Africans. In the wood at Delville the South African Infantry Brigade experienced its baptism of fire from German artillery in mid-July 1916. Of its 3,200 men only 143 returned unwounded. Behind the national monument dedicated in 1926, sixty years later the South African Government set up a museum recalling the deployment of (white) South Africans in the Great War and elsewhere. At Longueval there is a second memorial park and the Caterpillar Valley cemetery. These both recall the involvement of 1st New Zealand Division and its heavy losses in the autumn of 1916 when 1,560 soldiers were killed and 5,440 wounded in twenty-three days.

13 – The village of **Guillemont** was almost completely destroyed in the fighting. Two entrances to a preserved German concrete command post are found on the outskirts of the village.

14 – Rancourt is one of the few locations to have the cemeteries of various nationalities (German, French and British). The French chapel of remembrance resulted from a private initiative in memory of the only son of the du Bos family, fallen for France.

Other places in the Somme recall the fighting in the spring and summer of 1918. **Villers-Bretonneux** formed the outermost limit of the Germans' westward offensive. The Australians, who finally brought the German advance to a stop here, erected a memorial on this spot to their missing soldiers in 1938. It carried the names of their troops who have no grave (on D–23). The special relationship between the Départment of the Somme and the Australian continent became closer in 1993, after the exhumation of the remains of an unknown soldier from the Adélaide military cemetery and their transfer to Canberra. The small museum on the first floor of the local Victoria School was a gift from Australian schoolchildren in Victoria. It documents the deployment of Australian troops at the first tank battle in history with the use of models, photographs and uniforms.

The Australian memorial park at **Le Hamel** south of Albert (not to be confused with Beaumont-Hamel) recalls the fighting preceding the so-called Black Day of the German Army (8 August 1918 according to Ludendorff).

On 4 July 1918 General Monash succeeded, with US support, in a modern offensive using artillery, infantry, aircraft and tanks. The first significant attack by US units on the Somme took place at **Catigny** near Montdidiers on 28 May 1918. This operation is remembered by a monument to the 1st US Division (Big Red One). The graves of the US dead of 1917 and 1918 are found in the American Somme Cemetery at **Bony** (Aisne).

At **Noyelles-sur-Mer** north-east of Abbeville a small pagoda can be seen in the cemetery recalling the almost 100,000 Chinese non-combatant labourers used behind the front. According to the agreement between their Governements, the Chinese were allotted transport and trench work by the British and French from April 1917. After the war they performed clearance work on the Somme.

The variety of memorial and sites to visit in the region underlines the large number of nations sending troops to fight and die on the Somme. This applies particularly to Africans and Asians who worked there within the framework of the Allied war effort, often under the most appalling conditions. The preserved, or in part newly erected places of remembrance also indicate the great effort made by the Département of the Somme to keep alive the memory of the Great War, and so fulfil its obligation to history.

Note:
1   Susanne Brandt: *Vom Kriegsschauplatz zum Gedächtnisraum: Die Westfront 1914–1940*, Baden-Baden, 2000, p.129ff.